THE PROVINCE OF JURISPRUDENCE DETERMINED
BY JOHN AUSTIN

The Province of Jurisprudence Determined
by John Austin

Edited by
DAVID CAMPBELL and PHILIP THOMAS

With an Introduction by
W. L. MORISON

Routledge
Taylor & Francis Group
LONDON AND NEW YORK

First published 1998 by Dartmouth and Ashgate Publishing

Reissued 2018 by Routledge
2 Park Square, Milton Park, Abingdon, Oxon, OX14 4RN
52 Vanderbilt Avenue, New York, NY 10017

Routledge is an imprint of the Taylor & Francis Group, an informa business

Publisher's Note
The publisher has gone to great lengths to ensure the quality of this reprint but points out that some imperfections in the original copies may be apparent.

A Library of Congress record exists under LC control number:

ISBN 13: 978-0-367-02750-6 (hbk)
ISBN 13: 978-0-429-39801-8 (ebk)

CONTENTS

PREFACE

The Province of Jurisprudence Determined is the 'prefatory' first part of Austin's *Lectures on Jurisprudence or the Philosophy of Positive Laws*. *The Province* was published separately in 1832; the *Lectures* were first published, posthumously, in 1863. The standard text of *The Province* is taken from Robert Campbell's fifth edition of the *Lectures*, published in 1885, which had the benefit of being revised with the assistance of J. S. Mill's notes on Austin's original course of lectures delivered at the University of London in 1828. Campbell's edition formed the basis of H. L. A. Hart's edition of *The Province* published in 1955 and is the basis of this edition.

We have attempted to reproduce Campbell's text quite faithfully, with only four exceptions. We have taken advantage of word processing technology to give what we trust is a clearer layout to the text. We have silently corrected obvious errors. We have, in a very minor way, pruned some of what, to modern eyes, seems Austin's excessive punctuation. Most markedly, we have placed the relevant sections of Austin's 'Synopsis of Lectures' at the beginning of each lecture and attempted to break up the previously very long, unbroken text by using the parts of each synopsis as sub-headings. This has not always worked very elegantly at all, but we are confident that it does provide easier access to the text and is superior to the previous use of the parts of the synopsis as marginal annotations. The function of the 'Synopsis' was more or less duplicated by the 'Analysis of Lectures' which Austin also provided, and we have retained this 'Analysis' as a whole at the start of the book.

We are very grateful for the assistance of Rosita Chan, Loletta Tsang (and some of their colleagues) and Jennifer Yeadon in carrying the clerical burden of producing this book.

David Campbell
Philip Thomas

INTRODUCTION

W. L. Morison

Austin's History and Associations[1]

John Austin (1790–1859) was the first Professor of Jurisprudence at the University of London, now University College. His lecturing career appears to have been troubled and lasted only from 1828 to 1833 (at the longest). *The Province of Jurisprudence Determined*, consisting of his earliest lectures, was published in 1832. It was the only extensive monograph for which Austin himself was prepared to accept the responsibility of publishing. The manuscripts of his remaining lectures were edited by his wife, Sarah Austin, and published after his death.[2] *The Province* itself was out of print for many years before Austin's death, but Sarah had it reprinted in 1861 with some small additions, which she separated from the text itself. All of Austin's lectures were published by 1863. They were well received at Oxford and prescribed for the new Honours School of Jurisprudence. Interest in the lectures was further stimulated by John Stuart Mill's warm review of the work in the *Edinburgh Review*.[3] The lectures have since generated the widest interest. Overall, Austin's work has exerted influence as something of a time bomb, going off posthumously.

John Stuart Mill, most famous as a political philosopher, was a pupil of Austin when the latter was at the bar prior to being appointed to his chair. He also attended Austin's first course of lectures at the University of London. Mill was enthusiastic about Austin's teachings but was concerned by the lecturer's inability to communicate his material to others. Thomas Carlyle, the historian, described Austin as a lean, grey-headed, pained-looking man, with large, earnest, timid eyes and a clanging metallic voice.[4] Sarah described this same voice as bell-like.[5]

Austin's great intellectual advantage was his youthful success in commending himself to Jeremy Bentham, to whom Austin early wrote of his desire to convince the master that he was truly his disciple.[6] The newly-wed Austins took up residence near Bentham at Queen Square, London. Other neighbours were Bentham's close associates James Mill and his son, John Stuart Mill. Austin was something of a recluse, but Sarah was not, and those particularly attracted to her drawing room included Philosophic Radicals—persons of Benthamite persuasion who gained entry to Parliament after the Reform Act 1832 and were active in publications to which Austin contributed.[7]

The Benthamites' political stance derived from a formidable body of philosophical and social theory. They are known as utilitarians because of the central importance they attached to their utilitarian ethical theory. Bentham discovered the notion of utility in the work of Joseph Priestley, an eminent Unitarian divine. In Priestley's *Essay on Government*, which Bentham read in 1768, the principle appears in the form that 'the good and happiness of the members, that is of the majority of members, of any state is the great standard by which everything relating to that state must be finally determined'.[8] For Benthamites, the word 'good' might as well have been omitted from the expression 'good and happiness'. They recognised no qualitative distinction between pleasures. Alcohol was as good as poetry, their quantity of pleasure being equal. What was best was the greatest surplus, for the greatest number, of pleasure or happiness over pain or unhappiness, the measurement of the goodness or badness of anything being arrived at by a hedonistic calculus.

One appeal of utilitarianism to the Benthamites was its apparent consistency with their general philosophy. In general philosophy, the Benthamites are part of the long history of British empiricism. Shortly after Bentham's death, James Reddie classed Bentham's theory of law among those which regard law as belonging 'to that by far the largest and most important part of the domain of human knowledge, which the Germans denominate empirical, or *a posteriori*, which embraces all physical existence and events which is so far dependent on, or affected by, time and place, and which can only be acquired by observation and experience.'[9] Bentham's interest in law, in the first instance, was aroused by his strong reaction to the lectures of Sir William Blackstone, the first Vinerian Professor of English Law at the University of Oxford and the celebrated author of the *Commentaries on the Laws of England.*[10] Bentham considered the propositions that were centrally featured in Blackstone's exposition to be nothing better than ethical dogmas presented as law.[11] The Benthamites had two objections to Blackstone's exposition: the first was to his ethics, the propositions of which were not to be tested by justifications based on observation; the other was to a confusion between law and ethics which obscured the fact that the existing law might not, and in fact did not, measure up to intelligible ethical standards.[12] Empirical definitions were demanded of both ethics and law.

The notion of utility was the Benthamites' answer to what was a satisfactory, indeed the only satisfactory, ethical concept that would enable particular ethical propositions to be tested. Whether something was good or bad could be determined only by applying the hedonistic calculus to see whether it gave rise to the maximum of pleasure over pain for most people compared with alternatives. The 'something' to which the hedonistic calculus was to be applied was usually thought of as an existing or prospective legislative measure.

A major Benthamite objective was the codification of the laws of countries on the basis of maximum utility, comprehensiveness and clarity. Since, in the Benthamite view, laws were measures that imposed sanctions on their targets, laws were at an initial disadvantage from the point of view of utility. Hence a preliminary to codification was the repeal of laws which produced a balance of pain over pleasure, or less of a surplus of pleasure over pain than was possible. In practice, the Philosophical Radicals' activity was mainly directed to this end.

This activity and influence were felt particularly in the economic field—what was then known as political economy. For the Benthamites, economics was the epitome of a modern social science. It was closely related to the utilitarian objective, for they conceived it as the study of the conditions under which the greatest wealth of the greatest number could be achieved. The leading light among the utilitarians in this field was the banker, David Ricardo.[13] Bentham's right-hand man at the time, James Mill, summarised Ricardo's views for popular consumption.[14] This summary presented Ricardo as a *laissez faire* economist. Generally, free market forces could be expected to operate fairly—that is, with maximum utility. Laws that interfered with the free operation of market forces needed repeal. The major function of law in this area was to keep order, though a rather more complex question which Benthamites addressed was the framing of tax laws in a way that would not distort the operation of market forces. The positive tasks of law making had to take account of the characteristics of the targets of the laws—that is, of human psychology. In this respect, Bentham purported to observe in human beings a high degree of uniformity. When asked why he thought he could devise codes of law for countries to which he had never been, Bentham replied, in effect, that after you had seen a few human beings, you had seen them all.

The key to operating on human mental processes through laws was found in the association psychology that the Benthamites adopted.[15] Developed by David Hartley, the principal human emotions were thought to derive from the working of associative mechanisms upon our original experiences of pleasure and pain.[16] For Bentham, applying himself particularly to the criminal sphere, law operated by attaching pain to certain actions; this would act as a deterrent on the criminal as well as on others who observed his or her consequent suffering.

Bentham presented his definition in the context of working out what kind of analysis was needed to achieve a truly systematic exposition of law as a code for a particular country. His definition of a law was as follows:

> [Law is] an assemblage of signs, declaratory of a volition conceived or adopted by the sovereign in a state, concerning the conduct to be observed in a certain case by a certain person or class of persons, who in the case in question are or are supposed to be subject to his power, such volition trusting for its accomplishment to the expectation of certain events which it is intended such a declaration should upon occasion be a means of bringing to pass, and the prospect of which it is intended should act as a motive upon those whose conduct is in question.[17]

Austin's definition of law approximates to Bentham's in essentials and derives from it. It may therefore seem remarkable that this approach continues to be thought of as the Austinian rather than the Benthamite theory of law. In part, the explanation is that Bentham's major work on the character and structure of law was not published until 1945 and did not appear in a comprehensively scholarly edition until 1970. The 1945 edition was published under the title *The Limits of Jurisprudence Defined*, edited by C. W. Everett. H. L. A. Hart's 1970 edition is titled *Of Laws in General*. Nevertheless, even today, Austin's version continues to be read. There are factors that make Bentham's account more technically complex and, in places, obscure. Bentham's methods of analysis, through classification and sub-classification in relation to any topic, were doctrinaire—particularly in relation to law. An exercise of will was supposed to have a special logic about it, as distinct from matters that could be approached through the ordinary logic of the understanding.[18] Bentham's younger associates, on the other hand, regarded the notion of the will, as a psychological phenomenon with extraordinary features, as having been debunked.[19] Bentham's analysis of the expression of a legislative will was further complicated by his determination to expose what he saw as the complete expression of legislative will in relation to any legal offence, extending down to details of administration. Austin left most of these complexities out of *The Province*, reserving comment on them until his later lectures. This served to emphasise the crucial message of Bentham's central definition. Law was something *imposed* on subjects from above. Thus the Benthamites were utilitarians concerning ethics, but *positivists* concerning law.

The Province of Jurisprudence Determined[20]

Austin took great pride in his capacity to achieve clarity in delineating any field of study and, in particular, law. Some jurists take an engineering attitude when accommodating complex material to their definition of law: if it will not fit, bash it. But Austin's attitude was surgical: if it will not fit, cut it out. Austin thus presents a 'stripped' view of material central to law, with the additional assistance of simplifying assumptions that are now generally recognised as false. Nevertheless, Austin's work is still a convenient starting point for the study of jurisprudence. Much scientific and philosophical writing tends to oversimplify a field of study in the first instance for the sake of clarity, recognising that complicating corrections will have to be incorporated later on. In Austin's case, however, the corrections have to be made by studying the work of later writers[21] —while at the same time acknowledging that Austin may have got some things right that the purporting correctors got wrong.[22] Austin, moreover, did not lose interest in topics which he excluded from his field. This is something that gives *The Province* a rather scrappy structure. In it, Austin is rather like a housekeeper who seeks to reduce the house to strict order by giving things away to the neighbours, but then keeps visiting them to have a look at the jettisoned material.

Austin exercises himself, in the earlier part of *The Province*, by distinguishing law from what would now be called the social sciences. He decides that the term 'law', used simply and strictly, consists of rules laid down by political superiors to their inferiors in independent political societies. Austin confines the relevant rules to commands: significations of desire, with the power and purpose of inflicting an evil in case the desire be disregarded. The term 'rule' is in turn confined to those commands relating to acts or forbearances specified as a class. The term 'superiority' connotes superior might, having nothing to do with precedence or excellence. Austin concludes the first lecture in *The Province* by saying that some things that may appear to be excluded by this very strict set of definitions nevertheless turn out to be included. All laws impose duties on inferiors—because they subject them to sanctions—but rules that confer rights are laws too because they implicitly impose duties on others. Again, customary laws assume validity once they are enforced by the judges since they become the will of the sovereign (the politically superior legislator), either through the authority that the sovereign gives to the judges in that respect, or through sovereign acquiescence in what the judges have done.

In terms of our metaphor above, Austin spends the second of the six lectures that comprise *The Province* visiting the neighbour to whom he has disposed of the science of ethics. For Austin, divine laws are laws properly so called because they are addressed by a superior to inferiors, but not strictly and properly so called because God is not a political superior and therefore not within the area of jurisprudence as the science of law strictly requires. Since little divine law is revealed, the function of ethics is to provide an index to what God demands. Austin sneers at the suggestion that this index is to be found in the promptings of a moral sense, whether this be called practical reason, a moral sense, common sense, or whatever. Some of us, he indicates, are not equipped with 'that peculiar organ'; we are left to infer that it is generally in the category of the emperor's new clothes. The alternative is to find the index in considerations of utility that proves to be the answer. Austin is aware that critics argue that to calculate the utility of a proposed course of action in relation to alternatives is extremely difficult or even impossible in practical terms. But we do not have to rework the issues every time, he says. We can devise rules or maxims in relation to classes of action, giving rise to sentiments that immediately guide us. Occasionally, however, we may have to start from scratch when specific situations confront us.

Having disposed of one set of objections blocking the achievement of utilitarianism, Austin turns, in his third lecture, to another set of practical difficulties—the shortcomings of human beings whose co-operation would be required. Outside the charmed circle of the Benthamite elite he failed to make an impact on most people, and for this he blamed most people. 'His estimate of men was low', wrote Sarah Austin after her husband's death, 'and his solicitude for their approbation was consequently small.'[23] Those who raised problems for the achievement of utility fell, in Austin's view, into two classes. Firstly, there were scholars in the social science fields, whom he accused of venality towards the establishment as well as obtuseness. In the field of law, in particular, he said that the 'monstrous or crude productions of childish and imbecile intellect' had been cherished and perpetuated.

Proceeding from the shortcomings of scholars to those of the *hoi polloi*, Austin said it was important that at least some of the lower classes should be recruited as leaders by replacing their coarse and sordid pleasures with refined amusements and liberal curiosity. This would be accomplished through education. In matters of education, Benthamite theory called on Austin to be optimistic. In a broad sense, Benthamites regarded law as an effective instrument of education, since the public infliction of punishment on some would set up associations of wrongdoing with unpleasant consequence in the minds of people generally and thus induce psychological restraints. Bentham said that a man who was publicly hanged on Tyburn Hill should regard himself as a patriot dying for his country. But Austin is here concerned with educating the public through enlightenment in the principles of the social sciences. That human beings were perfectible through education was a plank of utilitarianism as derived from Priestley.[24] The Benthamites were impressed by this. Utilitarians were said to become Unitarians when they donned their Sunday best.[25] Accordingly, Austin claimed that the workers should find the fundamental truths of *laissez-faire* economic theory intelligible if properly instructed, and that, if they combined with this an understanding of Malthusian population theory and perceived that they should restrict the size of their families, they would see sense. So they would stop, for example, burning hay ricks. H. L. A. Hart has said that if Austin often went wrong, at least he usually went wrong clearly.[26] Having regard to workers' attitudes in times of economic recession to what is now called dry economic rationalism, this appears to be a conspicuous example of Austin having gone 'wrong clearly'.

In the fourth of the lectures comprising *The Province*, Austin moves to theoretical criticism of the view that what is good is what is dictated by the moral sense, a view that he had so far confined himself to deriding. This criticism, to the present writer, is an important matter on which Austin was right. But he was perhaps not as clearly right as he might have been had he made a systematic analysis of the different theories of moral sense. Austin's general criticism of moral sense theories was that they do not really offer any index to what is good in the way that utility does. They are *ipse dixit* in character—they suppose that our conscience directly tells us what it is right to do in each individual situation. A contrasting moral sense theory is rationalism: moral sense is reason that points out general principles applicable to individual situations. Although there is no necessary connection between these types of ethical theories and religious views, the former tends to be associated with dissenting Protestantism and the latter with Catholicism. So the dissenter's answer to Austin might be that what we apparently assert dogmatically in fact comes to us directly from our hotline to God. The rationalist, on the other hand, is able for the time being to give reasons if challenged: *Why do you consider X is right? Because it is Y. But why is Y right? Because it is Z.* But at some time the argument must stop when the most general principle, the one asserting the rightness of Z, has been reached. So Austin might fairly have argued that his criticism of arbitrariness applied, in the end, as much to ethical rationalist moral sense theory as to intuitionist moral sense theory. In fact Austin argues that what happens in practice is that, when called upon to make reasoned defences, moral sense theorists fall off their perch and tend to fall back on recognisable utilitarian arguments. He might have made this point whether the falling off the perch occurs immediately or at some point later in the moral argument. Austin is highly critical in this lecture of theories that tend to be composites of moral sense and utilitarianism, leading to unreal distinctions being made in order to rationalise the use of different ethical criteria according to supposed differences in the nature of the subject matter.

In the remainder of his fourth lecture Austin is unhappily on weaker ground when discussing the place of human motives in ethics. Here, at two extremes, are the views, first, that ethical behaviour is centrally a matter of compliance with moral *principles*, and second, that good and evil are opposite human *motives* with which what might be called right and wrong acts are connected. Austin naturally fell into the former approach, which critics claim is characteristic of legal positivists, Austinian and otherwise, because positivism appeals to authoritarian personalities or at least to those who are primarily concerned with *order*. Certainly Austin believed that it is better to have some system of law than live in a savage state of nature. On this last matter, as appears in the current lecture, Austin accepted the view of Thomas Hobbes.[27]

In thus setting himself against the view that ethics is a matter of variable human motives, Austin was tangling with much that exists in the background of religious, philosophical and legal traditions. In the extreme opposite approach to Austin's, goodness—like evil—is a matter of the state of the heart, in the sense of that word which has come down to us because the ancient Hebrews anatomically misplaced the seat of the emotions. When Jesus Christ said to his disciples 'The Kingdom of God is within you',[28] he scarcely appears to have been referring to a machine calculating considerations of utility that supposedly constituted part of their make-up. This is not to deny that the heart has its reasons, but they tend to be tentative, with any implications ready to be referred back to the heart. In the history of Greek philosophy, the account of goodness in the first book of the *Republic of Plato* is in terms of the opposition between constructive motives, spreading their influence by appealing to their own kind, and aggressive and appropriative ones, operating naturally through conflict with both constructive motives and other destructive ones.[29]

In his central field of law as a political phenomenon, Austin did not in his lifetime have to confront theories that regarded law not as something imposed from above, but as being somehow sustained from below by the spirit of the populace. The main English opposition to positivism came from historical jurists such as Sir Henry Maine, who were concerned with defining the patterns of technical development over long periods of time. It was German historical jurists like Friedrich von Savigny[30] who dug deeper, with theories of the influence of the developing *Volksgeist* on law, which in their view precluded satisfactory codification on a permanent basis at any given time. Although Austin visited Germany before giving his lectures, a German expert who examined his jottings and library has said that the lectures comprising *The Province* do not show German influence. Such influence seemed to operate only when Austin eventually got down to mapping out the legal system.[31]

Nevertheless, Austin was thoroughly familiar with criticisms of ethical utilitarianism on the grounds of its lack of humanity, and he makes some effort in this lecture to deal with them. He claims that the actions of utilitarians are not altogether governed through the utilitarian calculus. Kissing a woman is at any rate sometimes outside its field. Austin stresses that utilitarians regarded benevolence as an important factor in achieving the greatest happiness of the greatest number, though they might be in some uncertainty concerning how it is generated or whether it is a pristine human characteristic, as he himself thought. What, however, proved damaging to utilitarians on this issue was their theory of the utilitarian effectiveness of an economic system in which the market achieved optimum results through economic units, each of which maximised its own material interests. In Lady Thatcher's terms, it was an economic theory for 'dries'. When the political and social climate changed to wet, the Benthamites were savaged for their inhumanity in this area. Charles Dickens' novel *Hard Times* is an example. History repeats itself. Much of what is said now in a period of economic recession about the dry economic rationalism popular in the past period of expansion represents a great leap forward in thinking to the middle of the nineteenth century.

Positivist Developments from Austin[32]

In lectures V and VI, comprising nearly half of *The Province*, Austin goes into matters opened up in earlier lectures in substantially more detail (we cannot follow him in similar detail in an introduction of this length). In general terms, however, it becomes apparent as Austin progresses that he defines the political superiority which determines whence law emanates purely in terms of the superior power or force of persons or bodies. But when he tries to explain various legal phenomena in terms of this theory, he frequently finds himself using expressions that appear to make sense only if one assumes a background of *law*. Elements of circularity are evident and today no one would accept Austin's theory comprehensively. Nevertheless, some writers, such as Hart,[33] have developed their own views through detecting errors in Austin's and working out modified explanations of matters to which he pointed. The starting point is that, while it can scarcely be denied that effective functioning is to some degree a condition for the existence of law, a more important condition necessary for defining it is authority—properly explained.[34] If authority is not elucidated in a factual way without reference to law, then any competing theory is just as circular as Austin's.

While compliance through force may be described as imposed, compliance through authority is accorded, even if there is a degree of pressure influencing submission to authority (short of what would cause the regime to be described as one of naked power rather than of law) and even if the extent of that accord is more closely worked out by officials than by the general populace. In some degree, the authorities are recognised as legitimate, rather than as simply exacting submission. In a developed system, principles are likely to be formulated by the decision makers concerning what degree of authority it is proper to accord to what emerges from what processes. In this context, those officials who determine when coercion in the name of the community is to be exercised against particular individuals or bodies are especially significant, since they do the closest formulating for the purposes of their work. Those in this position are the judges.

The requirements of orderly judicial administration exert pressure on the judges to formulate these principles in a characteristic order, determining what sources (recognised as having authority for them and other officials) are to take priority over others. The principles concerning sources of authority—sources of law—form a hierarchy, otherwise the judges would be left in confusion when directions coming from different sources conflicted with one another. The authority of a particular source is made subject to the authority of another source or sources except in the case of the top source which is recognised by the judicial system—or even a multiplicity of top sources at some risk of conflict and resulting confusion.[35]

Austin's major error in describing a legal system was that he confused the top source of authority that emerges (as described above) with a body exercising coercive power. His followers had the greatest difficulty in reconciling this with the existence of federal systems where the top source is one or more constitutional document(s). They had to say that the constitutional amending body was sovereign. Since he was rarely called into existence, the ruler of the society was described as one who slumbered and slept. This was hardly conducive to the achievement of the realism based upon observation at which Austin aimed.[36] Further, Austin had somehow to attribute to other sources the authority that in practice is recognised as part of the power of the sovereign instead of being subject to the sovereign. This caused him to make artificial and strained claims that the sovereign adopted decisions taken outside the control of the person or body which Austin purported to find sovereign. It also contributed to what we have described as his surgical attitude in restricting the sources of law to bodies or persons over which the sovereign might be supposed to have control. His sources of law are restricted to officialdom within a State.

In fact, through the influence of their theories, Bentham and Austin contributed to the restriction of the sources of law recognised by English officialdom. An example is that 'Oxford textbooks' (e.g. those of Dicey and Cheshire[37]), while recognising custom as a source of law contrary to Austin's theory, declined to recognise international law as such a source. In Austin's view, the source of law could only be positive morality. By contrast to some others, English theory called for treaties to be recognised individually by local legislation before they acquired force, and then only as long as they continued to be recognised by local legislation. This kind of doctrinaire approach continues to create controversy, particularly in the circumstances of the European Union at the present time. Oxford texts have made a sharp distinction between Public International Law—merely positive morality—and Private International Law or Conflict of Laws in which, for them, foreign laws become part of domestic law only to the extent that local sources recognise them. This distinction is tortuous and artificial.[38]

In some twentieth-century theory such as that of Hart, which started from a consideration of Austin and proceeded to make modifications roughly in the direction we have traced above, the set of propositions designating the sources of law in a system is called its rule of recognition.[39] It *identifies* 'law', which we should interpret as what officialdom, and to some degree subjects, recognise as authoritative for them. Since, however, this set of rules is very complex, we might prefer to call it a country's constitutional theory. These writers also recognise principles of interpretation and principles of adjudication as part of the fundamentals of a system of law alongside the rules defining sources of law.[40]

But in fact principles of interpretation and adjudication also serve to identify what is authoritative in the system. The principles of adjudication, for example, give the order of a judge the same kind of authoritativeness for the individual case—recognised as proper to be applied by other officials as appropriate occasions may arise—as do general rules. The principles of interpretation influence what is to be done with the rules tendered to officials from various sources and so modify their authoritativeness in the course of application, just as in the case of rules of adjudication. The extent to which rules designating sources identify what is to be recognised as authoritative is *qualified*—their face value is affected—by reference to the rules now under consideration.

The effect of rules of adjudication on the degree of recognition accorded to accepted rules designating sources of law is readily seen where, as commonly, a rule of adjudication provides that, subject to appeal, the decision of a court is final for a particular case. It is expected to be enforced—and recognised for other purposes—even if it might seem to many to be plainly at variance with the logical result of the applicable rules identified by the relevant sources. But the rules of interpretation equally twist what comes from the application of the source of law rules. The rule of English law, that a statute must be clear to affect the common law, has enabled English judges to establish a measure of resistance to change of law by the latter even though Parliamentary legislation has been designated the paramount source by the source of law rules themselves. When something becomes clear is in itself unclear enough to give the judges a degree of latitude.

Both the Bentham–Austin approach to law and the more modern English theory to which we have been referring attach importance to the law being clear and certain. In the case of the former, once the structure of the law had been exposed by the analysis of its structure which was advocated, this clarity and certainty were to be achieved by proceeding to codification. The codification was expected to be permanently stable, requiring only minor modification from time to time. In the case of the more modern theory, a high degree of clarity was expected to reveal itself in the law once the structure of the identification rule, the interpretation rules and the rules of adjudication we have described was exposed. These fundamental rules in the system were considered to have a core of settled meaning, like the rules they identified as law, so that uncertainty in a developed legal system would be penumbral or peripheral—uncertainty being mainly involved in doubts about the precise limits of the meaning of the words involved in their formulation.[41]

Few nowadays would envisage the feasibility of a code of laws which did not require amendment on a continuing basis in response to changes in political, social and economic conditions. Nor does an examination of the history of the United Kingdom system support the proposition that fundamental changes in the rules concerning sources of law occur only in extraordinary times, when the old legal system is considered by more modern theory to need transformation. But, for example, over a period of hundreds of years the royal prerogative, as a United Kingdom source of law, has moved down the hierarchy of sources in ways that cannot be comprehensively tracked to cataclysmic system-changing events. Again, principles may have been somewhat tentatively worked out in which the source at the top of the hierarchy, traditionally the United Kingdom Parliament, may establish other sources of law by delegating authority. But what if it purports, wholly or in some degree, to sacrifice its own supremacy in favour of another body or bodies? There is really no answer to the question whether this is to be accorded authority by the settled principles of the system.

The more modern theory proceeding from an Austinian starting point considered his sharp distinction between the law as it 'is' and the law as it 'ought to be'—a vital feature of his theory which it was important to retain.[42] Of course the law that 'is' was understood in a different way, though the notion of the law as it 'ought to be' remained essentially utilitarian. Nevertheless, in the course of argument with opponents, concessions came to be made to the view that a system of law must at least be good enough, in some ethical sense, to be regarded as law.[43] But there is an argument that the concessions needed to be taken much further, in respects which Austin excluded from consideration by what we have called his surgical attitude, and which later theorists minimised through their view that the law was largely settled by authority. On the latter basis, what a system of law required to be done in cases of first impression was not as dominant a question as commonly supposed.[44]

Ethics Strikes Back at Law

Yet this topic has for long been prominent in general jurisprudential thinking. As a student, the writer was taught that 'common sense and the reason of the thing' can comprise a source of law where other recognised sources leave gaps. This was a reflection of English academic thinking about the development of the common law at the turn of the twentieth century. Writers of standard common law texts gave prominence to this notion. Sir Paul Vinogradoff, for example, wrote a book called *Common Sense in Law*.[45] Somehow this expression served to accommodate rationalist ethical notions to the British pride in being down to earth. At a later stage, the writer's Oxford supervisor, A. L. Goodhart, continued in somewhat the same vein by saying that the common law was not about reason, but about reasonableness.[46] As the twentieth century progressed, the Americans were quite candid about the ethical doctrinal roots of views about the appropriate approach of officials to the development of their system.

A visit to Harvard in the late 1950s disclosed former dean, Roscoe Pound, set up in a glass case arranged as an office in front of the Law School, not just for display, but as a place to write his multi-volume work *Jurisprudence*.[47] It was Pound who had shown a particular predilection in his jurisprudence for what he called German 'civilisation' theories of law.[48] His influence contributed to *Volksgeist* notions of the German historical jurists of Austin's time crossing the Atlantic. These theories were strongly reinforced by German evolutionary moral theory, though contrasting with specific well-known versions of that theory such as Hegelian dialectical spiritualism or Marxist dialectical materialism. The evolution of society that had taken place from lower to higher was seen to be gradual rather than abrupt, but following a defined pattern. Pound himself sought to trace legal developments, following evolutionary social developments, in a regular pattern[49] from preoccupation with problems of elementary order to the modern complex economically organized society.[50] A possible next development, he thought, was a law of the world.[51] But the supposition of movement away from preoccupation with order looks a little forlorn in the light of problems at the present time, while the elaborate presuppositions which he discerned at the current state of development seem hardly different from an acceptance of the old Benthamite and Austinian utilitarianism. Certainly he and others succeeded in convincing many Americans that legal problems could be solved by seeking conformity with the developing presuppositions of the society —especially in what might be treated as cases of the first impression. Harvard Professor of Philosophy, John Rawls, was to further emphasise the ethical influence on law with his *A Theory of Justice* (1972). At the beginning of the 1960s Ronald Dworkin[52] was still teaching at the Yale Law School, though shortly to bring to his post as Professor of Jurisprudence at Oxford the notion that there is a moral answer to every legal question. The Yale dean, Eugene V. Rostow, was to proceed in a different direction, as Secretary of State for Political Affairs under President Johnson. He was later to claim that he was the only incumbent of this post who went round telling the American people that they were suffering from a Jungian conflict.[53] It was Karl Llewellyn of Chicago who in particular fastened upon the notion attributed to Jung that there is a collective unconscious which develops refinement over time, just as the individual human embryo's development is said to reflect human biological development. This idea reinforced the kind of evolutionary moral theory transmitted by Pound. In his book *The Common Law Tradition*,[54] Llewellyn advocated the use of the Grand Style of treatment of legal authorities, which contrasted with the freedom of development of the law in the Formal Style. The right answers to legal questions were expected to 'well up' successively from the collective legal unconscious working through judges.

Certainly evolutionary moral ideas have continued to make a general impact on the popular consciousness with the increase of American global influence, and they still affect legal developments. The law must keep in tune with the moral development of society. The distinction between the law that is and the law that ought to be, regarded as vital by Austin and those who emulated him even into the second half of this century, is more than ever blurred by the wide insistence that judges, as well as other officials, should respond to the progress of society. If John Austin had been alive today he would undoubtedly have had a lot to say about this, even if he had been forced to concede that a judicially assumed duty to respond to social development *is* a source of law and an important one in practice. He would doubtless have found it necessary to defend his distinction in a different way.

Lon Fuller, one of Pound's successors in jurisprudence at Harvard, maintains that when a student is setting out his version of the continuing story of the common law it is important that he does not distinguish his own contribution in the development of the plot from that of others.[55] But Harold D. Lasswell and Myres S. McDougal of Yale, whose *Jurisprudence for a Free Society* appeared in 1992, take the opposite view. For them, it is vital to distinguish the standpoint of the observer, struggling for enlightenment, from the standpoint of the participants in the process being observed, with their variety of objectives in decision making.[56] While they put forward proposals of their own with reference to what, at a given time, the law should be, they stress that these are recommendations of their own to the *like minded*. There is no suggestion that there are universal objectives to which everyone must submit, whether by reference to the development of society or otherwise. This is moral authoritarianism, fraudulent in its pretence of objectivity in 'discovering' ideals, and intimidatory in the aggressiveness with which it demands conformity. And we can indeed observe that, in current society, whoever does not submit to current interpretations of the social developments embodying such sacred cows as multi-culturalism, feminism, environmentalism, valetudinarianism, health kicks etc. is beyond the pale.

Consistent with his general approach, Austin would have regarded the condemnation of those who are way out of the groove as immoral, as just another way of saying that they have no moral sense. This is a concept which he derided as a pretence of objective authority for subjective predilections, even if the latter were strongly supported by other people's predilections so as to represent current trends. It is that degree of support, however, which gives the operation of the moral sense its oppressive effect in the functioning of law and society. While Austin's notion of the law that 'is' (as being the command of the sovereign) has been condemned as authoritarian, and while he took the Hobbesian view that it is better to live under some legal system than none at all, he never postulated that it was the duty of a subject to accept even the law's leading ideas. He justified the American Revolution. He was not in a position to anticipate how oppressively modern notions of what the law ought to be could work as they filtered into the legal system. Continued recognition of the Austinian distinction between the actual state of the law and what it ought to be according to our *own* notions at least enables us to cut through the cant to some assessment of the degree of oppression under which we live.

Notes

1. See for a fuller account W. L. Morison, *John Austin* (1982) 7–63.
2. See J. Austin, *Lectures on Jurisprudence*, 2 vols, ed. R. Campbell (5th edn, 1885).
3. J. S. Mill, 'Austin on Jurisprudence' (1863) 118 *Edinburgh Review* 439.
4. J. A. Froude, Thomas Carlyle, *A History of the First Forty Years of His Life 1795–1835*, 2 vols (1882) II, 235.
5. In her introduction to Austin, *op cit. supra* n. 2.
6. Letter to Bentham, 20 July 1819, preserved by University College.
7. For example *The Westminster Review and Parliamentary History and Review*. See John Austin, 'Disposition of Property by Will—Primogeniture' (1824) 2, *The Westminster Review* 503 and John Austin, 'Joint Stock Companies' (1826) *Parliamentary History and Review* 709.
8. J. Priestley, *An Essay on the First Principles of Government* (1771) 17.
9. J. Reddie, *Inquiries Elementary and Historical in the Science of Law* (1840) 1–2.
10. W. Blackstone, *Commentaries on the Laws of England* (1770).
11. See generally J. Bentham, *A Comment on the Commentaries and a Fragment on Government*, ed. J. H. Burns and H. L. A. Hart (1977).
12. See H. L. A. Hart, 'Positivism and the Separation of Law and Morals' (1958) 71 *Harvard Law Review* 593, criticised by L. L. Fuller, 'Positivism and Fidelity to Law —a Reply to Professor Hart' (1958) 71 *Harvard Law Review* 630.
13. See D. Ricardo, 'On the Principles of Political Economy and Taxation', in *Works and Correspondence*, 11 vols, eds P. Sraffa and M. H. Dobb (1951ff) I.
14. J. Mill, *Elements of Political Economy* (1826).
15. See e.g. J. Mill (ed.), *Analysis of the Phenomena of the Human Mind*, 2 vols (1878).
16. D. Hartley, *Observations on Man, his Frame, his Duty and his Expectations* (1749). See further W. O'Neil, *Beginnings of Modern Psychology*, 2nd edn (1982) 15–16.

17. J. Bentham, *Of Laws in General*, ed. H. L. A. Hart (1970).
18. J. Bentham, *An Introduction to the Principles of Morals and Legislation*, eds J. H. Burns and H. L. A. Hart (1977) 8–9, 299–300 n. b2.
19. See e.g. Mill, *Analysis of the Phenomena of the Human Mind, op cit. supra* n. 15.
20. See for a fuller account Morison, *op cit. supra* n. 1, 64–91.
21. Earlier English and Commonwealth works showing Austinian influence but not slavish acceptance include W. Markby, *Elements of Law* (6th edn, 1905); T. E. Holland, *Elements of Jurisprudence* (13th edn, 1924); J. W. Salmond, *Jurisprudence or the Theory of Law* (7th edn, 1924); G. W. Paton, *A Textbook of Jurisprudence* (3rd edn, 1964). American works in this category include J. C. Gray, *The Nature and Sources of Law* (2nd edn, 1921); O. W. Holmes Jr, *The Common Law* (1887) and 'The Path of the Law' (1897) 10 *Harvard Law Review* 457; W. N. Hohfeld, *Fundamental Legal Conceptions as Applied in Judicial Reasoning*, eds W. W. Cook and A. L. Corbin (2nd edn, 1964); A. Kocourek, *Jural Relations* (1928) and A. Kocourek, 'The Century of Analytic Jurisprudence Since John Austin' in *Law, a Century of Progress 1835–1935*, 3 vols (1937) II, 195. The classical European positivist, Hans Kelsen (see e.g. *General Theory of Law and State* (1961), and *The Pure Theory of Law* (2nd edn, 1967)) proceeded independently of Austin and had to have the marked resemblances drawn to his attention. In fact, the first book about Austin appeared in continental Europe: A. Agnelli, *John Austin—alle origine de positivismo giuridico* (1959). References to recent works of Austinian relevance appear below.
22. Thus some have suggested that Austin's work is valid within narrow limits, as an 'analytical' study of law as distinct from a broader sociological approach. See e.g. J. Stone, *Legal Systems and Lawyers' Reasonings* (1964) ch. 2. This eliminates Austin's valuable empirical approach: see W. L. Morison, 'Some Myths about Positivism' (1958) 68 *Yale Law Journal* 212. Some descriptions of positivism include little that applies to Austin, e.g. R. S. Summers, 'The New Analytical Jurists' (1966) 41 *New York University Law Review* 861. This is not to suggest that the extent of Austin's empiricism cannot legitimately be questioned. See W. E. Rumble, 'The Legal Positivism of John Austin and the Realist Movement in American Jurisprudence' (1981) 66 *Cornell Law Review* 986. Again, more sophisticated versions of empiricism than Austin's exist among the more modern positivists. See e.g. H. L. A. Hart, 'Definition and Theory in Jurisprudence' (1954) 70 *Law Quarterly Review* 37.
23. Austin, *op cit. supra* n. 2, I, 20.
24. Priestley, *op cit. supra* n. 8, s. 1. Discussed in J. A. Passmore, *The Perfectibility of Man* (1970) 209–210.
25. L. Stephen, *The English Utilitarians*, 3 vols (1900) I, 169.
26. Discussed in C. Tapper, 'Austin on Sanctions' (1963) *Cambridge Law Journal* 270.
27. T. Hobbes, *Leviathan* (1651).
28. St Luke, ch. 17, v. 21.
29. Discussed in J. Anderson, *Studies in Empirical Philosophy* (1962) 223–224.
30. See e.g. F. F. von Savigny, *The History of Roman Law During the Middle Ages*, trans. E. Cathcart (1979).

31. A. B. Schwarz, 'John Austin and the German Jurisprudence of his Time' (1934–1935) 1 *Politica* 178.
32. See for a fuller account Morison, *op cit. supra* n. 1, 148–210.
33. See Hart, *op cit. supra* n. 12; H. L. A. Hart, *The Concept of Law*, rev. edn (1972). For further refinement of this development see N. MacCormick, H. L. A. Hart (1981). Compare J. Raz, *The Concept of a Legal System*, 2nd edn (1980). What follows in the text is, however, a composite picture of current positivism, and individual writers' views vary substantially from it.
34. For detailed consideration of the relations between the authority of law and control by law, see H. D. Lasswell and M. S. McDougal, *Jurisprudence for a Free Society* (1992) 63–92, 363–365, 400–404.
35. For models of sets of principles showing the hierarchy of sources in developed systems of law, see MacCormick, *op cit. supra* n. 33, 110–111.
36. See T. E. Holland's statement that it is convenient to recognise as laws only such rules as can count on the support of a sovereign political authority although, of course, in certain states of society, it is difficult to ascertain precisely what rules answer to this description: *op cit. supra* n. 21, 54.
37. See e.g. G. C. Cheshire and P. M. North, *Private International Law* (10th edn, 1979).
38. Positivism's history respecting international law is discussed in W. L. Morison, 'The Schools Revisited', in R. S. J. MacDonald and D. M. Johnston, *The Structure and Process of International Law* (1983) 141–162.
39. Hart, *op cit. supra* n. 32, 112.
40. See MacCormick, *op cit. supra* n. 33, 132–133.
41. Discussed *ibid.*, 20–21.
42. See Hart, *op cit. supra* n. 12 above; cf. MacCormick, *op cit. supra* n. 33, 162.
43. The thesis of Lon L. Fuller in his initial criticism of Hart, *op cit. supra* n. 12, to which Hart made some concessions in *The Concept of Law*, *op cit. supra* n. 32, 205–206.
44. See MacCormick, *op cit. supra* n. 33, 124–126.
45. P. Vinogradoff, *Common Sense in Law* (1913). See further W. L. Morison, 'Frames of Reference for Legal Ideals' (1975) 2 *Dalhousie Law Journal* 3–6.
46. As exemplified in A. L. Goodhart, 'Rescue and Voluntary Assumption of Risk' (1934) 5 *Cambridge Law Journal* 192.
47. R. Pound, *Jurisprudence*, 5 vols (1959).
48. *Ibid.*, I, 287.
49. *Ibid.*, 366.
50. *Ibid.*, 406–432.
51. *Ibid.*, 457.
52. See R. M. Dworkin, *Taking Rights Seriously*, rev. edn (1978) esp. chs 2–4. Dworkin took Austin as a starting point on some matters. See R. M. Dworkin, 'Is Law a System of Rules?' in R. M. Dworkin, ed., *The Philosophy of Law* (1977) 38–43.
53. E. V. Rostow, *Peace in the Balance* (1972) 77.
54. K. Llewellyn, *The Common Law Tradition – Deciding Appeals* (1960).
55. L. L. Fuller, *The Morality of Law* (1964) 106–107.
56. Laswell and McDougal, *op cit. supra* n. 34, 39–48, 898–902, 943–944.

ANALYSIS OF LECTURES

Laws proper, or properly so called, are commands; laws which are not commands are laws improper or improperly so called. Laws properly so called, with laws improperly so called, may be aptly divided into the four following kinds:

1. The divine laws, or the laws of God: that is to say, the laws which are set by God to his human creatures.
2. Positive laws: that is to say, laws which are simply and strictly so called, and which form the appropriate matter of general and particular jurisprudence.
3. Positive morality, rules of positive morality, or positive moral rules.
4. Laws metaphorical or figurative, or merely metaphorical or figurative.

The divine laws and positive laws are laws properly so called. Of positive moral rules, some are laws properly so called, but others are laws improper. The positive moral laws, which are laws improperly so called, may be styled laws or rules set or imposed by opinion: for they are merely opinions or sentiments held or felt by men in regard to human conduct. A law set by opinion and a law imperative and proper are allied by analogy merely; although the analogy by which they are allied is strong or close. Laws metaphorical or figurative, or merely metaphorical or figurative, are laws improperly so called. A law metaphorical or figurative and a law imperative and proper are allied by analogy merely; and the analogy by which they are allied is slender or remote.

Consequently, positive laws (the appropriate matter of jurisprudence) are related in the way of resemblance, or by close or remote analogies, to the following objects:

1. In the way of resemblance, they are related to the laws of God.
2. In the way of resemblance, they are related to those rules of positive morality which are laws properly so called. And by a close or strong analogy, they are related to those rules of positive morality which are laws set by opinion.
3. By a remote or slender analogy, they are related to laws metaphorical, or laws merely metaphorical.

The principal purpose or scope of the six ensuing lectures is to distinguish positive laws (the appropriate matter of jurisprudence) from the objects now enumerated: objects with which they are connected by ties of resemblance and analogy; with which they are further connected by the common name of 'laws'; and with which, therefore, they often are blended and confounded. And, since such is the principal purpose of the six ensuing lectures, I style them, considered as a whole, 'the province of jurisprudence determined'. For, since such is their principal purpose, they affect to describe the boundary which severs the province of jurisprudence from the regions lying on its confines.

The way which I take in order to the accomplishment of that purpose, may be stated shortly thus:

1. I determine the essence or nature which is common to all laws that are laws properly so called. In other words, I determine the essence or nature of a law imperative and proper.
2. I determine the respective characters of the four several kinds into which laws may be aptly divided. Or (changing the phrase) I determine the appropriate marks by which laws of each kind are distinguished from laws of the others.

And here I remark, by the by, that, examining the respective characters of those four several kinds, I found the following the order wherein I could explain them best. First, the characters or distinguishing marks of the laws of God; secondly, the characters or distinguishing marks of positive moral rules; thirdly, the characters or distinguishing marks of laws metaphorical or figurative; fourthly and lastly, the characters or distinguishing marks of positive law, or laws simply and strictly so called.

By determining the essence or nature of a law imperative and proper, and by determining the respective characters of those four several kinds, I determine positively and negatively the appropriate matter of jurisprudence. I determine positively what that matter is; and I distinguish it from various objects which are variously related to it, and with which it not unfrequently is blended and confounded. I show moreover its affinities with those various related objects:

affinities that ought to be conceived as precisely and clearly as may be, inasmuch as there are numerous portions of the *rationale* of positive law to which they are the only or principal key.

Having suggested the principal purpose of the following treatise, I now will indicate the topics with which it is chiefly concerned, and also the order wherein it presents them to the reader.

I. In the *first* of the six lectures which immediately follow, I state the essentials of a law or rule (taken with the largest signification that can be given to the term properly). In other words, I determine the essence or nature which is common to all laws that are laws properly so called.

Determining the essence or nature of a law imperative and proper, I determine implicitly the essence or nature of a command; and I distinguish such commands as are laws or rules from such commands as are merely occasional or particular. Determining the nature of a command, I fix the meanings of the terms which the term 'command' implies: namely, 'sanction' or 'enforcement of obedience'; 'duty' or 'obligation'; 'superior and inferior'.

II (a). In the beginning of the *second* lecture, I briefly determine the characters or marks by which the laws of God are distinguished from other laws.

In the beginning of the same lecture, I briefly divide the laws, and the other commands of the Deity, into two kinds: the revealed or express, and the unrevealed or tacit.

Having briefly distinguished his revealed from his unrevealed commands, I pass to the nature of the signs or index through which the latter are manifested to Man. Now, concerning the nature of the index to the tacit commands of the Deity, there are three theories or three hypotheses: first, the pure hypothesis or theory of general utility; secondly, the pure hypothesis or theory of a moral sense; thirdly, a hypothesis or theory mixed or compounded of the others. And with a statement and explanation of the three hypotheses or theories, the greater portion of the *second* lecture, and the whole of the *third* and *fourth* lectures, are exclusively or chiefly occupied.

The exposition of the three hypotheses or theories may seem somewhat impertinent to the subject and scope of my Course. But in a chain of systematical lectures concerned with the *rationale* of jurisprudence, such an exposition is a necessary link.

Of the principles and distinctions involved by the *rationale* of jurisprudence, or of the principles and distinctions occurring in the writings of jurists, there are many which could not be expounded correctly and clearly if the three hypotheses or theories had not been expounded previously. For example, positive law and morality are distinguished by modern jurists into law natural and law positive:

that is to say, into positive law and morality fashioned on the law of God, and positive law and morality of purely human origin. And this distinction of law and morality into law natural and law positive nearly tallies with a distinction which runs through the Pandects and Institutes, and which was taken by the compilers from the jurists who are styled 'classical'. By the jurists who are styled 'classical' (and of excerpts from whose writings the Pandects are mainly composed), *jus civile* is distinguished from *jus gentium*, or *jus omnium gentium*. For (say they) a portion of the positive law which obtains in a particular nation is peculiar to that community: and, being peculiar to that community, it may be styled *jus civile*, or *jus proprium ipsius civitatis*. But, besides such portions of positive law as are respectively peculiar to particular nations or states, there are rules of positive law which obtain in all nations, and rules of positive morality which all mankind observe. And since these legal rules obtain in all nations, and since these moral rules are observed by all mankind, they may be styled the *jus omnium gentium*, or the *commune omnium hominum jus*. Now these universal rules, being universal rules, cannot be purely or simply of human invention and position. They rather are made by men on laws coming from God, or from the intelligent and rational Nature which is the soul and the guide of the universe. They are not so properly laws of human device and institution, as divine or natural laws clothed with human sanctions. But the legal and moral rules which are peculiar to particular nations are purely or simply of human invention and position. Inasmuch as they are partial and transient, and not universal and enduring, they hardly are fashioned by their human authors on divine or natural models. Now, without a previous knowledge of the three hypotheses in question, the worth of the two distinctions to which I have briefly alluded cannot be known correctly, and cannot be estimated truly. Assuming the pure hypothesis of a moral sense, or assuming the pure hypothesis of general utility, those distinctions are absurd, or are purposeless and idle subtleties. But assuming the hypothesis compounded of the others, those distinctions are significant, and are also of considerable moment.

Besides, the divine law is the measure or test of positive law and morality: or (changing the phrase) law and morality, in so far as they *are* what they *ought* to be, conform, or are not repugnant, to the law of God. Consequently, an all-important object of the science of ethics (or, borrowing the language of Bentham, 'the science of deontology') is to determine the nature of the index to the tacit commands of the Deity, or the nature of the signs or proofs through which those commands may be known. I mean by 'the science of ethics' (or by 'the science of deontology'), the science of law and morality as they respectively *ought* to be, or (changing the phrase) the science of law and morality as they respectively *must* be *if they conform to their measure or test*. That department of the science of ethics, which is concerned especially with positive law as it ought to be, is styled the science of legislation: that department of the science of ethics, which is concerned especially with positive morality as it ought to be, has hardly gotten a name perfectly appropriate and distinctive. Now, though the science of legislation (or of positive law as it *ought* to be) is not the science of jurisprudence (or of positive law as it *is*), still the sciences are connected by numerous and indissoluble ties. Since, then, the nature of the index to the tacit command of the Deity is an all-important object of the science of legislation, it is a fit and important object of the kindred science of jurisprudence.

There are certain current and important misconceptions of the theory of general utility. There are certain objections resting on those misconceptions, which frequently are urged against it. There are also considerable difficulties with which it really is embarrassed. Labouring to rectify those misconceptions, to answer those objections, and to solve or extenuate those difficulties, I probably dwell upon the theory somewhat longer than I ought. Deeply convinced of its truth and importance, and therefore earnestly intent on commending it to the minds of others, I probably wander into ethical disquisitions which are not precisely in keeping with the subject and scope of my Course. If I am guilty of this departure from the subject and scope of my Course, the absorbing interest of the purpose which leads me from my proper path will excuse, to indulgent readers, my offence against rigorous logic.

II (b). At the beginning of the *fifth* lecture, I distribute laws or rules under two classes: first, laws properly so called, with such improper laws as are closely analogous to the proper; secondly, those improper laws which are remotely analogous to the proper, and which I style, therefore, laws metaphorical or figurative. I also distribute laws proper, with such improper laws as are closely analogous to the proper, under three classes: namely, the laws properly so called which I style the laws of God; the laws properly so called which I style positive laws; and the laws properly so called, with the laws improperly so called, which I style positive morality or positive moral rules. I assign moreover my reasons for marking those several classes with those respective names.

Having determined, in preceding lectures, the characters or distinguishing marks of the divine laws, I determine, in the fifth lecture, the characters or distinguishing marks of positive moral rules: that is to say, such of the laws or rules set by men to men as are not armed with legal sanctions; or such of those laws or rules as are not positive laws, or are not appropriate matter for general or particular jurisprudence. Having determined the distinguishing marks of positive moral rules, I determine the respective characters of their two dissimilar kinds: namely, the positive moral rules which are laws imperative and proper, and the positive moral rules which are laws set by opinion.

The divine law, positive law and positive morality are mutually related in various ways. To illustrate their mutual relations, I advert, in the fifth lecture, to the cases wherein they agree, wherein they disagree without conflicting, and wherein they disagree and conflict.

I show, in the same lecture, that my distribution of laws proper, and of such improper laws as are closely analogous to the proper, tallies, in the main, with a division of laws which is given incidentally by Locke in his *Essay on Human Understanding*.

II (c). At the end of the same lecture, I determine the characters or distinguishing marks of laws metaphorical or figurative. And I show that laws which are merely laws through metaphors are blended and confounded, by writers of celebrity, with laws imperative and proper.

II (d). In the *sixth* and *last* lecture, I determine the characters of laws positive: that is to say, laws which are simply and strictly so called, and which form the appropriate matter of general and particular jurisprudence.

Determining the characters of positive laws, I determine implicitly the notion of sovereignty with the implied or correlative notion of independent political society. For the essential difference of a positive law (or the difference that severs it from a law which is not a positive law) may be stated generally in the following manner. Every positive law, or every law simply and strictly so called, is set by a sovereign person, or a sovereign body of persons, to a member or members of the independent political society wherein that person or body is sovereign or supreme. Or (changing the phrase) it is set by a monarch, or sovereign number, to a person or persons in a state of subjection to its author.

To elucidate the nature of sovereignty, and of the independent political society that sovereignty implies, I examine various topics which I arrange under the following heads: first, the possible forms or shapes of supreme political government; secondly, the limits, real or imaginary, of supreme political power; thirdly, the origin or causes of political government and society. Examining those various topics, I complete my description of the limit or boundary by which positive law is severed from positive morality. For I distinguish them at certain points whereat they seemingly blend, or whereat the line which divides them is not easily perceptible.

The essential difference of a positive law (or the difference that severs it from a law which is not a positive law) may be stated generally as I have stated it above. But the foregoing general statement of that essential difference is open to certain correctives. And with a brief allusion to those correctives, I close the sixth and last lecture.

LECTURE I

SYNOPSIS OF LECTURE I

The *purpose* of the following attempt to determine the province of jurisprudence, stated or suggested
The *manner* of the following attempt to determine the province of jurisprudence
Law: what, in most comprehensive literal sense
Law of God
Human Laws. Two classes
First class. Laws set by political superiors
Second class. Laws set by men not political superiors
Objects improperly, but by close analogy, termed laws
The two last placed in one class under the name *positive morality*
Objects metaphorically termed laws
Laws or rules, *properly* so called, are a species of commands
The meaning of the term *command*
The meaning of the term *duty*
The terms *command* and *duty* are correlative
The meaning of the term *sanction*
To the existence of a command, a duty, and a sanction, a *violent* motive to compliance is not requisite
Rewards are not *sanctions*
The meaning of the term *command*, briefly restated
The inseparable connection of the three terms, *command*, *duty*, and *sanction*

TEXT OF LECTURE I

The purpose *of the following attempt to determine the province of jurisprudence, stated or suggested*

The matter of jurisprudence is positive law: law, simply and strictly so called, or law set by political superiors to political inferiors. But positive law (or law, simply and strictly so called) is often confounded with objects to which it is related by *resemblance*, and with objects to which it is related in the way of *analogy*: with objects which are *also* signified, *properly* and *improperly*, by the large and vague expression *law*. To obviate the difficulties springing from that confusion, I begin my projected Course with determining the province of jurisprudence, or with distinguishing the matter of jurisprudence from those various related objects: trying to define the subject of which I intend to treat, before I endeavour to analyse its numerous and complicated parts.

Law: what, in most comprehensive literal sense

A law, in the most general and comprehensive acceptation in which the term, in its literal meaning, is employed, may be said to be a rule laid down for the guidance of an intelligent being by an intelligent being having power over him. Under this definition are concluded, and without impropriety, several species. It is necessary to define accurately the line of demarcation which separates these species from one another, as much mistiness and intricacy has been infused into the science of jurisprudence by their being confounded or not clearly distinguished. In the comprehensive sense above indicated, or in the largest meaning which it has, without extension by metaphor or analogy, the term *law* embraces the following objects: laws set by God to his human creatures, and laws set by men to men.

Law of God

The whole or a portion of the laws set by God to men is frequently styled the law of nature, or natural law, being, in truth, the only natural law of which it is possible to speak without a metaphor, or without a blending of objects which ought to be distinguished broadly. But, rejecting the appellation Law of Nature as ambiguous and misleading, I name those laws or rules, as considered collectively or in a mass, the *Divine law*, or the *law of God*.

Human laws. Two classes

Laws set by men to men are of two leading or principal classes: classes which are often blended, although they differ extremely; and which, for that reason, should be severed precisely, and opposed distinctly and conspicuously.

First class. Laws set by political superiors

Of the laws or rules set by men to men, some are established by *political* superiors, sovereign and subject: by persons exercising supreme and subordinate *government*, in independent nations, or independent political societies. The aggregate of the rules thus established, or some aggregate forming a portion of that aggregate, is the appropriate matter of jurisprudence, general or particular. To the aggregate of the rules thus established, or to some aggregate forming a portion of that aggregate, the term *law*, as used simply and strictly, is exclusively applied. But, as contradistinguished to *natural* law, or to the law of *nature* (meaning by those expressions the law of God), the aggregate of the rules, established by political superiors, is frequently styled *positive* law, or law existing *by position*. As contradistinguished to the rules which I style *positive morality*, and on which I shall touch immediately, the aggregate of the rules, established by political superiors, may also be marked commodiously with the name of *positive law*. For the sake, then, of getting a name brief and distinctive at once, and agreeably to frequent usage, I style that aggregate of rules, or any portion of that aggregate, *positive law*: though rules, which are *not* established by political superiors, are also *positive*, or exist by *position*, if they be rules or laws, in the proper signification of the term.

Second class. Laws set by men not political superiors

Though *some* of the laws or rules, which are set by men to men, are established by political superiors, *others* are *not* established by political superiors, or are not established by political superiors, in that capacity or character.

Objects improperly but by close analogy termed laws

Closely analogous to human laws of this second class, are a set of objects frequently but *improperly* termed laws, being rules set and enforced by *mere opinion*, that is, by the opinions or sentiments held or felt by an indeterminate body of men in regard to human conduct. Instances of such a use of the term *law* are the expressions 'The law of honour'; 'The law set by fashion'; and rules of this species constitute much of what is usually termed 'International law'.

The two last placed in one class under the name positive morality

The aggregate of human laws properly so called belonging to the second of the classes above mentioned, with the aggregate of objects *improperly* but by *close analogy* termed laws, I place together in a common class, and denote them by the term *positive morality*. The name *morality* severs them from *positive law*, while the epithet *positive* disjoins them from the *law of God*. And to the end of obviating confusion, it is necessary or expedient that they *should* be disjoined from the latter by that distinguishing epithet. For the name *morality* (or *morals*), when standing unqualified or alone, denotes indifferently either of the following objects: namely, positive morality *as it is*, or without regard to its merits; and positive morality *as it would be*, if it conformed to the law of God, and were, therefore, deserving of *approbation*.

Objects metaphorically termed laws

Besides the various sorts of rules which are included in the literal acceptation of the term law, and those which are by a close and striking analogy, though improperly, termed laws, there are numerous applications of the term law, which rest upon a slender analogy and are merely metaphorical or figurative. Such is the case when we talk of *laws* observed by the lower animals; of *laws* regulating the growth or decay of vegetables; of *laws* determining the movements of inanimate bodies or masses. For where *intelligence* is not, or where it is too bounded to take the name of *reason*, and, therefore, is too bounded to conceive the purpose of a law, there is not the *will* which law can work on, or which duty can incite or restrain. Yet through these misapplications of a *name*, flagrant as the metaphor is, has the field of jurisprudence and morals been deluged with muddy speculation.

Having suggested the *purpose* of my attempt to determine the province of jurisprudence: to distinguish positive law, the appropriate matter of jurisprudence, from the various objects to which it is related by resemblance, and to which it is related, nearly or remotely, by a strong or slender analogy: I shall now state the essentials of *a law* or *rule* (taken with the largest signification which can be given to the term *properly*).

Laws or rules properly *so called, are a species of commands*

Every *law* or *rule* (taken with the largest signification which can be given to the term *properly*) is a *command*. Or, rather, laws or rules, properly so called, are a *species* of commands.

Now, since the term *command* comprises the term *law*, the first is the simpler as well as the larger of the two. But, simple as it is, it admits of explanation. And, since it is the *key* to the sciences of jurisprudence and morals, its meaning should be analysed with precision.

Accordingly, I shall endeavour, in the first instance, to analyse the meaning of '*command*': an analysis which I fear will task the patience of my hearers, but which they will bear with cheerfulness, or, at least, with resignation, if they consider the difficulty of performing it. The elements of a science are precisely the parts of it which are explained least easily. Terms that are the largest, and, therefore, the simplest of a series are without equivalent expressions into which we can resolve them *concisely*. And when we endeavour to *define* them, or to translate them into terms which we suppose are better understood, we are forced upon awkward and tedious circumlocutions.

The meaning of the term command

If you express or intimate a wish that I shall do or forbear from some act, and if you will visit me with an evil in case I comply not with your wish, the *expression* or *intimation* of your wish is a *command*. A command is distinguished from other significations of desire, not by the style in which the desire is signified, but by the power and the purpose of the party commanding to inflict an evil or pain in case the desire be disregarded. If you cannot or will not harm me in case I comply not with your wish, the expression of your wish is not a command, although you utter your wish in imperative phrase. If you are able and willing to harm me in case I comply not with your wish, the expression of your wish amounts to a command, although you are prompted by a spirit of courtesy to utter it in the shape of a request. '*Preces* erant, sed *quibus contradici non posset*'. Such is the language of Tacitus, when speaking of a petition by the soldiery to a son and lieutenant of Vespasian.

A command, then, is a signification of desire. But a command is distinguished from other significations of desire by this peculiarity: that the party to whom it is directed is liable to evil from the other, in case he comply not with the desire.

The meaning of the term duty

Being liable to evil from you if I comply not with a wish which you signify, I am *bound* or *obliged* by your command, or I lie under a *duty* to obey it. If, in spite of that evil in prospect, I comply not with the wish which you signify, I am said to disobey your command, or to violate the duty which it imposes.

The terms command *and* duty *are correlative*

Command and duty are, therefore, correlative terms: the meaning denoted by each being implied or supposed by the other. Or (changing the expression) wherever a duty lies, a command has been signified; and whenever a command is signified, a duty is imposed.

Concisely expressed, the meaning of the correlative expressions is this. He who will inflict an evil in case his desire be disregarded, utters a command by expressing or intimating his desire: he who is liable to the evil in case he disregard the desire, is bound or obliged by the command.

The meaning of the term sanction

The evil which will probably be incurred in case a command be disobeyed or (to use an equivalent expression) in case a duty be broken, is frequently called a *sanction*, or an *enforcement of obedience*. Or (varying the phrase) the command or the duty is said to be *sanctioned* or *enforced* by the chance of incurring the evil.

Considered as thus abstracted from the command and the duty which it enforces, the evil to be incurred by disobedience is frequently styled a *punishment*. But, as punishments, strictly so called, are only a *class* of sanctions, the term is too narrow to express the meaning adequately.

To the existence of a command, a duty, and a sanction, a violent *motive to compliance is not requisite*

I observe that Dr Paley, in his analysis of the term *obligation*, lays much stress upon the *violence* of the motive to compliance. In so far as I can gather a meaning from his loose and inconsistent statement, his meaning appears to be this: that unless the motive to compliance be *violent* or *intense*, the expression or intimation of a wish is not a *command*, nor does the party to whom it is directed lie under a *duty* to regard it.

If he means, by a *violent* motive, a motive operating with certainty, his proposition is manifestly false. The greater the evil to be incurred in case the wish be disregarded, and the greater the chance of incurring it on that same event, the greater, no doubt, is the *chance* that the wish will *not* be disregarded. But no conceivable motive will *certainly* determine to compliance, or no conceivable motive will render obedience inevitable. If Paley's proposition be true, in the sense which I have now ascribed to it, commands and duties are simply impossible. Or, reducing his proposition to absurdity by a consequence as manifestly false, commands and duties are possible, but are never disobeyed or broken.

If he means by a *violent* motive, an evil which inspires fear, his meaning is simply this: that the party bound by a command is bound by the prospect of an evil. For that which is not feared is not apprehended as an evil: or (changing the shape of the expression) is not an evil in prospect.

The truth is that the magnitude of the eventual evil, and the magnitude of the chance of incurring it, are foreign to the matter in question. The greater the eventual evil, and the greater the chance of incurring it, the greater is the efficacy of the command, and the greater is the strength of the obligation: or (substituting expressions exactly equivalent), the greater is the *chance* that the command will be obeyed, and that the duty will not be broken. But where there is the smallest chance of incurring the smallest evil, the expression of a wish amounts to a command, and, therefore, imposes a duty. The sanction, if you will, is feeble or insufficient; but still there *is* a sanction, and, therefore, a duty and a command.

Rewards are not sanctions

By some celebrated writers (by Locke, Bentham, and, I think, Paley), the term *sanction*, or *enforcement of obedience*, is applied to conditional good as well as to conditional evil: to reward as well as to punishment. But, with all my habitual veneration for the names of Locke and Bentham, I think that this extension of the term is pregnant with confusion and perplexity.

Rewards are, indisputably, *motives* to comply with the wishes of others. But to talk of commands and duties as *sanctioned* or *enforced* by rewards, or to talk of rewards as *obliging* or *constraining* to obedience, is surely a wide departure from the established meaning of the terms.

If *you* expressed a desire that *I* should render a service, and if you proffered a reward as the motive or inducement to render it, *you* would scarcely be said to *command* the service, nor should *I*, in ordinary language, be *obliged* to render it. In ordinary language, *you* would *promise* me a reward, on condition of my rendering the service, whilst *I* might be *incited* or *persuaded* to render it by the hope of obtaining the reward.

Again: if a law hold out a *reward* as an inducement to do some act, an eventual *right* is conferred, and not an *obligation* imposed, upon those who shall act accordingly, the *imperative* part of the law being addressed or directed to the party whom it requires to *render* the reward.

In short, I am determined or inclined to comply with the wish of another, by the fear of disadvantage or evil. I am also determined or inclined to comply with the wish of another, by the hope of advantage or good. But it is only by the chance of incurring *evil*, that I am *bound* or *obliged* to compliance. It is only by conditional *evil*, that duties are *sanctioned* or *enforced*. It is the power and the purpose of inflicting eventual *evil*, and *not* the power and the purpose of imparting eventual *good*, which gives to the expression of a wish the name of a *command*.

If we put *reward* into the import of the term *sanction*, we must engage in a toilsome struggle with the current of ordinary speech; and shall often slide unconsciously, notwithstanding our efforts to the contrary, into the narrower and customary meaning.

The meaning of the term command, *briefly restated*

It appears, then, from what has been premised, that the ideas or notions comprehended by the term *command* are the following:

1. A wish or desire conceived by a rational being, that another rational being shall do or forbear.
2. An evil to proceed from the former, and to be incurred by the latter, in case the latter comply not with the wish.
3. An expression or intimation of the wish by words or other signs.

The inseparable connection of the three terms, command, duty, *and* sanction

It also appears from what has been premised, that *command*, *duty*, and *sanction* are inseparably connected terms: that each embraces the same ideas as the others, though each denotes those ideas in a peculiar order or series.

'A wish conceived by one, and expressed or intimated to another, with an evil to be inflicted and incurred in case the wish be disregarded', are signified directly and indirectly by each of the three expressions. Each is the name of the same complex notion.

The manner of that connection

But when I am talking *directly* of the expression or intimation of the wish, I employ the term *command*: the expression or intimation of the wish being presented *prominently* to my hearer; whilst the evil to be incurred, with the chance of incurring it, are kept (if I may so express myself) in the background of my picture.

When I am talking *directly* of the chance of incurring the evil, or (changing the expression) of the liability or obnoxiousness to the evil, I employ the term *duty*, or the term *obligation*: the liability or obnoxiousness to the evil being put foremost, and the rest of the complex notion being signified implicitly.

When I am talking *immediately* of the evil itself, I employ the term *sanction*, or a term of the like import, the evil to be incurred being signified directly; whilst the obnoxiousness to that evil, with the expression or intimation of the wish, are indicated indirectly or obliquely.

To those who are familiar with the language of logicians (language unrivalled for brevity, distinctness, and precision), I can express my meaning accurately in a breath: each of the three terms *signifies* the same notion; but each *denotes* a different part of that notion, and *connotes* the residue.

Laws *or* rules *distinguished from* commands *which are* occasional *or* particular

Commands are of two species. Some are *laws* or *rules*. The others have not acquired an appropriate name, nor does language afford an expression which will mark them briefly and precisely. I must, therefore, note them as well as I can by the ambiguous and inexpressive name of '*occasional* or *particular* commands'.

The term *laws* or *rules* being not unfrequently applied to occasional or particular commands, it is hardly possible to describe a line of separation which shall consist in every respect with established forms of speech. But the distinction between laws and particular commands may, I think, be stated in the following manner.

By every command, the party to whom it is directed is obliged to do or to forbear.

Now where it obliges *generally* to acts or forbearances of a *class*, a command is a law or rule. But where it obliges to a *specific* act or forbearance, or to acts or forbearances which it determines *specifically* or *individually*, a command is occasional or particular. In other words, a class or description of acts is determined by a law or rule, and acts of that class or description are enjoined or forbidden generally. But where a command is occasional or particular, the act or acts, which the command enjoins or forbids, are assigned or determined by their specific or individual natures as well as by the class or description to which they belong.

The statement which I have given in abstract expressions I will now endeavour to illustrate by apt examples.

If you command your servant to go on a given errand, or *not* to leave your house on a given evening, or to rise at such an hour on such a morning, or to rise at that hour during the next week or month, the command is occasional or particular. For the act or acts enjoined or forbidden are specially determined or assigned.

But if you command him *simply* to rise at that hour, or to rise at that hour *always*, or to rise at that hour *till further orders*, it may be said, with propriety, that you lay down a *rule* for the guidance of your servant's conduct. For no specific act is assigned by the command, but the command obliges him generally to acts of a determined class.

If a regiment be ordered to attack or defend a post, or to quell a riot, or to march from their present quarters, the command is occasional or particular. But an order to exercise daily till further orders shall be given would be called a *general* order, and *might* be called a *rule*.

If Parliament prohibited simply the exportation of corn, either for a given period or indefinitely, it would establish a law or rule: a *kind* or *sort* of acts being determined by the command, and acts of that kind or sort being *generally* forbidden. But an order issued by Parliament to meet an impending scarcity, and stopping the exportation of corn *then shipped and in port*, would not be a law or rule, though issued by the sovereign legislature. The order regarding exclusively a specified quantity of corn, the negative acts or forbearances, enjoined by the command, would be determined specifically or individually by the determinate nature of their subject.

As issued by a sovereign legislature, and as wearing the form of a law, the order which I have now imagined would probably be *called* a law. And hence the difficulty of drawing a distinct boundary between laws and occasional commands.

Again: an act which is not an offence, according to the existing law, moves the sovereign to displeasure and, though the authors of the act are legally innocent or unoffending, the sovereign commands that they shall be punished. As enjoining a specific punishment in that specific case, and as not enjoining generally acts or forbearances of a class, the order uttered by the sovereign is not a law or rule.

Whether such an order would be *called* a law, seems to depend upon circumstances which are purely immaterial: immaterial, that is, with reference to the present purpose, though material with reference to others. If made by a sovereign assembly deliberately, and with the forms of legislation, it would probably be called a law. If uttered by an absolute monarch, without deliberation or ceremony, it would scarcely be confounded with acts of legislation, and would be styled an arbitrary command. Yet, on either of these suppositions, its nature would be the same. It would not be a law or rule, but an occasional or particular command of the sovereign One or Number.

To conclude with an example which best illustrates the distinction, and which shows the importance of the distinction most conspicuously, *judicial commands* are commonly occasional or particular, although the commands which they are calculated to enforce are commonly laws or rules.

For instance, the lawgiver commands that thieves shall be hanged. A specific theft and a specified thief being given, the judge commands that the thief shall be hanged, agreeably to the command of the lawgiver.

Now the lawgiver determines a class or description of acts; prohibits acts of the class generally and indefinitely; and commands, with the like generality, that punishment shall follow transgression. The command of the lawgiver is, therefore, a law or rule. But the command of the judge is occasional or particular. For he orders a specific punishment, as the consequence of a specific offence.

According to the line of separation which I have now attempted to describe, a law and a particular command are distinguished thus: acts or forbearances of a *class* are enjoined *generally* by the former. Acts *determined specifically*, are enjoined or forbidden by the latter.

A different line of separation has been drawn by Blackstone and others. According to Blackstone and others, a law and a particular command are distinguished in the following manner: a law obliges *generally* the members of the given community, or a law obliges *generally* persons of a given class. A particular command obliges a *single* person, or persons whom it determines *individually*.

That laws and particular commands are not to be distinguished thus, will appear on a moment's reflection.

For, *first*, commands which oblige generally the members of the given community, or commands which oblige generally persons of given classes, are not always laws or rules.

Thus, in the case already supposed; that in which the sovereign commands that all corn actually shipped for exportation be stopped and detained; the command is obligatory upon the whole community, but as it obliges them only to a set of acts individually assigned, it is not a law. Again, suppose the sovereign to issue an order, enforced by penalties, for a general mourning, on occasion of a public calamity. Now, though it is addressed to the community at large, the order is scarcely a rule, in the usual acceptation of the term. For, though it obliges generally the members of the entire community, it obliges to acts which it assigns specifically, instead of obliging generally to acts or forbearances of a class. If the sovereign commanded that *black* should be the dress of his subjects, his command would amount to a law. But if he commanded them to wear it on a specified occasion, his command would be merely particular.

And, *secondly*, a command which obliges exclusively persons individually determined may amount, notwithstanding, to a law or a rule.

For example, a father may set a *rule* to his child or children; a guardian, to his ward; a master, to his slave or servant. And certain of God's *laws* were as binding on the first man, as they are binding at this hour on the millions who have sprung from his loins.

Most, indeed, of the laws which are established by political superiors, or most of the laws which are simply and strictly so called, oblige generally the members of the political community, or oblige generally persons of a class. To frame a system of duties for every individual of the community were simply impossible; and if it were possible, it were utterly useless. Most of the laws established by political superiors are, therefore, *general* in a twofold manner: as enjoining or forbidding generally acts of kinds or sorts; and as binding the whole community, or, at least, whole classes of its members.

But if we suppose that Parliament creates and grants an office, and that Parliament binds the grantee to services of a given description, we suppose a law established by political superiors, and yet exclusively binding a specified or determinate person.

Laws established by political superiors, and exclusively binding specified or determinate persons, are styled, in the language of the Roman jurists, *privilegia*. Though that, indeed, is a name which will hardly denote them distinctly: for, like most of the leading terms in actual systems of law, it is not the name of a definite class of objects, but of a heap of heterogeneous objects.[1]

The definition of a law or rule, properly *so called*

It appears, from what has been premised, that a law, properly so called, may be defined in the following manner.

A law is a command which obliges a person or persons.

But, as contradistinguished or opposed to an occasional or particular command, a law is a command which obliges a person or persons, and obliges *generally* to acts or forbearances of a *class*.

In language more popular but less distinct and precise, a law is a command which obliges a person or persons to a *course* of conduct.

The meaning of the correlative terms superior *and* inferior

Laws and other commands are said to proceed from *superiors*, and to bind or oblige *inferiors*. I will, therefore, analyse the meaning of those correlative expressions; and will try to strip them of a certain mystery, by which that simple meaning appears to be obscured.

Superiority is often synonymous with *precedence* or *excellence*. We talk of superiors in rank; of superiors in wealth; of superiors in virtue: comparing certain persons with certain other persons; and meaning that the former precede or excel the latter in rank, in wealth or in virtue.

But, taken with the meaning wherein I here understand it, the term *superiority* signifies *might*: the power of affecting others with evil or pain, and of forcing them, through fear of that evil, to fashion their conduct to one's wishes.

For example, God is emphatically the *superior* of Man. For his power of affecting us with pain, and of forcing us to comply with his will, is unbounded and resistless.

To a limited extent, the sovereign One or Number is the superior of the subject or citizen: the master, of the slave or servant; the father, of the child.

In short, whoever can *oblige* another to comply with his wishes, is the *superior* of that other, so far as the ability reaches: the party who is obnoxious to the impending evil, being, to that same extent, the *inferior*.

The might or superiority of God, is simple or absolute. But in all or most cases of human superiority, the relation of superior and inferior, and the relation of inferior and superior, are reciprocal. Or (changing the expression) the party who is the superior, as viewed from one aspect, is the inferior as viewed from another.

For example, to an indefinite, though limited extent, the monarch is the superior of the governed: his power being commonly sufficient to enforce compliance with his will. But the governed, collectively or in mass, are also the superior of the monarch who is checked in the abuse of his might by his fear of exciting their anger; and of rousing to active resistance the might which slumbers in the multitude.

A member of a sovereign assembly is the superior of the judge: the judge being bound by the law which proceeds from that sovereign body. But, in his character of citizen or subject, he is the inferior of the judge: the judge being the minister of the law, and armed with the power of enforcing it.

It appears, then, that the term *superiority* (like the terms *duty* and *sanction*) is implied by the term *command*. For superiority is the power of enforcing compliance with a wish: and the expression or intimation of a wish, with the power and the purpose of enforcing it, are the constituent elements of a command.

'That *laws* emanate from *superiors*' is, therefore, an identical proposition. For the meaning which it affects to impart is contained in its subject.

If I mark the peculiar source of a given law, or if I mark the peculiar source of laws of a given class, it is possible that I am saying something which may instruct the hearer. But to affirm of laws universally 'that they flow from *superiors*', or to affirm of laws universally 'that *inferiors* are bound to obey them', is the merest tautology and trifling.

*Laws (*improperly *so called) which are not commands*

Like most of the leading terms in the sciences of jurisprudence and morals, the term *laws* is extremely ambiguous. Taken with the largest signification which can be given to the term properly, *laws* are a species of *commands*. But the term is improperly applied to various objects which have nothing of the imperative character: to objects which are *not* commands; and which, therefore, are *not* laws, properly so called.

Accordingly, the proposition 'that laws are commands' must be taken with limitations. Or, rather, we must distinguish the various meanings of the term *laws*; and must restrict the proposition to that class of objects which is embraced by the largest signification that can be given to the term properly.

I have already indicated, and shall hereafter more fully describe, the objects improperly termed laws, which are *not* within the province of jurisprudence (being either rules enforced by opinion and closely analogous to laws properly so called, or being laws so called by a metaphorical application of the term merely). There are other objects improperly termed laws (not being commands) which yet may properly be included within the province of jurisprudence. These I shall endeavour to particularise:

One. Acts on the part of legislatures to *explain* positive law, can scarcely be called laws, in the proper signification of the term. Working no change in the actual duties of the governed, but simply declaring what those duties *are*, they properly are acts of *interpretation* by legislative authority. Or, to borrow an expression from the writers on the Roman Law, they are acts of *authentic* interpretation.

But, this notwithstanding, they are frequently styled laws; *declaratory* laws, or declaratory statutes. They must, therefore, be noted as forming an exception to the proposition 'that laws are a species of commands'.

It often, indeed, happens (as I shall show in the proper place), that laws declaratory in name are imperative in effect: legislative, like judicial interpretation, being frequently deceptive; and establishing new law, under guise of expounding the old.

Two. Laws to repeal laws, and to release from existing duties, must also be excepted from the proposition 'that laws are a species of commands'. In so far as they release from duties imposed by existing laws, they are not commands, but revocations of commands. They authorise or permit the parties, to whom the repeal extends, to do or to forbear from acts which they were commanded to forbear from or to do. And, considered with regard to *this*, their immediate or direct purpose, they are often named *permissive laws*, or, more briefly and more properly, *permissions*.

Remotely and indirectly, indeed, permissive laws are often or always imperative. For the parties released from duties are restored to liberties or rights: and duties answering those rights are, therefore, created or revived.

But this is a matter which I shall examine with exactness, when I analyse the expressions 'legal right', 'permission by the sovereign or state', and 'civil or political liberty'.

Three. Imperfect laws, or laws of imperfect obligation, must also be excepted from the proposition 'that laws are a species of commands'.

An imperfect law (with the sense wherein the term is used by the Roman jurists) is a law which wants a sanction, and which, therefore, is not binding. A law declaring that certain acts are crimes, but annexing no punishment to the commission of acts of the class, is the simplest and most obvious example.

Though the author of an imperfect law signifies a desire, he manifests no purpose of enforcing compliance with the desire. But where there is not a purpose of enforcing compliance with the desire, the expression of a desire is not a command. Consequently, an imperfect law is not so properly a law, as counsel, or exhortation, addressed by a superior to inferiors.

Examples of imperfect laws are cited by the Roman jurists. But with us in England, laws professedly imperative are always (I believe) perfect or obligatory. Where the English legislature affects to command, the English tribunals not unreasonably presume that the legislature exacts obedience. And, if no specific sanction be annexed to a given law, a sanction is supplied by the courts of justice, agreeably to a general maxim which obtains in cases of the kind.

The imperfect laws, of which I am now speaking, are laws which are imperfect, in the sense of the *Roman jurists*: that is to say, laws which speak the desires of political superiors, but which their authors (by oversight or design) have not provided with sanctions. Many of the writers on *morals*, and on the so-called *law of nature*, have annexed a different meaning to the term *imperfect*. Speaking of imperfect obligations, they commonly mean duties which are *not legal*: duties imposed by commands of God, or duties imposed by positive morality, as contradistinguished to duties imposed by positive law. An imperfect obligation, in the sense of the Roman jurists, is exactly equivalent to no obligation at all. For the term *imperfect* denotes simply that the law wants the sanction appropriate to laws of the kind. An imperfect obligation, in the other meaning of the expression, is a religious or a moral obligation. The term *imperfect* does not denote that the law imposing the duty wants the appropriate sanction. It denotes that the law imposing the duty is *not* a law established by a political superior: that it wants that *perfect*, or that surer or more cogent sanction, which is imparted by the sovereign or state.

Laws (properly *so called) which may* seem *not imperative*

I believe that I have now reviewed all the classes of objects, to which the term *laws* is improperly applied. The laws (improperly so called) which I have here lastly enumerated, are (I think) the only laws which are not commands, and which yet may be properly included within the province of jurisprudence. But though these, with the so-called laws set by opinion and the objects metaphorically termed laws, are the only laws which *really* are not commands, there are certain laws (properly so called) which may *seem* not imperative. Accordingly, I will subjoin a few remarks upon laws of this dubious character.

One. There are laws, it may be said, which *merely* create *rights*, and, seeing that every command imposes a *duty*, laws of this nature are not imperative.

But, as I have intimated already, and shall show completely hereafter, there are no laws *merely* creating *rights*. There are laws, it is true, which *merely* create *duties*: duties not correlating with correlating rights, and which, therefore may be styled *absolute*. But every law, really conferring a right, imposes expressly or tacitly a *relative* duty, or a duty correlating with the right. If it specify the remedy to be given, in case the right shall be infringed, it imposes the relative duty expressly. If the remedy to be given be not specified, it refers tacitly to pre-existing law, and clothes the right which it purports to create with a remedy provided by that law. Every law, really conferring a right, is, therefore, imperative: as imperative, as if its only purpose were the creation of a duty, or as if the relative duty, which it inevitably imposes, were merely absolute.

The meanings of the term *right*, are various and perplexed; taken with its proper meaning, it comprises ideas which are numerous and complicated; and the searching and extensive analysis, which the term, therefore, requires, would occupy more room than could be given to it in the present lecture. It is not, however, necessary, that the analysis should be performed here. I purpose, in my earlier lectures, to determine the province of jurisprudence; or to distinguish the laws established by political superiors, from the various laws, proper and improper, with which they are frequently confounded. And this I may accomplish exactly enough, without a nice inquiry into the import of the term *right*.

Two. According to an opinion which I must notice *incidentally* here, though the subject to which it relates will be treated *directly* hereafter, *customary laws* must be excepted from the proposition 'that laws are a species of commands'.

By many of the admirers of customary laws (and, especially, of their German admirers), they are thought to oblige legally (independently of the sovereign or state), *because* the citizens or subjects have observed or kept them. Agreeably to this opinion, they are not the *creatures* of the sovereign or state, although the sovereign or state may abolish them at pleasure. Agreeably to this opinion, they are positive law (or law, strictly so called), inasmuch as they are enforced by the courts of justice. But, that notwithstanding, they exist *as positive law* by the spontaneous adoption of the governed, and not by position or establishment on the part of political superiors. Consequently, customary laws, considered as positive law, are not commands. And, consequently, customary laws, considered as positive law, are not laws or rules properly so called.

An opinion less mysterious, but somewhat allied to this, is not uncommonly held by the adverse party: by the party which is strongly opposed to customary law; and to all law made judicially, or in the way of judicial legislation. According to the latter opinion, all judge-made law, or all judge-made law established by *subject* judges, is purely the creature of the judges by whom it is established immediately. To impute it to the sovereign legislature, or to suppose that it speaks the will of the sovereign legislature, is one of the foolish or knavish *fictions* with which lawyers, in every age and nation, have perplexed and darkened the simplest and clearest truths.

I think it will appear, on a moment's reflection, that each of these opinions is groundless: that customary law is *imperative*, in the proper signification of the term; and that all judge-made law is the creature of the sovereign or state.

At its origin, a custom is a rule of conduct which the governed observe spontaneously, or not in pursuance of a law set by a political superior. The custom is transmuted into positive law, when it is adopted as such by the courts of justice, and when the judicial decisions fashioned upon it are enforced by the power of the state. But before it is adopted by the courts, and clothed with the legal sanction, it is merely a rule of positive morality: a rule generally observed by the citizens or subjects; but deriving the only force, which it can be said to possess, from the general disapprobation falling on those who transgress it.

Now when judges transmute a custom into a legal rule (or make a legal rule not suggested by a custom), the legal rule which they establish is established by the sovereign legislature. A subordinate or subject judge is merely a minister. The portion of the sovereign power which lies at his disposition is merely delegated. The rules which he makes derive their legal force from authority given by the state: an authority which the state may confer expressly, but which it commonly imparts in the way of acquiescence. For, since the state may reverse the rules which he makes, and yet permits him to enforce them by the power of the political community, its sovereign will 'that his rules shall obtain as law' is clearly evinced by its conduct, though not by its express declaration.

The admirers of customary law love to trick out their idol with mysterious and imposing attributes. But to those who can see the difference between positive law and morality, there is nothing of mystery about it. Considered as rules of positive morality, customary laws arise from the consent of the governed, and not from the position or establishment of political superiors. But, considered as moral rules turned into positive laws, customary laws are established by the state: established by the state directly, when the customs are promulged in its statutes; established by the state circuitously, when the customs are adopted by its tribunals.

The opinion of the party which abhors judge-made laws springs from their inadequate conception of the nature of commands.

Like other significations of desire, a command is express or tacit. If the desire be signified by *words* (written or spoken), the command is express. If the desire be signified by conduct (or by any signs of desire which are *not* words), the command is tacit.

Now when customs are turned into legal rules by decisions of subject judges, the legal rules which emerge from the customs are *tacit* commands of the sovereign legislature. The state, which is able to abolish, permits its ministers to enforce them: and it, therefore, signifies its pleasure, by that its voluntary acquiescence, 'that they shall serve as a law to the governed'.

My present purpose is merely this: to prove that the positive law styled *customary* (and all positive law made judicially) is established by the state directly or circuitously, and, therefore, is *imperative*. I am far from disputing that law made judicially (or in the way of improper legislation) and law made by statute (or in the properly legislative manner) are distinguished by weighty differences. I shall inquire, in future lectures, what those differences are; and why subject judges, who are properly ministers of the law, have commonly shared with the sovereign in the business of making it.

Laws which are not commands enumerated

I assume, then, that the only laws which are not imperative, and which belong to the subject-matter of jurisprudence, are the following:

1. Declaratory laws, or laws explaining the import of existing positive law.
2. Laws abrogating or repealing existing positive law.
3. Imperfect laws, or laws of imperfect obligation (with the sense wherein the expression is used by the Roman jurists).

But the space occupied in the science by these improper laws is comparatively narrow and insignificant. Accordingly, although I shall take them into account so often as I refer to them directly, I shall throw them out of account on other occasions. Or (changing the expression) I shall limit the term *law* to laws which are imperative, unless I extend it expressly to laws which are not.

Note

1. Where a *privilegium* merely imposes a duty, it exclusively obliges a determinate person or persons. But where a *privilegium* confers a right, and the right conferred *avails against the world at large*, the law is *privilegium* as viewed from a certain aspect, but is also *a general law* as viewed from another aspect. In respect of the right conferred, the law exclusively regards a determinate person, and, therefore, is *privilegium*. In respect of the duty imposed, and corresponding to the right conferred, the law regards generally the members of the entire community.

   This I shall explain particularly at a subsequent point of my Course, when I consider the peculiar nature of so-called *privilegia*, or of so-called *private laws*.

LECTURE II

SYNOPSIS OF LECTURE II

The connection of the second with the first lecture
The Divine laws, or the laws of God
Of the Divine laws, some are *revealed*, and others are *unrevealed*
Such of the Divine laws as are *revealed*
Such of the Divine laws as are *unrevealed*
What is the *index* to such of the Divine laws as are unrevealed?
The *hypotheses* or *theories* which regard the nature of that index
The hypothesis or theory of a *moral sense*, or *innate practical principles*; of a *practical reason*; of a *common sense*, etc. etc.
The theory or hypothesis of *utility*
A brief summary of the theory of utility
The following explanations of that summary briefly introduced
The true *tendency* of a human action, and the true *test* of that tendency
According to the theory of utility, God's commands are mostly *rules*
It does not follow from the theory of utility that *every* useful action is the object of a Divine injunction; and *every* pernicious action the object of a Divine prohibition
A current and specious objection to the theory of utility, introduced and stated
The *two* apt answers to the foregoing objection briefly introduced
The *first* answer to the foregoing objection stated
The *second* answer to the foregoing objection briefly introduced

If our conduct were truly adjusted to the principle of general utility, our conduct would conform, for the most part, to *rules*: rules which emanate from the Deity, and to which the tendencies of human actions are the guide or index

Theory and *practice* are inseparable

If our conduct were truly adjusted to the principle of general utility, our conduct would be guided, for the most part, by *sentiments* associated with *rules*: rules which emanate from the Deity, and to which the tendencies of human actions are the guide or index

If our conduct were truly adjusted to the principle of general utility, our conduct would conform, for the most part, to Divine *rules*, and would also be guided, for the most part, by *sentiments* associated with those rules. But, in anomalous and excepted cases (of comparatively rare occurrence) our conduct would be fashioned *directly* on the principle of general utility, or guided by a conjecture and comparison of *specific* or *particular* consequences

The *second* answer to the foregoing objection briefly resumed

TEXT OF LECTURE II

The connection of the second with the first lecture

In my first lecture, I stated or suggested the purpose and the manner of my attempt to determine the province of jurisprudence: to distinguish positive law, the appropriate matter of jurisprudence, from the various objects to which it is related by resemblance, and to which it is related, nearly or remotely, by a strong or slender analogy.

In pursuance of that purpose, and agreeably to that manner, I stated the essentials of a law or rule (taken with the largest signification which can be given to the term *properly*).

In pursuance of that purpose, and agreeably to that manner, I proceed to distinguish laws set by men to men from those Divine laws which are the ultimate test of human.

The Divine laws or the laws of God

The Divine laws, or the laws of God, are laws set by God to his human creatures. As I have intimated already, and shall show more fully hereafter, they are laws or rules, *properly* so called.

As distinguished from duties imposed by human laws, duties imposed by the Divine laws may be called *religious duties*.

As distinguished from violations of duties imposed by human laws, violations of religious duties are styled *sins*.

As distinguished from sanctions annexed to human laws, the sanctions annexed to the Divine laws may be called *religious sanctions*. They consist of the evils, or pains, which we may suffer here or hereafter, by the immediate appointment of God, and as *consequences* of breaking his commandments.

Of the Divine laws, some are revealed, *and others are* unrevealed

Of the Divine laws, or the laws of God, some are *revealed* or promulged, and others are *unrevealed*. Such of the laws of God as are unrevealed are not unfrequently denoted by the following names or phrases: 'the law of nature'; 'natural law'; 'the law manifested to man by the light of nature or reason'; 'the laws, precepts, or dictates of natural religion'.

The *revealed* law of God, and the portion of the law of God which is *unrevealed*, are manifested to men in different ways, or by different sets of signs.

Such of the Divine laws as are revealed

With regard to the laws which God is pleased to *reveal*, the way wherein they are manifested is easily conceived. They are *express* commands: portions of the *word* of God: commands signified to men through the medium of human language and uttered by God directly, or by servants whom he sends to announce them.

Such of the Divine laws as are unrevealed

Such of the Divine laws as are *unrevealed* are laws set by God to his human creatures, but not through the medium of human language, or not expressly.

These are the only laws which he has set to that portion of mankind who are excluded from the light of Revelation.

These laws are binding upon us (who have access to the truths of Revelation) in so far as the revealed law has left our duties undetermined. For, though his express declarations are the clearest evidence of his will, we must look for many of the duties, which God has imposed upon us, to the marks or signs of his pleasure which are styled the *light of nature*. Paley and other divines have proved beyond a doubt that it was not the purpose of Revelation to disclose the *whole* of those duties. Some we could not know without the help of Revelation; and these the revealed law has stated distinctly and precisely. The rest we may know, if we will, by the light of nature or reason; and these the revealed law supposes or assumes. It passes them over in silence, or with a brief and incidental notice.

What is the index *to such of the Divine laws as are unrevealed?*

But if God has given us laws which he has not revealed or promulged, how shall we know them? What are those signs of his pleasure, which we style the *light of nature*; and oppose, by that figurative phrase, to express declarations of his will?

The hypotheses *or* theories *which regard the nature of that index*

The hypotheses or theories which attempt to resolve this question may be reduced, I think, to two.

The hypothesis or theory of a moral sense, *or* innate practical principles; *of a* practical reason; *of a* common sense, *etc. etc.*

According to one of them, there are human actions which all mankind approve, human actions which all men disapprove; and these universal sentiments arise at the thought of those actions, spontaneously, instantly, and inevitably. Being common to all mankind and inseparable from the thoughts of those actions, these sentiments are marks or signs of the Divine pleasure. They are proofs that the actions which excite them are enjoined or forbidden by the Deity.

The rectitude or pravity of human conduct, or its agreement or disagreement with the laws of God, is instantly inferred from these sentiments, without the possibility of mistake. He has resolved that our happiness shall depend on our keeping his commandments: and it manifestly consists with his manifest wisdom and goodness that we should know them promptly and certainly. Accordingly, he has not committed us to the guidance of our slow and fallible *reason*. He has wisely endowed us with *feelings*, which warn us at every step and pursue us, with their importunate reproaches, when we wander from the path of our duties.

These simple or inscrutable feelings have been compared to those which we derive from the outward senses, and have been referred to a peculiar faculty called the *moral sense*: though, admitting that the feelings exist, and are proofs of the Divine pleasure, I am unable to discover the analogy which suggested the comparison and the name. The objects or appearances which properly are perceived through the senses are perceived immediately, or without an inference of the understanding. According to the hypothesis which I have briefly stated or suggested, there is always an inference of the understanding, though the inference is short and inevitable. From feelings which arise within us when we think of certain actions, we infer that those actions are enjoined or forbidden by the Deity.

The hypothesis, however, of a *moral sense*, is expressed in other ways.

The laws of God, to which these feelings are the index, are not unfrequently named *innate practical principles*, or *postulates of practical reason*: or they are said to be written on our hearts, by the finger of their great Author, in broad and indelible characters.

Common sense (the most yielding and accommodating of phrases) has been moulded and fitted to the purpose of expressing the hypothesis in question. In all their decisions on the rectitude or pravity of conduct (its agreement or disagreement with the unrevealed law), mankind are said to be determined by *common sense*: this same *common sense* meaning, in this instance, the simple or inscrutable sentiments which I have endeavoured to describe.

Considered as affecting the soul, when the man thinks especially of *his own* conduct, these sentiments, feelings, or emotions, are frequently styled his *conscience*.

The theory or hypothesis of utility

According to the other of the adverse theories or hypotheses, the laws of God, which are not revealed or promulged, must be gathered by man from the goodness of God and from the tendencies of human actions. In other words, the benevolence of God, with the principle of general utility, is our only index or guide to his unrevealed law.

A brief summary of the theory of utility

God designs the happiness of all his sentient creatures. Some human actions forward that benevolent purpose, or their tendencies are beneficent or useful. Other human actions are adverse to that purpose, or their tendencies are mischievous or pernicious. The former, as promoting his purpose, God has enjoined. The latter, as opposed to his purpose, God has forbidden. He has given us the faculty of observing, of remembering, of reasoning: and, by duly applying those faculties, we may collect the tendencies of our actions. Knowing the tendencies of our actions, and knowing his benevolent purpose, we know his tacit commands.

The following explanations of that summary briefly introduced

Such is a brief summary of this celebrated theory. I should wander to a measureless distance from the main purpose of my lectures if I stated all the explanations with which that summary must be received. But, to obviate the principal misconceptions to which the theory is obnoxious, I will subjoin as many of those explanations as my purpose and limits will admit.

The theory is this: inasmuch as the goodness of God is boundless and impartial, he designs the greatest happiness of all his sentient creatures; he wills that the aggregate of their enjoyments shall find no nearer limit than that which is inevitably set to it by their finite and imperfect nature. From the probable effects of our actions on the greatest happiness of all, or from the tendencies of human actions to increase or diminish that aggregate, we may infer the laws which he has given, but has not expressed or revealed.

The true tendency *of a human action, and the true* test *of that tendency*

Now the *tendency* of a human action (as its tendency is thus understood) is the whole of its tendency: the sum of its probable consequences, in so far as they are important or material: the sum of its remote and collateral, as well as of its direct consequences, in so far as any of its consequences may influence the general happiness.

Trying to collect its tendency (as its tendency is thus understood) we must not consider the action as if it were *single* and *insulated*, but must look at the *class* of actions to which it belongs. The probable *specific* consequences of doing that single act, of forbearing from that single act, or of omitting that single act, are not the objects of the inquiry. The question to be solved is this: if acts of the *class* were *generally* done, or *generally* forborne or omitted, what would be the probable effect on the general happiness or good?

Considered by itself, a mischievous act may seem to be useful or harmless. Considered by itself, a useful act may seem to be pernicious.

For example, if a poor man steal a handful from the heap of his rich neighbour, the act, considered by itself, is harmless or positively good. One man's poverty is assuaged with the superfluous wealth of another.

But suppose that thefts were general (or that the useful right of property were open to frequent invasions) and mark the result.

Without security for property, there were no inducement to save. Without habitual saving on the part of proprietors, there were no accumulation of capital. Without accumulation of capital, there were no fund for the payment of wages, no division of labour, no elaborate and costly machines: there were none of those helps to labour which augment its productive power, and, therefore, multiply the enjoyments of every individual in the community. Frequent invasions of property would bring the rich to poverty and, what were a greater evil, would aggravate the poverty of the poor.

If a single and insulated theft seem to be harmless or good, the fallacious appearance merely arises from this: that the vast majority of those who are tempted to steal abstain from invasions of property; and the detriment to security, which is the end produced by a single theft, is overbalanced and concealed by the mass of wealth, the accumulation of which is produced by general security.

Again: if I evade the payment of a tax imposed by a good government, the *specific* effects of the mischievous forbearance are indisputably useful. For the money which I unduly withhold is convenient to myself and, compared with the bulk of the public revenue, is a quantity too small to be missed. But the regular payment of taxes is necessary to the existence of the government. And I, and the rest of a community, enjoy the security which it gives, because the payment of taxes is rarely evaded.

In the cases now supposed, the act or omission is good, considered as single or insulated; but, considered with the rest of its class, is evil. In other cases, an act or omission is evil, considered as single or insulated; but, considered with the rest of its class, is good.

For example, a punishment, as a solitary fact, is an evil: the pain inflicted on the criminal being added to the mischief of the crime. But, considered as part of a system, a punishment is useful or beneficent. By a dozen or score of punishments, thousands of crimes are prevented. With the sufferings of the guilty few, the security of the many is purchased. By the lopping of a peccant member, the body is saved from decay.

It, therefore, is true generally (for the proposition admits of exceptions) that, to determine the true tendency of an act, forbearance, or omission, we must resolve the following question: what would be the probable effect on the general happiness or good, if *similar* acts, forbearances, or omissions were general or frequent?

Such is the *test* to which we must usually resort, if we would try the true *tendency* of an act, forbearance, or omission: meaning, by the true *tendency* of an act, forbearance, or omission, the sum of its probable effects on the general happiness or good, or its agreement or disagreement with the principle of general utility.

According to the theory of utility, God's commands are mostly rules

But, if this be the ordinary test for trying the tendencies of actions, and if the tendencies of actions be the index to the will of God, it follows that most of his commands are general or universal. The useful acts which he enjoins and the pernicious acts which he prohibits, he enjoins or prohibits, for the most part, not singly, but by classes: not by commands which are particular or directed to insulated cases, but by laws or rules which are general and commonly inflexible.

For example, certain acts are pernicious, considered as a class: or (in other words) the frequent repetition of the act were adverse to the general happiness, though, in this or that instance, the act might be useful or harmless. Further, such are the motives or inducements to the commission of acts of the class that, unless we were determined to forbearance by the fear of punishment, they *would* be frequently committed. Now, if we combine these *data* with the wisdom and goodness of God, we must infer that he forbids such acts and forbids them *without exception*. In the tenth or the hundredth case, the act might be useful: in the nine, or the ninety and nine, the act would be pernicious. If the act were permitted or tolerated in the rare and anomalous case, the motives to forbear in the others would be weakened or destroyed. In the hurry and tumult of action, it is hard to distinguish justly. To grasp at present enjoyment and to turn from present uneasiness, is the habitual inclination of us all. And thus, through the weakness of our judgments and the more dangerous infirmity of our wills, we should frequently *stretch* the exception to cases embraced by the rule.

Consequently, where acts, considered as a class, are useful or pernicious, we must conclude that he enjoins or forbids them, and by a *rule* which probably is inflexible.

It does not follow from the theory of utility that every *useful action is the object of a Divine injunction; and* every *pernicious action the object of a Divine prohibition*

Such, I say, is the conclusion at which we must arrive, supposing that the fear of punishment be necessary to incite or restrain.

For the tendency of an act is one thing: the utility of enjoining or forbidding it is another thing. There are classes of useful acts which it were useless to enjoin; classes of mischievous acts which it were useless to prohibit. Sanctions were superfluous. We are sufficiently prone to the useful, and sufficiently averse from the mischievous acts, without the motives which are presented to the will by a lawgiver. Motives *natural* or spontaneous (or motives *other* than those which are created by injunctions and prohibitions) impel us to action in the one case and hold us to forbearance in the other. In the language of Mr Locke, 'The mischievous omission or action would bring down evils upon us, which are its *natural* products or consequences; and which, as *natural* inconveniences, operate *without a law*.'

A current and specious objection to the theory of utility, introduced and stated

Now, if the measure or test which I have endeavoured to explain be the ordinary measure or test for trying the tendencies of our actions, the most current and specious of the objections which are made to the theory of utility is founded in gross mistake and is open to triumphant refutation.

The theory, be it always remembered, is this:

Our motives to obey the laws which God has given us are paramount to all others. For the transient pleasures which we may snatch, or the transient pains which we may shun, by violating the duties which they impose are nothing in comparison with the pains by which those duties are sanctioned.

The greatest possible happiness of all his sentient creatures is the purpose and effect of those laws. For the benevolence by which they were prompted, and the wisdom with which they were planned, equal the might which enforces them.

But, seeing that such is their purpose, they embrace the *whole* of our conduct: so far, that is, as our conduct may promote or obstruct that purpose, and so far as injunctions and prohibitions are necessary to correct our desires.

In so far as the laws of God are clearly and indisputably revealed, we are bound to guide our conduct by the plain meaning of their terms. In so far as they are not revealed, we must resort to another guide: namely, the probable effect of our conduct on that *general happiness* or *good* which is the object of the Divine Lawgiver in all his laws and commandments.

In each of these cases the *source* of our duties is the same, though the *proofs* by which we know them are different. The principle of general utility is the *index* to many of these duties; but the principle of general utility is not their *fountain* or *source*. For duties or obligations arise from commands and sanctions. And commands, it is manifest, proceed not from abstractions, but from living and rational beings.

Admit these premises and the following conclusion is inevitable: the *whole* of our conduct should be guided by the principle of utility, in so far as the conduct to be pursued has not been determined by Revelation. For, to conform to the principle or maxim with which a law coincides is equivalent to obeying that law.

Such is the theory which I have repeated in various forms and, I fear, at tedious length, in order that my younger hearers might conceive it with due distinctness.

The current and specious objection to which I have adverted may be stated thus:

> Pleasure and pain (or good and evil) are inseparably connected. Every positive act, and every forbearance or omission, is followed by *both*: immediately or remotely, directly or collaterally, to ourselves or to our fellow creatures.
>
> Consequently, if we shape our conduct justly to the principle of general utility, every election which we make between doing or forbearing from an act will be preceded by the following process. *First*: we shall conjecture the consequences of the act, and also the consequences of the forbearance. For these are the competing elements of that *calculation*, which, according to our guiding principle, we are bound to make. *Secondly*: we shall compare the consequences of the act with the consequences of the forbearance, and determine the set of consequences which gives the *balance* of advantage: which yields the larger residue of probable good, or (adopting a different, though exactly equivalent, expression) which leaves the smaller residue of probable evil.

Now let us suppose that we actually tried this process before we arrived at our resolves. And then let us mark the absurd and mischievous effects which would inevitably follow our attempts.

Generally speaking, the period allowed for deliberation is brief and to lengthen deliberation beyond that limited period is equivalent to forbearance or omission. Consequently, if we performed this elaborate process completely and correctly, we should often defeat its purpose. We should abstain from action altogether, though utility required us to act; or the occasion for acting *usefully* would slip through our fingers whilst we weighed, with anxious scrupulosity, the merits of the act and the forbearance.

But feeling the necessity of resolving promptly, we should *not* perform the process completely and correctly. We should guess or conjecture hastily the effects of the act and the forbearance, and compare their respective effects with equal precipitancy. Our premises would be false or imperfect; our conclusions badly deduced. Labouring to adjust our conduct to the principle of general utility, we should work inevitable mischief.

And such were the consequences of following the principle of utility, though we sought the true and the useful with simplicity and in earnest. But, as we commonly prefer our own to the interests of our fellow creatures, and our own immediate to our own remote interests, it is clear that we should warp the principle to selfish and sinister ends.

The final cause or purpose of the Divine laws is the general happiness or good. But to trace the effect of our conduct on the general happiness or good is not the way to know them. By consulting and obeying the laws of God we promote our own happiness and the happiness of our fellow creatures. But we should *not* consult his laws, we should *not* obey his laws, and, so far as in us lay, we should thwart their benevolent design, if we made the general happiness our object or end. In a breath, we should widely deviate *in effect* from the principle of general utility by taking it as the *guide* of our conduct.

The two *apt answers to the foregoing objection briefly introduced*

Such, I believe, is the meaning of those—if they have a meaning—who object to the meaning of utility 'that it were a *dangerous* principle of conduct'.

As the objectors are generally persons little accustomed to clear and determinate thinking, I am not quite certain that I have conceived the objection exactly. But I have endeavoured with perfectly good faith to understand their meaning, and as forcibly as I can to state it, or to state the most rational meaning which their words can be supposed to import.

It has been said, in answer to this objection, that it involves a contradiction in terms. *Danger* is another name for *probable mischief*: and, surely, we best avert the probable mischiefs of our conduct, by conjecturing and estimating its probable consequences. To say 'that the principle of utility were a *dangerous* principle of conduct', is to say 'that it were contrary to utility to consult utility'.

Now, though this is so brief and pithy that I heartily wish it were conclusive, I must needs admit that it scarcely touches the objection, and falls far short of a crushing reduction to absurdity. For the objection obviously assumes that we *cannot* foresee and estimate the probable effects of our conduct: that if we attempted to calculate its good and its evil consequences, our presumptuous attempt at calculation would lead us to error and sin. What is contended is that, by the attempt to act according to utility, an attempt which would not be successful, we should deviate from utility. A proposition involving, when fairly stated, nothing like a contradiction.

But, though this is not the refutation, there *is* a refutation.

The first *answer to the foregoing objection stated*

And first, if utility be our only index to the tacit commands of the Deity, it is idle to object to its imperfections. We must even make the most of it.

If we were endowed with a *moral sense*, or with a *common sense*, or with a *practical reason*, we scarcely should construe his commands by the principle of general utility. If our souls were furnished out with *innate practical principles* we scarcely should read his commands in the tendencies of human actions. For, by the supposition, man would be gifted with a peculiar organ for acquiring a knowledge of his duties. The duties imposed by the Deity would be subjects of immediate consciousness, and completely exempted from the jurisdiction of observation and induction. An attempt to displace that invincible consciousness, and to thrust the principle of utility into the vacant seat, would be simply impossible and manifestly absurd. An attempt to taste or smell by force of syllogism were not less hopeful or judicious.

But, if we are not gifted with that peculiar organ, we must take to the principle of utility, let it be never so defective. We must gather our duties, as we can, from the tendencies of human actions, or remain, at our own peril, in ignorance of our duties. We must pick our scabrous way with the help of a glimmering light, or wander in profound darkness.

The second *answer to the foregoing objection briefly introduced*

Whether there be any ground for the hypothesis of a *moral sense* is a question which I shall duly examine in a future lecture, but which I shall not pursue in the present place. For the present is a convenient place for the introduction of another topic: namely, that they who advance the objection in question misunderstand the theory which they presume to impugn.

Their objection is founded on the following assumption: that, if we adjusted our conduct to the principle of general utility, every election which we made between doing and forbearing from an act would be preceded by a *calculation*, by an attempt to conjecture and compare the respective probable consequences of action and forbearance.

Or (changing the expression) their assumption is this: that, if we adjusted our conduct to the principle of general utility, our conduct would always be determined by an immediate or direct resort to it.

And, granting their assumption, I grant their inference. I grant that the principle of utility were a halting and purblind guide.

But their assumption is groundless. They are battering (and most effectually) a misconception of their own, whilst they fancy they are hard at work demolishing the theory which they hate.

For, according to that theory, our conduct would conform to *rules* inferred from the tendencies of actions, but would not be determined by a direct resort to the principle of general utility. Utility would be the test of our conduct, ultimately, but not immediately: the immediate test of the rules to which our conduct would conform, but not the immediate test of specific or individual actions. Our rules would be fashioned on utility; our conduct on our rules.

Recall the true test for trying the tendency of an action and, by a short and easy deduction, you will see that their assumption is groundless.

If our conduct were truly adjusted to the principle of general utility, our conduct would conform, for the most part, to rules*: rules which emanate from the Deity, and to which the tendencies of human actions are the guide or index*

If we would try the tendency of a specific or individual act, we must not contemplate the act as if it were single and insulated, but must look at the class of acts to which it belongs. We must suppose that acts of the class were generally done or omitted, and consider the probable effect upon the general happiness or good.

We must guess the consequences which would follow if acts of the class were general; and also the consequences which would follow if they were generally omitted. We must then compare the consequences on the positive and negative sides and determine on which of the two the *balance* of advantage lies.

If it lie on the positive side, the tendency of the act is good: or (adopting a wider, yet exactly equivalent expression) the general happiness requires that *acts* of the *class* shall be done. If it lie on the negative side, the tendency of the act is bad: or (again adopting a wider, yet exactly equivalent expression) the general happiness requires that *acts* of the *class* shall be forborne.

In a breath, if we truly try the tendency of a specific or individual act, we try the tendency of the class to which that act belongs. The *particular* conclusion which we draw, with regard to the single act, implies a *general* conclusion embracing all similar acts.

But, concluding that acts of the class are useful or pernicious, we are forced upon a further inference. Adverting to the known wisdom and the known benevolence of the Deity, we infer that He enjoins or forbids them by a general and inflexible *rule*.

Such is the inference at which we inevitably arrive, supposing that the acts be *such* as to call for the intervention of a lawgiver.

To *rules* thus inferred and lodged in the memory, our conduct would conform *immediately* if it were truly adjusted to utility. To consider the specific consequences of single or individual acts would seldom consist with that ultimate principle. And our conduct would, therefore, be guided by *general* conclusions, or (to speak more accurately) by *rules* inferred from those conclusions.

But, this being admitted, the necessity of pausing and calculating, which the objection in question supposes, is an imaginary necessity. To preface each act or forbearance by a conjecture and comparison of consequences were clearly superfluous and mischievous. It were clearly superfluous, inasmuch as the result of that process would be embodied in a known *rule*. It were clearly mischievous, inasmuch as the *true* result would be expressed by that rule, whilst the process would probably be faulty if it were done on the spur of the occasion.

Theory *and* practice *are inseparable*

Speaking generally, human conduct, including the human conduct which is subject to the Divine commands, is inevitably guided by *rules*, or by *principles* or *maxims*.

If our experience and observation of particulars were not *generalised*, our experience and observation of particulars would seldom avail us in *practice*. To review on the spur of the occasion a host of particulars, and to obtain from those particulars a conclusion applicable to the case, were a process too slow and uncertain to meet the exigencies of our lives. The inferences suggested to our minds by repeated experience and observation are, therefore, drawn into *principles*, or compressed into *maxims*. These we carry about us ready for use, and apply to individual cases promptly or without hesitation, without reverting to the process by which they were obtained; or without recalling, and arraying before our minds, the numerous and intricate considerations of which they are handy abridgments.

This is the main, though not the only, use of *theory* which ignorant and weak people are in a habit of *opposing* to practice, but which is essential to practice guided by experience and observation.

''Tis true in *theory*; but, then, 'tis false in *practice*.' Such is a common talk. This says Noodle, propounding it with a look of the most ludicrous profundity.

But, with due and discreet deference to this worshipful and weighty personage, *that* which is true in *theory* is *also* true in *practice*.

Seeing that a true theory is a *compendium* of particular truths, it is necessarily true as applied to particular cases. The terms of the theory are general and abstract, or the particular truths which the theory implies would not be abbreviated or condensed. But, unless it be true of particulars and, therefore, true in practice, it has no *truth* at all. *Truth* is always particular, though *language* is commonly general. Unless the terms of a theory can be resolved into particular truths, the theory is mere jargon: a coil of those senseless abstractions which often ensnare the *instructed*; and in which the wits of the ignorant are certainly caught and entangled when they stir from the track of authority and venture to think for themselves.

They who talk of theory as if it were the antagonist of practice, or of a thing being true in *theory* but not true in *practice*, mean (if they have a meaning) that the theory in question is false: that the particular truths which it concerns are treated imperfectly or incorrectly; and that, if it were applied in practice, it might, therefore, mislead. They *say* that truth in theory is not truth in practice. They *mean* that a false theory is not a true one, and might lead us to practical errors.

If our conduct were truly adjusted to the principle of general utility, our conduct would be guided, for the most part, by sentiments *associated with* rules: *rules which emanate from the Deity, and to which the tendencies of human actions are the guide or index*

Speaking, then, generally, human conduct is inevitably guided by *rules*, or by *principles* or *maxims*.

The human conduct which is subject to the Divine commands is not only guided by *rules*, but also by *moral sentiments* associated with those rules.

If I believe (no matter why) that acts of a class or description are enjoined or forbidden by the Deity, a moral sentiment or feeling (or a sentiment or feeling of approbation or disapprobation) is inseparably connected in my mind with the thought or conception of such acts. And by this I am urged to do, or restrained from doing, such acts, although I advert not to the reason in which my belief originated, nor recall the Divine rule which I have inferred from that reason.

Now, if the reason in which my belief originated be the useful or pernicious tendency of acts of the class, my conduct is truly adjusted to the principle of general utility, but my conduct is not determined by a direct resort to it. It is directly determined by a *sentiment* associated with acts of the class, and with the rule which I have inferred from their tendency.

If my conduct be truly adjusted to the principle of general utility, my conduct is guided remotely by *calculation*. But, immediately, or at the moment of action, my conduct is determined by *sentiment*. I am swayed by *sentiment* as imperiously as I *should* be swayed by it, supposing I were utterly unable to produce a reason for my conduct, and were ruled by the capricious feelings which are styled the moral sense.

For example, reasons which are quite satisfactory, but somewhat numerous and intricate, convince me that the institution of property is necessary to the general good. Convinced of this, I am convinced that thefts are pernicious. Convinced that thefts are pernicious, I infer that the Deity forbids them by a general and inflexible rule.

Now the train of induction and reasoning by which I arrive at this rule is somewhat long and elaborate. But I am not compelled to repeat the process before I can know with certainty that I should forbear from taking your purse. Through my previous habits of thought and by my education, *a sentiment of aversion* has become associated in my mind with the thought or conception of *a theft*. And, without adverting to the reasons which have convinced me that thefts are pernicious, or without adverting to the rule which I have inferred from their pernicious tendency, I am determined by that ready emotion to keep my fingers from your purse.

To think that the theory of utility would *substitute* calculation for sentiment is a gross and flagrant error: the error of a shallow, precipitate understanding. He who *opposes* calculation and sentiment opposes the rudder to the sail, or to the breeze which swells the sail. Calculation is the guide and not the antagonist of sentiment. Sentiment without calculation were blind and capricious; but calculation without sentiment were inert.

To crush the moral sentiments is not the scope or purpose of the true theory of utility. It seeks to impress those sentiments with a just or beneficent direction: to free us of *groundless* likings, and from the tyranny of senseless antipathies; to fix our love upon the useful, our hate upon the pernicious.

If our conduct were truly adjusted to the principle of general utility, our conduct would conform, for the most part, to Divine rules, *and would also be guided, for the most part, by* sentiments *associated with those rules. But, in anomalous and excepted cases (of comparatively rare occurrence) our conduct would be fashioned* directly *on the principle of general utility, or guided by a conjecture and comparison of* specific *or* particular *consequences*

If, then, the principle of utility were the presiding principle of our conduct, our conduct would be determined immediately by Divine *rules*, or rather by moral *sentiments* associated with those rules. And, consequently, the application of the principle of utility to particular or individual cases would neither be attended by the errors, nor followed by the mischiefs, which the current objection in question supposes. But these conclusions (like most conclusions) must be taken with limitations.

There certainly are cases (of comparatively rare occurrence) wherein the specific considerations balance or outweigh the general: cases which (in the language of Bacon) are 'immersed in matter'; cases perplexed with peculiarities from which it were dangerous to abstract them, and to which our attention would be directed, if we were true to our presiding principle. It were mischievous to depart from a rule which regarded any of these cases since every departure from a rule tends to weaken its authority. But so important were the *specific* consequences which would follow our resolves, that the evil of observing the rule might surpass the evil of breaking it. Looking at the reasons from which we had inferred the rule, it were absurd to think it inflexible. We should, therefore, dismiss the *rule*; resort directly to the *principle* upon which our rules were fashioned; and calculate *specific* consequences to the best of our knowledge and ability.

For example, if we take the principle of utility as our index to the Divine commands, we must infer that obedience to established government is enjoined generally by the Deity. For, without obedience to 'the powers which be', there were little security and little enjoyment. The ground, however, of the inference is the *utility* of government, and if the protection which it yields be *too costly*, or if it vex us with *needless* restraints and load us with *needless* exactions, the principle which points at submission as our general duty may counsel and justify resistance. Disobedience to an established government, let it be never so bad, is an evil: for the mischiefs inflicted by a bad government are less than the mischiefs of anarchy. So momentous, however, is the difference between a bad and a good government, *that if it would lead to a good one*, resistance to a bad one would be useful. The anarchy attending the transition were an extensive, but a passing, evil: the good which would follow the transition were extensive and lasting. The peculiar good would outweigh the generic evil: the good which would crown the change in the insulated and eccentric case would more than compensate the evil which is inseparable from rebellion.

Whether resistance to government be useful or pernicious, be consistent or inconsistent with the Divine pleasure, is, therefore, an *anomalous* question. We must try it by a direct resort to the ultimate or presiding *principle*, and not by the Divine *rule* which the principle clearly indicates. To consult the rule were absurd. For, the rule being general and applicable to ordinary cases, it ordains obedience to governments and excludes the question.

The members of a political society who resolve this momentous question must, therefore, dismiss the rule and calculate specific consequences. They must measure the mischief wrought by the actual government; the chance of getting a better, by resorting to resistance; the evil which must attend resistance, whether it prosper or fail; and the good which may follow resistance, in case it be crowned with success. And, then, by comparing these, the elements of their moral calculation, they must solve the question before them to the best of their knowledge and ability.

And in this eccentric or anomalous case, the application of the principle of utility would probably be beset with the difficulties which the current objection in question imputes to it generally. To measure and compare the evils of submission and disobedience, and to determine which of the two would give the balance of advantage, would probably be a difficult and uncertain process. The numerous and competing considerations by which the question must be solved might well perplex and divide the wise and the good and the brave. A Milton or a Hampden might animate their countrymen to resistance, but a Hobbes or a Falkland would counsel obedience and peace.

But, though the principle of utility would afford no certain solution, the community would be fortunate if their opinions and sentiments were formed upon it. The pretensions of the opposite parties being tried by an intelligible test, a peaceable compromise of their difference would, at least, be possible. The adherents of the established government might think it the most *expedient*: but, as their liking would depend upon reasons, and not upon names and phrases, they might possibly prefer innovations, of which they would otherwise disapprove, to the mischiefs of a violent contest. They might chance to see the absurdity of upholding the existing order with a stiffness which must end in anarchy. The party affecting reform, being also intent upon *utility*, would probably accept concessions short of their notions and wishes, rather than persist in the chase of a greater possible good through the evils and the hazards of a war. In short, if the object of each party were measured by the standard of utility, each might compare the worth of its object with the cost of a violent pursuit.

But, if the parties were led by their ears, and not by the principle of utility: if they appealed to unmeaning abstractions, or to senseless fictions; if they mouthed of 'the rights of man', or 'the sacred rights of sovereigns', of 'unalienable liberties', or 'eternal and immutable justice'; of an 'original contract or covenant', or 'the principles of an inviolable constitution'; neither could compare its object with the cost of a violent pursuit, nor would the difference between them admit of a peaceable compromise. A sacred or unalienable right is truly and indeed *invaluable*: for, seeing that it means nothing, there is nothing with which it can be measured. Parties who rest their pretensions on the jargon to which I have adverted, must inevitably push to their objects through thick and thin, though their objects be straws or feathers as weighed in the balance of utility. Having bandied their fustian phrases and 'bawled till their lungs be spent', they must even take to their weapons and fight their difference out.

It really *is* important (though I feel the audacity of the paradox) that men should think distinctly and speak with a meaning.

In most of the domestic broils which have agitated civilised communities, the result has been determined or seriously affected by the nature of the prevalent *talk*: by the nature of the topics or phrases which have figured in the war of words. These topics or phrases have been more then pretexts; more than varnish; more than distinguishing cockades mounted by the opposite parties.

For example, if the bulk of the people of England had thought and reasoned with Mr Burke, had been imbued with the spirit and had seized the scope of his arguments, her needless and disastrous war with her American colonies would have been stifled at the birth. The stupid and infuriate majority who rushed into that odious war could perceive and discourse of nothing but the *sovereignty* of the mother country, and her so-called *right* to tax her colonial subjects.

But, granting that the mother country was properly the sovereign of the colonies, granting that the fact of her sovereignty was proved by invariable practice, and granting her so-called *right* to tax her colonial subjects, this was hardly a topic to move an enlightened people.

Is it the interest of England to insist upon her sovereignty? Is it her interest to exercise her right without the approbation of the colonists? For the chance of a slight revenue to be wrung from her American subjects, and of a trifling relief from the taxation which now oppresses herself, shall she drive those reluctant subjects to assert their alleged independence, visit her own children with the evil of war, squander her treasures and soldiers in trying to keep them down, and desolate the very region from which the revenue must be drawn? These and the like considerations would have determined the people of England, if their dominant opinions and sentiments had been fashioned on the principle of utility.

And, if these and the like considerations had determined the public mind, the public would have damned the project of taxing and coercing the colonies and the government would have abandoned the project. For, it is only in the ignorance of the people, and in their consequent mental imbecility, that governments or demagogues can find the means of mischief.

If these and the like considerations had determined the public mind, the expenses and miseries of the war would have been avoided; the connection of England with America would not have been torn asunder; and, in case their common interests had led them to dissolve it quietly, the relation of sovereign and subject, or of parent and child, would have been followed by an equal, but intimate and lasting, alliance. For the interests of the two nations perfectly coincide; and the open and the covert hostilities, with which they plague one another, are the offspring of a bestial antipathy begotten by their original quarrel.

But arguments drawn from utility were not to the dull taste of the stupid and infuriate majority. The rabble, great and small, would hear of nothing but their *right*. 'They'd a *right* to tax the colonists, and tax 'em they would: Ay, *that* they would.' Just as if a *right* were worth a rush of itself, or a something to be cherished and asserted independently of the good that it may bring.

Mr Burke would have taught them better: would have purged their muddled brains, and 'laid the fever in their souls', with the healing principle of utility. He asked them what they would get if the project of coercion should succeed, and implored them to compare the advantage with the hazard and the cost. But the sound practical men still insisted on the *right*, and sagaciously shook their heads at him as a refiner and a theorist.

If a serious difference shall arise between themselves and Canada, or if a serious difference shall arise between ourselves and Ireland, an attempt will probably be made to cram us with the same stuff. But, such are the mighty strides which reason has taken in the interval, that I hope we shall not swallow it with the relish of our good ancestors. It will probably occur to us to ask whether she be worth keeping, and whether she be worth keeping at the cost of a war? I think there is nothing romantic in the hope which I now express, since an admirable speech of Mr Baring, advising the relinquishment of Canada, was seemingly received, a few years ago, with general assent and approbation.[1]

The second *answer to the foregoing objection briefly resumed*

There are, then, cases, which are anomalous or eccentric; and to which the man, whose conduct was fashioned on utility, would apply that ultimate principle immediately or directly. And, in these anomalous or eccentric cases, the application of the principle would probably be beset with the difficulties which the current objection in question imputes to it generally.

But, even in these cases, the principle would afford an intelligible test and a likelihood of a just solution: a probability of discovering the conduct required by the general good, and, therefore, required by the commands of a wise and benevolent Deity.

And the anomalies, after all, are comparatively few. In the great majority of cases, the general happiness requires that *rules* shall be observed, and that *sentiments* associated with rules shall be promptly obeyed. If our conduct were truly adjusted to the principle of general utility, our conduct would seldom be determined by an immediate or direct resort to it.

Note

1. The *rationale* of the so-called rights of sovereign governments is treated in more detail in Lecture VI. *post.*

LECTURE III

SYNOPSIS OF LECTURE III

Apology for introducing the principle of utility
The connection of the third with the second lecture
A second objection to the theory of utility, stated
An answer to that second objection, introduced
An objection to the foregoing answer, stated
The foregoing objection to the foregoing answer, solved or extenuated
The second objection to the theory of utility, together with the foregoing answer to that second objection, briefly restated

TEXT OF LECTURE III

Apology for introducing the principle of utility

Although it is not the object of this course of lectures to treat of the science of legislation, but to evolve and expound the principles and distinctions involved in the idea of law, it was not a deviation from my subject to introduce the principle of utility. For I shall often have occasion to refer to that principle in my course, as that which not only ought to guide, but has commonly in fact guided, the legislator. The principle of utility, well or ill understood, has usually been the principle consulted in making laws; and I therefore should often be unable to explain distinctly and precisely the scope and purport of a law, without having brought the principle of utility directly before you. I have therefore done so, not pretending to expound the principle in its various applications, which would be a subject of sufficient extent for many courses of lectures; but attempting to give you a general notion of the principle, and to obviate the most specious of the objections which are commonly made to it.

The connection of the third with the second lecture

In my second lecture, I examined a current and specious objection to the theory of general utility.

The drift of the objection, you undoubtedly remember; and you probably remember the arguments by which I attempted to refute it.

Accordingly, I merely resume that general conclusion which I endeavoured to establish by the second of my two answers.

The conclusion may be stated briefly, in the following manner. If our conduct were truly adjusted to the principle of general utility, our conduct would conform, for the most part, to laws or rules: *laws* or *rules* which are set by the Deity, and to which the tendencies of *classes* of actions are the guide or index.

A second objection to the theory of utility stated

But here arises a difficulty which certainly is most perplexing, and which scarcely admits of a solution that will perfectly satisfy the mind.

If the Divine laws must be gathered from the tendencies of action, how can they, who are bound to keep them, know them fully and correctly?

So numerous are the classes of actions to which those laws relate that no single mind can mark the whole of those classes and examine completely their respective tendencies. If every single man must learn their respective tendencies, and thence infer the rules which God has set to mankind, every man's scheme of ethics will embrace but a *part* of those rules, and, on many or most of the occasions which require him to act or forbear, he will be forced on the dangerous process of calculating specific consequences.

Besides, ethical, like other wisdom, 'cometh by opportunity of leisure': and, since they are busied with earning the means of living, the many are unable to explore the field of ethics and to learn their numerous duties by learning the tendencies of actions.

If the Divine laws must be gathered from the tendencies of actions, the inevitable conclusion is absurd and monstrous. God has given us laws which no man can know completely and to which the great bulk of mankind has scarcely the slightest access.

The considerations suggested by this and the next discourse may solve or extenuate the perplexing difficulty to which I have now adverted.

An answer to that second objection introduced

In so far as law and morality are what they *ought* to be (or in so far as law and morality accord with their ultimate test, or in so far as law and morality accord with the Divine commands), legal and moral rules have been fashioned on the principle of utility, or obtained by observation and induction from the tendencies of human actions. But, though they have been fashioned on the principle of utility, or obtained by observation and induction from the tendencies of human actions, it is not necessary that all whom they bind should know or advert to the process through which they have been gotten. If all whom they bind keep or observe them, the ends to which they exist are sufficiently accomplished, though most of those who observe them be unable to perceive their ends, and be ignorant of the reasons on which they were founded, or of the proofs from which they were inferred.

According to the theory of utility, the science of Ethics or Deontology (or the science of Law and Morality, as they *should* be, or *ought* to be) is one of the sciences which rest upon observation and induction. The science has been formed, through a long succession of ages, by many and separate contributions from many and separate discoverers. No single mind could explore the whole of the fields, though each of its numerous departments has been explored by numerous inquirers.

If positive law and morality were exactly what they *ought* to be (or if positive law and morality were exactly fashioned to utility) sufficient reasons might be given for each of their constituent rules, and each of their constituent rules would *in fact* have been founded on those reasons. But no single mind could have found the whole of those rules, nor could any single mind compass the whole of their proofs. Though all the evidence would be known, the several parts of the evidence would be known by different men. Every single man might master a *portion* of the evidence: a portion commensurate with the attention which he gave to the science of ethics, and with the mental perspicacity and vigour which he brought to the study. But no single man could master *more* than a portion: and many of the rules of conduct, which were actually observed or admitted, would be taken by the most instructed on *authority*, *testimony*, or *trust*.

In short, if a system of law and morality were exactly fashioned to utility, all its constituent *rules* might be known by all or most. But all the numerous *reasons*, upon which the system would rest, could scarcely be compassed by any: while most must limit their inquiries to a few of those numerous reasons; or, without an attempt to examine the reasons, must receive the whole of the rules from the teaching and example of others.

But this inconvenience is not peculiar to law and morality. It extends to all the sciences and to all the arts.

Many mathematical truths are probably taken upon trust by deep and searching mathematicians: and of the thousands who apply arithmetic to daily and hourly use, not one in a hundred knows or surmises the reasons upon which its rules are founded. Of the millions who till the earth and ply the various handicrafts, few are acquainted with the grounds of their homely but important arts, though these arts are generally practised with passable expertness and success.

The powers of single individuals are feeble and poor, though the powers of conspiring numbers are gigantic and admirable. Little of any man's knowledge is gotten by original research. It mostly consists of *results* gotten by the researches of others, and taken by himself upon *testimony*.

And in many departments of science we may safely rely upon testimony: though the knowledge which we thus obtain is less satisfactory and useful than that which we win for ourselves by direct examination of the proofs.

In the mathematical and physical sciences, and in the arts which are founded upon them, we may commonly trust the conclusions which we take upon authority. For the adepts in these sciences and arts mostly agree in their results, and lie under no temptation to cheat the ignorant with error. I firmly believe (for example) that the earth moves round the sun, though I know not a tittle of the evidence from which the conclusion is inferred. And my belief is perfectly rational, though it rests upon mere authority. For there is nothing in the alleged fact contrary to my experience of nature: whilst all who have scrutinised the evidence concur in affirming the fact, and have no conceivable motive to assert and diffuse the conclusion, but the liberal and beneficent desire of maintaining and propagating truth.

An objection to the foregoing answer stated

But the case is unhappily different with the important science of ethics, and also with the various sciences such as legislation, politics, and political economy which are nearly related to ethics. Those who have inquired, or affected to inquire into ethics, have rarely been impartial, and, therefore, have differed in their results. Sinister interests, or prejudices begotten by such interests, have mostly determined them to embrace the opinions which they have laboured to impress upon others. Most of them have been advocates rather than inquirers. Instead of examining the evidence and honestly pursuing its consequences, most of them have hunted for arguments in favour of *given* conclusions, and have neglected or purposely suppressed the unbending and incommodious considerations which pointed at opposite inferences.

Now how can the bulk of mankind, who have little opportunity for research, compare the respective merits of these varying and hostile opinions, and hit upon those of the throng which accord with utility and truth? Here, testimony is not to be trusted. There is not *that concurrence or agreement of numerous and impartial inquirers*, to which the most cautious and erect understanding readily and wisely defers. With regard to the science of ethics, and to all the various sciences which are nearly related to ethics, invincible doubt, or blind and prostrate belief, would seem to be the doom of the multitude. Anxiously busied with the means of earning a precarious livelihood, they are debarred from every opportunity of carefully surveying the *evidence*: whilst every *authority*, whereon they may hang their faith, wants that mark of trustworthiness which justifies reliance on authority.

Accordingly, the science of ethics, with all the various sciences which are nearly related to ethics, lag behind the others. So few are the sincere inquirers who turn their attention to these sciences, and so difficult is it for the multitude to perceive the worth of their labours, that the advancement of the sciences themselves is comparatively slow; whilst the most perspicuous of the truths, with which they are occasionally enriched, are either rejected by the many as worthless or pernicious paradoxes, or win their laborious way to general assent through a long and dubious struggle with established and obstinate errors.

Many of the legal and moral rules which obtain in the most civilized communities rest upon brute custom, and not upon manly reason. They have been taken from preceding generations without examination and are deeply tinctured with barbarity. They arose in early ages, and in the infancy of the human mind, partly from caprices of the fancy (which are nearly omnipotent with barbarians), and partly from the imperfect apprehension of general utility which is the consequence of narrow experience. And so great and numerous are the obstacles to the diffusion of ethical truth that these monstrous or crude productions of childish and imbecile intellect have been cherished and perpetuated, through ages of advancing knowledge, to the comparatively enlightened period in which it is our happiness to live.

The foregoing objection to the foregoing answer, solved or extenuated

It were idle to deny the difficulty. The *diffusion* and the *advancement* of ethical truth are certainly prevented or obstructed by great and peculiar obstacles.

But these obstacles, I am firmly convinced, will gradually disappear. In two causes of slow but sure operation, we may clearly perceive a cure or, at least, a palliative of the evil. In every civilised community of the Old and New World, the *leading principles* of the science of ethics, and also of the various sciences which are nearly related to ethics, are gradually finding their way, in company with other knowledge, amongst the great mass of the people: whilst those who accurately study, and who labour to advance these sciences, are proportionally increasing in number and waxing in zeal and activity. From the combination of these two causes we may hope for a more rapid progress both in the discovery and in the diffusion of moral truth.

Profound knowledge of these, as of the other sciences, will always be confined to the comparatively few who study them long and assiduously. But the multitude are fully competent to conceive the leading principles, and to apply those *leading principles* to particular cases. And, if they were imbued with those principles, and were practised in the art of applying them, they would be docile to the voice of reason and armed against sophistry and error. There is a wide and important difference between ignorance of principles and ignorance of particulars or details. The man who is ignorant of principles, and unpractised in right reasoning, is imbecile as well as ignorant. The man who is simply ignorant of particulars or details can reason correctly from premises which are *suggested* to his understanding, and can justly estimate the consequences which are drawn from those premises by others. If the minds of the many were informed and invigorated, so far as their position will permit, they could distinguish the statements and reasonings of their instructed and judicious friends from the lies and fallacies of those who would use them to sinister purposes, and from the equally pernicious nonsense of their weak and ignorant well-wishers. Possessed of directing principles, able to reason rightly, helped to the requisite premises by accurate and comprehensive inquirers, they could examine and fathom the questions which it most behoves them to understand: though the leisure which they can snatch from their callings is necessarily so limited that their opinions upon numerous questions of subordinate importance would continue to be taken from the mere *authority* of others.

The shortest and clearest illustrations of this most cheering truth are furnished by the inestimable science of political economy, which is so interwoven with every consideration belonging to morals, politics, and legislation that it is impossible to treat any one of these sciences without a continual reference to it.

The broad or leading principles of the science of political economy may be mastered, with moderate attention, in a short period. With these simple, but commanding principles, a number of important questions are easily resolved. And if the multitude (as they can and will) shall ever understand these principles, many pernicious prejudices will be extirpated from the popular mind, and truths of ineffable moment planted in their stead.

For example, in many or all countries (the least uncivilised not excepted) the prevalent opinions and sentiments of the working people are certainly not consistent with the complete security of property. To the *ignorant* poor, the inequality which inevitably follows the beneficent institution of property is necessarily invidious. That they who toil and produce should fare scantily, whilst others, who 'delve not nor spin', batten on the fruits of labour, seems, to the jaundiced eyes of the poor and the ignorant, a monstrous state of things: an arrangement upheld by the few at the *cost* of the many, and flatly inconsistent with the benevolent purposes of Providence.

A statement of the numerous evils which flow from this single prejudice would occupy a volume. But they cast so clear a light on the mischiefs of popular ignorance, and show so distinctly the advantages of popular instruction, that I will briefly touch upon a few of them, though at the risk of tiring your patience.

In the first place, this prejudice blinds the people to the cause of their sufferings, and to the only remedy or palliative which the case will admit.

Want and labour spring from the niggardliness of nature, and not from the inequality which is consequent on the institution of property. These evils are inseparable from the condition of man upon earth; and are lightened, not aggravated, by this useful, though invidious institution. Without *capital*, and the arts which depend upon capital, the reward of labour would be far scantier than it is; and capital, with the arts which depend upon it, are creatures of the institution of property. The institution is good for the many, as well as for the few. The poor are not stripped by it of the produce of their labour; but it gives them a part of the enjoyment of wealth which it calls into being. In effect, though not in law, the labourers are co-proprietors with the capitalists who hire their labour. The reward which they get for their labour is principally drawn from *capital*; and they are not less interested than the legal owners in protecting the fund from invasion.

It is certainly to be wished that their reward were greater; and that they were relieved from the incessant drudgery to which they are now condemned. But the condition of the working people (whether their wages shall be high or low; their labour, moderate or extreme) depends upon their own will, and not upon the will of the rich. In *the true principle of population*, detected by the sagacity of Mr Malthus, they must look for the cause and the remedy of their penury and excessive toil. There they may find the means which would give them comparative affluence; which would give them the degree of leisure necessary to knowledge and refinement which would raise them to personal dignity and political influence, from grovelling and sordid subjection to the arbitrary rule of a few.

And these momentous truths are deducible from plain principles, by short and obvious inferences. Here, there is no need of large and careful research, or of subtle and sustained thinking. If the people understood distinctly a few indisputable propositions, and were capable of going correctly through an easy process of reasoning, their minds would be purged of the prejudice which blinds them to the cause of their sufferings, and they would see and apply the remedy which is suggested by the principle of population. Their repinings at the affluence of the rich would be appeased. Their murmurs at the injustice of the rich would be silenced. They would scarcely break machinery, or fire barns and corn ricks, to the end of raising wages or the rate of parish relief. They would see that violations of property are mischievous to *themselves*: that such violations weaken the motives to accumulation and, therefore, diminish the fund which yields the labourer his subsistence. They would see that they are deeply interested in the *security* of property: that, if they adjusted their numbers to the demands for their labour, they would share abundantly, with their employers, in the blessings of that useful institution.

Another of the numerous evils which flow from the prejudice in question is the frequency of crimes.

Nineteen offences out of twenty are offences against property. And most offences against property may be imputed to the prejudice in question.

The authors of such offences are commonly of the poorer sort. For the most part, poverty is the incentive. And this prejudice perpetuates poverty amongst the great body of the people by blinding them to the cause and the remedy.

And whilst it perpetuates the ordinary incentive to crime it weakens the restraints.

As a check or deterring motive, as an inducement to abstain from crime, the fear of public disapprobation, with its countless train of evils, is scarcely less effectual than the fear of legal punishment. To the purpose of forming the moral character, of rooting in the soul a prompt aversion from crime, it is infinitely more effectual.

The help of the hangman and the gaoler would seldom be called for if the *opinion* of the great body of the people were cleared of the prejudice in question and, therefore, fell heavily upon all offenders against property. If the *general opinion* were thoroughly cleared of that prejudice, it would greatly weaken the temptations to crime by its salutary influence on the moral character of the multitude: the motives which it would oppose to those temptations would be scarcely less effectual than the motives which are presented by the law; and it would heighten the terrors, and strengthen the restraints of the law, by engaging a countless host of eager and active volunteers in the service of criminal justice. If the people saw distinctly the tendencies of offences against property; if the people saw distinctly the tendencies and the grounds of the punishments; and if they were, therefore, bent upon pursuing the criminals to justice, the laws which prohibit these offences would seldom be broken with impunity and, by consequence, would seldom be broken. An enlightened people were a better auxiliary to the judge than an army of policemen.

But, in consequence of the prejudice in question, the fear of public disapprobation scarcely operates upon the poor to the end of restraining them from offences against the property of the wealthier classes. For every man's public is formed of his own class: of those with whom he associates; of those whose favourable or unfavourable opinion sweetens or embitters his life. The poor man's public is formed of the poor. And the crimes, which affect merely the property of the wealthier classes, are certainly regarded with little, or rather with no, abhorrence by the indigent and ignorant portion of the working people. Not perceiving that such crimes are pernicious to *all* classes, but considering property to be a benefit in which they have no share and which is enjoyed by others at their expense, the indigent and ignorant portion of the working people are prone to consider such crimes as *reprisals* made upon usurpers and enemies. They regard the criminal with sympathy rather than with indignation. They rather incline to favour or, at least, to wink at his escape, than to lend their hearty aid towards bringing him to justice.

Those who have inquired into the causes of crimes, and into the means of lessening their number, have commonly expected magnificent results from an improved system of *punishments*. And I admit that something might be done by a judicious mitigation of punishments, and by removing that frequent inclination to abet the escape of a criminal which springs from their repulsive severity. Something might also be accomplished by improvements in prison-discipline and by providing a refuge for criminals who have *suffered* their punishments. For the stigma of legal punishment is commonly indelible; and, by debarring the unhappy criminal from the means of living honestly, forces him on further crimes.

But nothing but *the diffusion of knowledge through the great mass of the people* will go to the root of the evil. Nothing but this will cure or alleviate the poverty which is the ordinary incentive to crime. Nothing but this will extirpate their prejudices and correct their moral sentiments: will lay them under the restraints which are imposed by enlightened opinion, and which operate so potently on the higher and more cultivated classes.

The evils which I have now mentioned, with many which I pass in silence, flow from *one* of the prejudices which enslave the popular mind. The advantages at which I have pointed, with many which I leave unnoticed, would follow the emancipation of the multitude from that *single* error.

And this, with other prejudices, might be expelled from their understandings and affections, if they had mastered the broad principles of the science of political economy, and could make the easiest applications of those simple, though commanding, truths.

The functions of paper money, the incidence of taxes, with other of the *nicer* points which are presented by this science, the multitude, it is probable, will never understand distinctly: and their opinions on such points (if ever they shall think of them at all) will, it is most likely, be always taken from *authority*. But the importance of those nicer points dwindles to nothing when they are compared with the true reasons which call for the institution of property, and with the effect of the principle of population on the price of labour. For if these (which are *not* difficult) were clearly apprehended by the many, they would be raised from penury to comfort: from the necessity of toiling like cattle, to the enjoyment of sufficient leisure: from ignorance and brutishness, to knowledge and refinement: from abject subjection, to the independence which *commands* respect.

If my limits would permit me to dwell upon the topic at length, I could show, by many additional and pregnant examples, that the multitude might clearly apprehend the *leading principles* of ethics and also of the various sciences which are nearly related to ethics and that, if they had seized these principles, and could reason distinctly and justly, all the more momentous of the derivative practical truths would find access to their understandings and expel the antagonist errors.

And the multitude (in civilised communities) would soon apprehend these principles, and would soon acquire the talent of reasoning distinctly and justly, if one of the weightiest of the duties, which God has laid upon governments, were performed with fidelity and zeal. For, if we must construe those duties by the principles of general utility, it is not less incumbent on governments to forward the diffusion of knowledge than to protect their subjects from one another by a due administration of justice, or to defend them by a military force from the attacks of external enemies. A small fraction of the sums which are squandered in needless war would provide complete instruction for the working people: would give this important class that portion in the knowledge of the age which consists with the nature of their callings and with the necessity of toiling for a livelihood.

It appears, then, that the ignorance of the multitude is not altogether invincible, though the principle of general utility be the index to God's commands, and, therefore, the proximate test of positive law and morality.

If ethical science must be gotten by consulting the principle of utility, if it rest upon observation and induction applied to the tendencies of actions, if it be matter of acquired knowledge and not of immediate consciousness, much of it (I admit) will ever be hidden from the multitude or will ever be taken by the multitude on authority, testimony, or trust. For an inquiry into the tendencies of actions embraces so spacious a field, that none but the comparatively few, who study the science assiduously, can apply the principle extensively to received or positive rules and determine how far they accord with its genuine suggestions or dictates.

But the multitude might clearly understand the elements or groundwork of the science, together with the more momentous of the derivative practical truths. To that extent, they might be freed from the dominion of authority: from the necessity of blindly persisting in hereditary opinions and practices; or of turning and veering, for want of directing principles, with every wind of doctrine.

Nor is this the only advantage which would follow the spread of those elements amongst the great body of the people.

If the elements of ethical science were widely *diffused*, the science would *advance* with proportionate rapidity.

If the minds of the many were informed and invigorated, their coarse and sordid pleasures, and their stupid indifference about knowledge, would be supplanted by refined amusements and by liberal curiosity. A numerous body of recruits from the lower of the middle classes, and even from the higher classes of the working people, would thicken the slender ranks of the reading and reflecting public: the public which occupies its leisure with letters, science and philosophy; whose opinion determines the success or failure of books; and whose notice and favour are naturally courted by the writers.

And until that public shall be much extended, shall embrace a considerable portion of the middle and working people, the science of ethics, with all the various sciences which are nearly related to ethics, will advance slowly.

It was the opinion of Mr Locke, and I fully concur in the opinion, that there is no peculiar uncertainty in the *subject* or *matter* of these sciences: that the great and extraordinary difficulties by which their advancement is impeded, are *extrinsick*; are opposed by sinister interests, or by prejudices which are the offspring of such interests, that, if they who seek or affect to seek the truth, would pursue it with obstinate application and with due '*indifferency*', they might frequently hit upon the object which they profess to look for.

Now a few of them *will* pursue it with this requisite 'indifferency' or impartiality, so long as the bulk of the public, which determines the fate of their labours, shall continue to be formed from the classes which are elevated by rank or opulence, and from the peculiar professions or callings which are distinguished by the name of 'liberal'.

In the science of ethics, and in all the various sciences which are nearly related to ethics, your only sure guide is *general* utility. If thinkers and writers would stick to it honestly and closely, they would frequently enrich these sciences with additional truths, or would do them good service by weeding them of nonsense and error. But, since the *peculiar* interests of particular and narrow classes are always somewhat adverse to the interests of the great majority, it is hardly to be expected of writers, whose reputation depends upon such classes, that they should fearlessly tread the path which is indicated by the general well-being. The *indifferency* in the pursuit of truth, which is so earnestly inculcated by Mr Locke, is hardly to be expected of writers who occupy so base a position. Knowing that a fraction of the community can make or mar their reputation, they unconsciously or purposely accommodate their conclusions to the prejudices of that narrower public. Or, to borrow the expressive language of this greatest and best of philosophers, 'they begin with espousing the *well-endowed* opinions in fashion, and then seek arguments to show their beauty, or to varnish and disguise their deformity'.

The treatise by Dr Paley on Moral and Political Philosophy exemplifies the natural tendency of narrow and domineering interests to pervert the course of inquiry from its legitimate purpose.

As men go, this celebrated and influential writer was a wise and a virtuous man. By the qualities of his head and heart, by the cast of his talents and affections, he was fitted, in a high degree, to seek for ethical truth and to expound it successfully to others. He had a clear and just understanding; a hearty contempt of paradox, and of ingenious but useless refinements; no fastidious disdain of the working people, but a warm sympathy with their homely enjoyments and sufferings. He knew that they are more numerous than all the rest of the community, and he felt that they are more important than all the rest of the community to the eye of unclouded reason and impartial benevolence.

But the sinister influence of the position which he unluckily occupied cramped his generous affections and warped the rectitude of his understanding.

A steady pursuit of the consequences indicated by *general* utility was not the most obvious way to professional advancement, nor even the short cut to extensive reputation. For there was no impartial public, formed from the community at large, to reward and courage, with its approbation, an inflexible adherence to truth.

If the bulk of the community had been instructed, so far as their position will permit, he might have looked for a host of readers from the middle classes. He might have looked for a host of readers from those classes of the working people whose wages are commonly high, whose leisure is not inconsiderable, and whose mental powers are called into frequent exercise by the natures of their occupations or callings. To readers of the middle classes, and of all the higher classes of the working people, a well made and honest treatise on Moral and Political Philosophy, in his clear, vivid, downright, *English* style, would have been the most easy and attractive, as well as instructive and useful, of abstract or scientific books.

But those numerous classes of the community were commonly too coarse and ignorant to care for books of the sort. The great majority of the readers who were likely to look into his book belonged to the classes which are elevated by rank or opulence, and to the peculiar professions or callings which are distinguished by the name of 'liberal'. And the character of the book which he wrote betrays the position of the writer. In almost every chapter, and in almost every page, his fear of offending the prejudices commonly entertained by such readers, palpably suppresses the suggestions of his clear and vigorous reason and masters the better affections which inclined him to the *general* good.

He was one of the greatest and best of the great and excellent writers who, by the strength of their philosophical genius, or by their large and tolerant spirit, have given imperishable lustre to the Church of England, and extinguished or softened the hostility of many who reject her creed. He may rank with the Berkeleys and Butlers, with the Burnets, Tillotsons and Hoadlys.

But, in spite of the esteem with which I regard his memory, truth compels me to add that the book is unworthy of the man. For there is much ignoble truckling to the dominant and influential few. There is a deal of shabby sophistry in defence or extenuation of abuses which the few are interested in upholding.

If there were a reading public numerous, discerning, and *impartial*, the science of ethics, and all the various sciences which are nearly related to ethics, would advance with unexampled rapidity.

By the hope of obtaining the approbation which it would bestow upon genuine merit, writers would be incited to the patient research and reflection which are not less requisite to the improvement of ethical, than to the advancement of mathematical, science.

Slight and incoherent thinking would be received with general contempt, though it were cased in polished periods studded with brilliant metaphors. Ethics would be considered by readers, and therefore treated by writers, as the matter or subject of a *science*: as a subject for persevering and accurate investigation, and not as a theme for childish and babbling rhetoric.

This general demand for truth (though it were clothed in homely guise), and this general contempt of falsehood and nonsense (though they were decked with rhetorical graces), would improve the method and style of inquiries into ethics, and into the various sciences which are nearly related to ethics. The writers would attend to the suggestions of Hobbes and of Locke, and would imitate the method so successfully pursued by geometers: though such is the variety of the premises which some of their inquiries involve, and such are the complexity and ambiguity of some of the terms, that they would often fall short of the perfect exactness and coherency, which the fewness of his premises, and the simplicity and definiteness of his expressions, enable the geometer to reach. But, though they would often fall short of geometrical exactness and coherency, they might always approach, and would often attain to them. They would acquire the art and the habit of defining their leading terms; of steadily adhering to the meanings announced by the definitions; of carefully examining and distinctly stating their premises; and of deducing the consequences of their premises with logical rigour. Without rejecting embellishments which might happen to fall in their way, the only excellencies of style for which they would seek are precision, clearness, and conciseness: the first being absolutely requisite to the successful prosecution of inquiry; whilst the others enable the reader to seize the meaning with certainty and spare him unnecessary fatigue.

And, what is equally important, the protection afforded by this public to diligent and honest writers would inspire into writers upon ethics, and upon the nearly related sciences, the spirit of dispassionate inquiry: 'the indifferency' or impartiality in the pursuit of truth, which is just as requisite to the detection of truth as continued and close attention, or sincerity and simplicity of purpose. Relying on the discernment and the justice of a numerous and powerful public, shielded by its countenance from the shafts of the hypocrite and the bigot, indifferent to the idle whistling of that harmless storm, they would scrutinise established institutions and current or received opinions, fearlessly, but coolly; with the freedom which is imperiously demanded by general utility, but without the antipathy which is begotten by the dread of persecution, and which is scarcely less adverse than 'the love of things ancient' to the rapid advancement of science.

This patience in investigation, this distinctness and accuracy of method, this freedom and 'indifferency' in the pursuit of the useful and the true, would thoroughly dispel the obscurity by which the science is clouded and would clear it from most of its uncertainties. The wish, the hope, the prediction of Mr Locke would, in time, be accomplished; and 'ethics would rank with the sciences which are *capable of demonstration*'. The adepts in ethical, as well as in mathematical science, would commonly agree in their results: and, as the jar of their conclusions gradually subsided, a body of doctrine and authority to which the *multitude* might trust would emerge from the existing chaos. The direct examination of the multitude would only extend to the elements and to the easier, though more momentous, of the derivative practical truths. But none of their opinions would be adopted blindly, nor would any of their opinions be obnoxious to groundless and capricious change. Though most or many of their opinions would still be taken from *authority*, the authority to which they would trust might satisfy the most scrupulous reason. In the *unanimous or general consent of numerous and impartial inquirers*, they would find that mark of trustworthiness which justifies reliance on authority, wherever we are debarred from the opportunity of examining the evidence for ourselves.

The second objection to the theory of utility, together with the foregoing answer to that second objection, briefly restated

With regard, then, to the perplexing difficulty which I am trying to solve or extenuate, the case stands thus:

If utility be the proximate test of positive law and morality, it is simply impossible that positive law and morality should be free from defects and errors. Or (adopting a different, though exactly equivalent expression) if the principle of general utility be our guide to the Divine commands, it is impossible that the rules of *conduct actually obtaining amongst mankind* should accord completely and correctly with *the laws established by the Deity*. The index to his will is imperfect and uncertain. His laws are signified obscurely to those upon whom they are binding, and are subject to inevitable and involuntary misconstruction.

For, *first*, positive law and morality, fashioned on the principle of utility, are gotten by observation and induction from the tendencies of human actions: from what can be known or conjectured, by means of observation and induction, of their uniform or customary effects on the general happiness or good. Consequently, till these actions shall be marked and classed with perfect completeness, and their effects observed and ascertained with similar completeness, positive law and morality, fashioned on the principle of utility, must be more or less defective, and more or less erroneous. And these actions being infinitely various, and their effects being infinitely diversified, the work of classing them completely, and of collecting their effects completely, transcends the limited faculties of created and finite beings. As the experience of mankind enlarges, as they observe more extensively and accurately and reason more closely and precisely, they may gradually mend the defects of their legal and moral rules, and may gradually clear their rules from the errors and nonsense of their predecessors. But, though they may constantly approach, they certainly will never attain to a faultless system of ethics: to a system perfectly in unison with the dictates of general utility and, therefore, perfectly in unison with the benevolent wishes of the Deity.

And, *secondly*, if utility be the proximate test of positive law and morality, the defects and errors of *popular* or *vulgar* ethics will scarcely admit of a remedy. For, if ethical truth be matter of science, and not of immediate consciousness, most of the ethical maxims, which govern the sentiments of the multitude, must be taken, without examination, from human authority. And where is the ***human*** authority upon which they can safely rely? Where is the ***human*** authority bearing such marks of trustworthiness, that the ignorant may hang their faith upon it with reasonable assurance? Reviewing the various ages and the various nations of the world, reviewing the various sects which have divided the opinions of mankind, we find conflicting maxims taught with equal confidence, and received with equal docility. We find the guides of the multitude moved by sinister interests, or by prejudices which are the offspring of such interests. We find them stifling inquiry according to the measure of their means: upholding with fire and sword, or with sophistry, declamation and calumny, the theological and ethical dogmas which they impose upon their prostrate disciples.

Such is the difficulty. The only solution of which this difficulty seems to admit is suggested by the remarks which I have already submitted to your attention, and which I will now repeat in an inverted and compendious form.

In the *first* place, the *diffusion* of ethical science amongst the great bulk of mankind will gradually remove the obstacles which prevent or retard its *advancement*. The field of human conduct being infinite or immense, it is impossible that human understanding should embrace and explore it completely. But, by the general diffusion of knowledge amongst the great bulk of mankind, by the impulse and the direction which the diffusion will give to inquiry, many of the defects and errors in existing law and morality will in time be supplied and corrected.

Secondly, though the many must trust to authority for a number of subordinate truths, they are competent to examine the elements which are the groundwork of the science of ethics, and to infer the more momentous of the derivative practical consequences.

And, *thirdly*, as the science of ethics advances and is cleared of obscurity and uncertainties, they who are debarred from opportunities of examining the science extensively will find an authority, whereon they may rationally rely, in the unanimous or general agreement of searching and impartial inquirers.

LECTURE IV

SYNOPSIS OF LECTURE IV

The connection of the fourth with the third lecture
The second objection to the theory of utility, resumed
A further answer to that second objection
The hypothesis of a *moral sense*, briefly introduced
'A moral sense', 'a common sense', 'a moral instinct', 'a principle of reflection or conscience', 'a practical reason', 'innate practical principles', 'connate practical principles', etc., are various expressions for one and the same hypothesis
The hypothesis in question involves two assumptions
The first of the two assumptions involved by the hypothesis in question, stated in general expressions
The foregoing statement of the first assumption, exemplified and explained by an imaginary case
The first of the two assumptions involved by the hypothesis in question, briefly restated in general expressions
The second of the two assumptions involved by the hypothesis in question, briefly stated
As an index to God's commands, a moral sense were less fallible than the principle of general utility
But is there any *evidence* to sustain the hypothesis in question?
The hypothesis in question is disproved by the negative state of our consciousness

TEXT OF LECTURE IV

The connection of the fourth with the third lecture

In my last lecture, I endeavoured to answer an objection which may be urged against the theory of utility. And to the purpose of linking my present with my last lecture, I will now restate, in a somewhat abridged shape, that summary of the objection and the answer with which I concluded my discourse.

The objection may be put briefly in the following manner.

If utility be the proximate test of positive law and morality, it is impossible that the rules of conduct *actually obtaining amongst mankind* should accord completely and correctly with the laws *established by the Deity*. The index to his will is imperfect and uncertain. His laws are signified obscurely to those upon whom they are binding, and are subject to inevitable and involuntary misconstruction.

For, *first*, positive law and morality, fashioned on the principle of utility, are gotten by observation and induction from the tendencies of human actions. Consequently, till these actions shall be marked and classed with perfect completeness, and their effects observed and ascertained with similar completeness, positive law and morality, fashioned on the principle of utility, must be more or less defective, and more or less erroneous. And, these actions being infinitely various, and their effects being infinitely diversified, the work of classing them completely and of collecting their effects completely, transcends the limited faculties of created and finite beings.

And, *secondly*, if utility be the proximate test of positive law and morality, the defects and errors of *popular* or *vulgar* ethics will scarcely admit of a remedy. For if ethical truth be matter of science, and not of immediate consciousness, most of the ethical maxims which govern the sentiments of the multitude must be taken, without examination, from human authority.

Such is the objection. The only answer of which the objection will admit, is suggested by the remarks which I offered in my last lecture, and which I repeated at its close, and here repeat in an inverted and compendious form.

In the *first* place, the *diffusion* of ethical science amongst the great bulk of mankind will gradually remove the obstacles which prevent or retard its *advancement*. The field of human conduct being infinite or immense, it is impossible that human understanding should embrace and explore it completely. But, by the general diffusion of knowledge among the great bulk of mankind, by the impulse and the direction which the diffusion will give to inquiry, many of the defects and errors in existing law and morality will in time be supplied and corrected.

Secondly, though the many must trust to authority for a number of subordinate truths, they are competent to examine the elements which are the groundwork of the science of ethics and to infer the more momentous of the derivative practical consequences.

And, *thirdly*, as the science of ethics advances and is cleared of obscurity and uncertainties, they, who are debarred from opportunities of examining the science extensively, will find an authority whereon they may rationally rely, in the unanimous or general agreement of searching and impartial inquirers.

The second objection to the theory of utility, resumed

But this answer, it must be admitted, merely *extenuates* the objection. It shows that law and morality fashioned on the principle of utility might approach continually and indefinitely to absolute perfection. But it grants that law and morality fashioned on the principle of utility is inevitably defective and erroneous: that, if the laws established by the Deity must be construed by the principle of utility, the most perfect system of ethics which the wit of man could conceive were a partial and inaccurate copy of the Divine original or pattern.

And this (it may be urged) disproves the theory which makes the principle of utility the index to the Divine pleasure. For it consists not with the known wisdom and the known benevolence of the Deity, that he should signify his commands defectively and obscurely to those upon whom they are binding.

A further answer to that second objection

But admitting the imperfection of utility as the index to the Divine pleasure, it is impossible to argue, from this its admitted imperfection, 'that utility is *not* the index'.

Owing to causes which are hidden from human understanding, all the works of the Deity which are open to human observation are alloyed with imperfection or evil. That the Deity should signify his commands defectively and obscurely is strictly in keeping or unison with the rest of his inscrutable ways. The objection now in question proves too much, and, therefore, is untenable. If you argue 'that the principle of utility is *not* the index to his laws, *because* the principle of utility were an *imperfect* index to his laws', you argue 'that all his works are in fact exempt from evil, *because* imperfection or evil is inconsistent with his wisdom and goodness'. The former of these arguments *implies* the latter, or is merely an application of the sweeping position to *one* of innumerable cases.

Accordingly, if the objection now in question will lie to the theory of utility, a similar objection will lie to *every* theory of ethics which supposes that any of our duties are set or imposed by the Deity.

The objection is founded on the alleged inconsistency of evil with his perfect wisdom and goodness. But the notion or idea of evil or imperfection is involved in the connected notions of law, duty, and sanction. For, seeing that every law imposes a restraint, every law is an evil of itself: and, unless it be the work of malignity, or proceed from consummate folly, it also supposes an evil which it is designed to prevent or remedy. Law, like medicine, is a preventive or remedy of *evil*: and, if the world were free from evil, the notion and the name would be unknown.

'That his laws are signified obscurely, if utility be the index to his laws' is rather a presumption in favour of the theory which makes utility our guide. Analogy might lead us to expect that they would be signified obscurely. For laws or commands suppose the existence of evils which they are designed to remedy: let them be signified as they may, they remedy those evils imperfectly; and the imperfection which they are designed to remedy, and of which the remedy partakes, might naturally be expected to show itself in the mode by which they are manifested.

My answer to the objection is the very argument which the excellent Butler, in his admirable *Analogy*, has wielded in defence of Christianity with the vigour and the skill of a master.

Considered as a system of rules for the guidance of human conduct, the Christian religion is defective. There are also circumstances, regarding the manner of its promulgation, which human reason vainly labours to reconcile with the wisdom and goodness of God. Still it were absurd to argue 'that the religion is not of God, *because* the religion is defective, and is imperfectly revealed to mankind'. For the objection is founded on the alleged inconsistency of evil with his perfect wisdom and goodness. And, since evil pervades the universe, in so far as it is open to our inspection, a similar objection will lie to *every* system of religion which ascribes the existence of the universe to a wise and benevolent Author. Whoever believes that the universe is the work of benevolence and wisdom, is concluded, or *estopped*, by his own religious creed, from taking an objection of the kind to the creed or system of another.

Analogy (as Butler has shown) would lead us to expect the imperfection upon which the objection is founded. Something of the imperfection which runs through the frame of the universe would probably be found in a revelation emanating from the Author of the universe.

And here my solution of the difficulty necessarily stops. A complete solution is manifestly impossible. To reconcile the existence of evil with the wisdom and goodness of God is a task which surpasses the powers of our narrow and feeble understandings. This is a deep which our reason is too short to fathom. From the decided predominance of good which is observable in the order of the world, and from the manifold marks of wisdom which the order of the world exhibits, we may draw the cheering inference 'that its Author is good and wise'. Why the world which he has made is not altogether perfect, or why a benevolent Deity tolerates the existence of evil, or what (if I may so express myself) are the obstacles in the way of his benevolence, are clearly questions which it were impossible to solve, and which it were idle to agitate although they admitted a solution. It is enough for us to know that the Deity is perfectly good; and that, since he is perfectly good, he wills the happiness of his creatures. *This* is a truth of the greatest *practical* moment. For the cast of the affections, which we attribute to the Deity, determines, for the most part, the cast of our moral sentiments.

The hypothesis of a moral sense, briefly introduced

I admit, then, that God's commands are imperfectly signified to man, supposing we must gather his commands from the tendencies of human actions. But I deny that this imperfection is a conclusive objection to the theory which makes the principle of utility our guide or index to his will. Whoever would disprove the theory which makes utility our guide must produce another principle that were a surer and a better guide.

Now, if we reject *utility* as the index to God's commands we must assent to the theory or hypothesis which supposes *a moral sense*. One of the adverse theories, which regard the nature of that index, is certainly true. He has left us to *presume* his commands from the tendencies of human actions, or he has given us a peculiar *sense* of which his commands are the objects.

'A moral sense', 'a common sense', 'a moral instinct', 'a principle of reflection or conscience', 'a practical reason', 'innate practical principles', 'connate practical principles', etc., are various expressions for one and the same hypothesis

All the hypotheses, regarding the nature of that index, which discard the principle of utility, are built upon the supposition of a peculiar or appropriate sense. The language of each of these hypotheses differs from the language of the others, but the import of each resembles the import of the rest.

By '*a moral sense*', with which my understanding is furnished, I discern the human actions which the Deity enjoins and forbids: and, since you and the rest of the species are provided with a like organ, it is clear that this sense of mine is 'the *common* sense of mankind'. By '*a moral instinct*', with which the Deity has endowed me, I am urged to some of these actions, and am warned to forbear from others. '*A principle of reflection or conscience*', which Butler assures me I possess, informs me of their rectitude or pravity. Or '*the innate practical principles*', which Locke has presumed to question, define the duties, which God has imposed upon me, with infallible clearness and certainty.

These and other phrases are various but equivalent expressions for one and the same hypothesis. The only observable difference between these various expressions consists in this: that some denote *sentiments* which are excited by human actions, whilst others denote the *commands* to which those sentiments are the index.

The hypothesis in question involves two assumptions

The hypothesis of a moral sense, or the hypothesis which is variously signified by these various but equivalent expressions, involves two assumptions.

The first of the two assumptions involved by the hypothesis in question, stated in general expressions

The first of the two assumptions involved by the hypothesis in question may be stated, in general expressions, thus:

Certain sentiments or feelings of approbation or disapprobation accompany our conceptions of certain human actions. They are neither effects of reflection upon the tendencies of the actions which excite them, nor are they effects of education. A conception of any of these actions would be accompanied by certain of these sentiments, although we had not adverted to its good or evil tendency, nor knew the opinions of others with regard to actions of the class.

In a word, that portion of the hypothesis in question which I am now stating is purely *negative*. We are gifted with moral sentiments which are *ultimate or inscrutable facts*: which are *not* the consequences of reflection upon the tendencies of human actions, which are *not* the consequences of the education that we receive from our fellowmen, which are *not* the consequences or effects of any antecedents or causes placed within the reach of our inspection. Our conceptions of certain actions are accompanied by certain sentiments, and *there* is an end of our knowledge.

For the sake of brevity, we may say that these sentiments are 'instinctive', or we may call them 'moral instincts'.

For the terms 'instinctive', and 'instinct', are merely *negative* expressions. They merely denote our own ignorance. They mean that the phenomena of which we happen to be talking are *not* preceded by causes which man is able to perceive. For example, the bird, it is commonly said, builds her nest by 'instinct': or the skill which the bird evinces in the building of her nest, is commonly styled 'instinctive'. That is to say, it is not the product of experiments made by the bird herself; it has not been imparted to the bird by the teaching or example of others; nor is it the consequence or effect of any antecedent or cause open to our observation.

The remark which I have now made upon the terms 'instinctive' and 'instinct', is not interposed needlessly. For, though their true import is extremely simple and trivial, they are apt to dazzle and confound us (unless we advert to it steadily) with the false and cheating appearance of a mysterious and magnificent meaning.

The foregoing statement of the first assumption, exemplified and explained by an imaginary case

In order that we may clearly apprehend the nature of these 'moral instincts', I will descend from general expressions to an imaginary case.

I will not imagine the case which is fancied by Dr Paley: for I think it ill fitted to bring out the meaning sharply. I will merely take the liberty of borrowing his solitary savage: a child abandoned in the wilderness immediately after its birth, and growing to the age of manhood in estrangement from human society.

Having gotten my subject, I proceed to deal with him after my own fashion.

I imagine that the savage, as he wanders in search of prey, meets, for the first time in his life, with a man. This man is a hunter, and is carrying a deer which he has killed. The savage pounces upon it. The hunter holds it fast. And, in order that he may remove this obstacle to the satisfaction of his gnawing hunger, the savage seizes a stone and knocks the hunter on the head. Now, according to the hypothesis in question, the savage is affected with *remorse* at the thought of the deed which he has done. He is affected with more than the *compassion* which is excited by the sufferings of another, and which, considered by itself, amounts not to a moral sentiment. He is affected with the more complex emotion of *self-condemnation* or *remorse*: with a consciousness of *guilt*: with the feeling that haunts and tortures civilised or cultivated men whenever they violate rules which accord with their notions of utility, or which they have learned from others to regard with habitual veneration. He feels as you would feel in case you had committed a murder: in case you had killed another, in an attempt to rob him of his goods: or in case you had killed another under *any* combination of circumstances, which, agreeably to your notions of utility, would make the act a pernicious one or, agreeably to the moral impressions which you have passively received from others, would give to the act of killing the quality and the name of an *injury*.

Again, shortly after the incident which I have now imagined, he meets with a second hunter whom he also knocks on the head. But, in this instance, he is not the aggressor. He is attacked, beaten, wounded, without the shadow of a provocation: and to prevent a deadly blow which is aimed at his own head he kills the wanton assailant. Now here, according to the hypothesis, he is *not* affected with remorse. The sufferings of the dying man move him, perhaps, to *compassion*: but his *conscience* (as the phrase goes) is tranquil. He feels as you would feel after a justifiable homicide, after you had shot a highwayman in defence of your goods and your life, or after you had killed another under *any* combination of circumstances which, agreeably to your notions of utility, would render killing innocuous, or agreeably to the current morality of your age and country, would render the killing of another a just or lawful action.

That *you* should feel remorse if you kill in an attempt to rob, and should not be affected with remorse if you kill a murderous robber, is a difference which I readily account for without the supposition of an instinct. The law of your country distinguishes the cases: and the current morality of your country accords with the law.

Supposing that you have never adverted to the reasons of that distinction, the difference between your feelings is easily explained by imputing it to *education*: meaning, by the term *education*, the influence of authority and example on opinions, sentiments, and habits.

Supposing that you have ever adverted to the reasons of that distinction, you, of course, have been struck with its obvious utility. Generally speaking, the intentional killing of another is an act of pernicious tendency. If the act were frequent, it would annihilate that general security, and that general feeling of security, which are, or should be, the principal ends of political society and law. But to this there are exceptions: and the intentional killing of a robber who aims at your property and life is amongst those exceptions. Instead of being adverse to the principal ends of law, it rather promotes those ends. It answers the purpose of the punishment which the law inflicts upon murderers: and it also accomplishes a purpose which punishment is too tardy to reach. The death inflicted on the aggressor tends, as his punishment would tend, to deter from the crime of murder: and it also prevents, what his punishment would not prevent, the completion of the murderous design in the specific or particular instance. Supposing that you have ever adverted to these and similar reasons, the difference between your feelings is easily explained by imputing it to a *perception of utility*. You see that the tendencies of the act vary with the circumstances of the act, and your sentiments in regard to the act vary with those varying tendencies.

But the difference, supposed by the hypothesis, between the feelings of the *savage* cannot be imputed to *education*. For the savage has lived in estrangement from human society.

Nor can the supposed difference be imputed to *a perception of utility*. He knocks a man on the head, that he may satisfy his gnawing hunger. He knocks another on the head, that he may escape from wounds and death. So far, then, as these different actions exclusively regard himself, they are equally good: and so far as these different actions regard the men whom he kills, they are equally bad. As tried by the test of utility, *and with the lights which the savage possesses*, the moral qualities of the two actions are precisely the same. If we suppose it possible that he adverts to considerations of utility, and that his sentiments in respect to these actions are determined by considerations of utility, we must infer that he remembers both of them with similar feelings: with similar feelings of complacency, as the actions regard himself; with similar feelings of regret, as they regard the sufferings of the slain.

To the social man the difference between these actions, as tried by the test of utility, were immense. The general happiness or good demands the institution of property: that the exclusive enjoyment conferred by the law upon the owner shall not be disturbed by private and unauthorised persons: that no man shall take from another the product of his labour or saving, without the permission of the owner previously signified, or without the authority of the sovereign acting for the common weal. Were want, however intense, an excuse for violations of property; could every man who hungers take from another with impunity, and slay the owner with impunity if the owner stood on his possession; that beneficent institution would become nugatory, and the ends of government and law would be defeated. And, on the other hand, the very principle of utility, which demands the institution of property, requires that an attack upon the body shall be repelled at the instant: that, if the impending evil cannot be averted otherwise, the aggressor shall be slain on the spot by the party whose life is in jeopardy.

But these are considerations which would not present themselves to the solitary savage. They involve a number of notions with which his mind would be unfurnished. They involve the notions of political society; of supreme government; of positive law; of legal right; of legal duty; of legal injury. The good and the evil of the two actions, in so far as the two actions would affect the immediate parties, is all that the savage could perceive.

The difference, supposed by the hypothesis, between the feelings of the savage must, therefore, be ascribed to *a moral sense*, or to *innate practical principles*. Or (speaking in homelier but plainer language) he would regard the two actions with different sentiments, *we know not why*.

The first of the two assumptions involved by the hypothesis in question, briefly restated in general expressions

The first of the two assumptions involved by the hypothesis in question is, therefore, this: certain inscrutable sentiments of approbation or disapprobation accompany our conceptions of certain human actions. They are not begotten by reflection upon the tendencies of the actions which excite them, nor are they instilled into our minds by our intercourse with our fellowmen. They are simple elements of our nature. They are ultimate facts. They are not the effects of causes, or are not the consequents of antecedents, which are open to human observation.

And, thus far, the hypothesis in question has been embraced by sceptics as well as by religionists. For example, it is supposed by David Hume, in his *Essay on the Principles of Morals*, that *some* of our moral sentiments spring from *a perception of utility*: but he also appears to imagine that *others* are not to be analysed or belong exclusively to the province of *taste*. Such, I say, *appears* to be his meaning. For, in this essay, as in all his writings, he is rather acute and ingenious than coherent and profound: handling detached topics with signal dexterity, but evincing an utter inability to grasp his subject as a whole. When he speaks of *moral sentiments* belonging to the province of *taste*, he may, perhaps, be adverting to the origin of *benevolence*, or to the origin of our *sympathy* with the pleasures and pains of others: a feeling that differs as broadly as the appetite of hunger or thirst from the sentiments of approbation or disapprobation which accompany our judgments upon actions.

The second of the two assumptions involved by the hypothesis in question, briefly stated

That these inscrutable sentiments are signs of the Divine will, or the proofs that the actions which excite them are enjoined or forbidden by God, is the second of the two assumptions involved by the hypothesis in question.

In the language of the admirable Butler (who is the ablest advocate of the hypothesis) the human actions by which these feelings are excited are their direct and appropriate objects: just as things visible are the direct and appropriate objects of the sense of seeing.

In homelier but plainer language, I may put his meaning thus: as God has given us eyes, in order that we may see therewith; so has he gifted or endowed us with the feelings or sentiments in question, in order that we may distinguish directly, by means of these feelings or sentiments, the actions which he enjoins or permits, from the actions which he prohibits.

Or, if you like it better, I may put the meaning thus: that these inscrutable sentiments are signs of the Divine will is an inference which we necessarily deduce from our consideration of *final causes*. Like the rest of our appetites or aversions, these sentiments were designed by the Author of our being to answer an appropriate end. And the only pertinent end which we can possibly ascribe to them, is the end or final cause at which I have now pointed.

As an index to God's commands, a moral sense were less fallible than the principle of general utility

Now, supposing that the Deity has endowed us with a moral sense or instinct, we are free of the difficulty to which we are subject, if we must construe his laws by the principle of general utility. According to the hypothesis in question, the inscrutable feelings which are styled the moral sense arise directly and inevitably with the thoughts of their appropriate objects. We cannot mistake the laws which God has prescribed to mankind, although we may often be seduced by the blandishments of present advantage from the plain path of our duties. The understanding is never at a fault, although the will may be frail.

But is there any evidence *to sustain the hypothesis in question?*

But here arises a small question: is there any *evidence* that we are gifted with feelings of the sort?

The hypothesis in question is disproved by the negative state of our consciousness

That this question is possible, or is seriously asked and agitated, would seem of itself a sufficient proof that we are *not* endowed with such feelings. According to the hypothesis of a moral sense, we are conscious of the feelings which indicate God's commands, as we are conscious of hunger or thirst. In other words, the feelings which indicate God's commands are ultimate facts. But, since they are ultimate facts, these feelings or sentiments must be indisputable, and must also differ obviously from the other elements of our nature. If I were really gifted with feelings or sentiments of the sort, I could no more seriously question whether I had them or not, and could no more blend and confound them with my other feelings or sentiments, than I can seriously question the existence of hunger or thirst, or can mistake the feeling which affects me when I am hungry for the different feeling which affects me when I am thirsty. All the parts of our nature which are ultimate, or incapable of analysis, are certain and distinct, as well as inscrutable. We know and discern them with unhesitating and invincible assurance.

The two current arguments in favour of the hypothesis in question, briefly stated

The two current arguments in favour of the hypothesis in question are raised on the following assertions.

1. The judgments which we pass internally upon the rectitude or pravity of actions are immediate and involuntary. In other words, our moral sentiments or feelings arise directly and inevitably with our conceptions of the actions which excite them.
2. The moral sentiments of all men are precisely alike.

The first argument in favour of the hypothesis in question, examined

Now the first of these venturous assertions is not universally true. In numberless cases, the judgments which we pass internally upon the rectitude or pravity of actions are hesitating and slow. And it not unfrequently happens that we cannot arrive at a conclusion, or are utterly at a loss to determine whether we shall praise or blame.

And, granting that our moral sentiments are always instantaneous and inevitable, this will not demonstrate that our moral sentiments are instinctive. Sentiments which are factitious, or begotten in the way of association, are not less prompt and involuntary than feelings which are instinctive or inscrutable. For example, we begin by loving money for the sake of the enjoyment which it purchases: and, that enjoyment apart, we care not a straw for money. But, in time, our love of enjoyment is extended to money itself, or our love of enjoyment becomes inseparably associated with the thought of the money which procures it. The conception of money suggests a wish for money, although we think not of the uses to which we should apply it. Again, we begin by loving knowledge as a means to ends. But, in time, the love of the ends becomes inseparably associated with the thought or conception of the instrument. Curiosity is instantly roused by every unusual appearance, although there is no purpose which the solution of the appearance would answer, or although we advert not to the purpose which the solution of the appearance might subserve.

The promptitude and decision with which we judge of actions are impertinent to the matter in question: for our moral sentiments would be prompt and inevitable, although they arose from a perception of utility, or although they were impressed upon our minds by the authority of our fellow-men. Supposing that a moral sentiment sprang from a perception of utility, or supposing that a moral sentiment were impressed upon our minds by authority, it would hardly recur spontaneously until it had recurred frequently. Unless we recalled the *reasons* which had led us to our opinion, or unless we adverted to the *authority* which had determined our opinion, the sentiment, at the outset, would hardly be excited by the thought of the corresponding action. But, in time, the sentiment would adhere inseparably to the thought of the corresponding action. Although we recalled not the ground of our moral approbation or aversion, the sentiment would recur directly and inevitably with the conception of its appropriate object.

The second argument in favour of the hypothesis in question, examined

But, to prove that moral sentiments are instinctive or inscrutable, it is bodily asserted, by the advocates of the hypothesis in question, that the moral sentiments of all men are precisely alike.

The argument, in favour of the hypothesis, which is raised on this hardy assertion, may be stated briefly in the following manner: no opinion or sentiment which is a result of observation and induction is held or felt by all mankind. Observation and induction, as applied to the same subject, lead different men to different conclusions. But the judgments which are passed internally upon the rectitude or pravity of actions, or the moral sentiments or feelings which actions excite, are precisely alike with all men. Consequently, our moral sentiments or feelings were not gotten by our inductions from the tendencies of the actions which excite them: nor were these sentiments or feelings gotten by inductions of others, and then impressed upon our minds by human authority and example. Consequently, our moral sentiments are instinctive or are ultimate or inscrutable facts.

Now, though the assertion were granted, the argument raised on the assertion would hardly endure examination. Though the moral sentiments of all men were precisely alike, it would hardly follow that moral sentiments are instinctive.

But an attempt to confute the argument were superfluous labour: for the assertion whereon it is raised is groundless. The respective moral sentiments of different ages and nations, and of different men in the same age and nation, have differed to infinity. This proposition is so notoriously true, and to every instructed mind the facts upon which it rests are so familiar, that I should hardly treat my hearers with due respect if I attempted to establish it by proof. I therefore assume it without an attempt at proof; and I oppose it to the assertion which I am now considering, and to the argument which is raised on that assertion.

But, before I dismiss the assertion which I am now considering, I will briefly advert to a difficulty attending the hypothesis in question which that unfounded assertion naturally suggests. Assuming that moral sentiments are instinctive or inscrutable, they are either different with different men, or they are alike with all men. To affirm 'that they are alike with all men' is merely to hazard a bold assertion contradicted by notorious facts. If they are different with different men, it follows that God has not set to men a *common* rule. If they are different with different men, there is no *common* test of human conduct: there is no test by which one man may try the conduct of another. It were folly and presumption to *me* to sit in judgment upon *you*. That which were pravity in *me* may, for aught I can know, be rectitude in *you*. The moral sense which *you* allege may be just as good and genuine as that of which *I* am conscious. Though *my* instinct points one way, *yours* may point another. There is no broad sun destined to illumine the world but every single man must walk by his own candle.

A brief statement of the fact whereon the second argument in favour of the hypothesis in question is founded

Now what is the fact whereon the second argument in favour of the hypothesis in question is founded? The plain and glaring fact is this: with regard to actions of a few classes, the moral sentiments of most, though not of all men, have been alike. But, with regard to actions of other classes, their moral sentiments have differed, through every shade or degree, from slight diversity to direct opposition.

The fact accords exactly with the hypothesis or theory of utility

And this is what might be expected, supposing that the principle of general utility is our only guide or index to the tacit commands of the Deity. The fact accords exactly with that hypothesis or theory. For, first, the positions wherein men, in different ages and nations, are, in many respects, widely different: whence it inevitably follows that much which was useful there and then were useless or pernicious here and now. And, secondly, since human tastes are various, and since human reason is fallible, men's moral sentiments must often widely differ even in respect of the circumstances wherein their positions are alike. But, with regard to actions of a few classes, the dictates of utility are the same at all times and places, and are also so obvious that they hardly admit of mistake or doubt. And hence would naturally ensue what observation shows us is the fact: namely, a general resemblance, with infinite variety, in the systems of law and morality which have actually obtained in the world.

A brief statement of the intermediate hypothesis which is compounded of the hypothesis of utility and the hypothesis of a moral sense

According to the hypothesis which I have now stated and examined, the moral sense is our *only* index to the tacit commands of the Deity. According to an intermediate hypothesis, compounded of the hypothesis of utility and the hypothesis of a moral sense, the moral sense is our index to *some* of his tacit commands, but the principle of general utility is our index to *others*.

In so far as I can gather his opinion from his admirable sermons, it would seem that the compound hypothesis was embraced by Bishop Butler. But of this I am not certain: for, from many passages in those sermons, we may perhaps infer that he thought the moral sense our only index or guide.

The compound hypothesis now in question naturally arose from the fact to which I have already adverted. With regard to actions of a few classes, the moral sentiments of most, though not of all men, have been alike. With regard to actions of other classes, their moral sentiments have differed, through every shade or degree, from slight diversity to direct opposition. In respect to the classes of actions, with regard to which their moral sentiments have agreed, there was some show of reason for the supposition of a moral sense. In respect to the classes of action, with regard to which their moral sentiments have differed, the supposition of a moral sense seemed to be excluded.

But the modified or mixed hypothesis now in question is not less halting than the pure hypothesis of a moral sense or instinct. With regard to actions of a few classes, the moral sentiments of *most* men have concurred or agreed. But it were hardly possible to indicate a single class of actions with regard to which *all* men have thought and felt alike. And it is clear that every objection to the simple or pure hypothesis may be urged, with slight adaptions, against the modified or mixed.

The division of positive law into law natural *and* law positive, *and the division of* jus civile *into* jus gentium *and* jus civile, *suppose or involve the intermediate hypothesis which is compounded of the hypothesis of utility and the hypothesis of a moral sense*

By modern writers on jurisprudence, positive law (or law, simply and strictly so-called) is divided into *law natural* and *law positive*. By the classical Roman jurists, borrowing from the Greek philosophers, *jus civile* (or positive law) is divided into *jus gentium* and *jus civile*. Which two divisions of positive law are exactly equivalent.

By modern writers on jurisprudence, and by the classical Roman jurists, positive morality is also divided into *natural* and *positive*. For, through the frequent confusion (to which I shall advert hereafter) of positive law and positive morality, a portion of positive morality, as well as of positive law, is embraced by the *law natural* of modern writers on jurisprudence, and by the equivalent *jus gentium* of the classical Roman jurists.

By reason of the division of positive law into *law natural* and *law positive*, crimes are divided by modern writers on jurisprudence into crimes which are 'mala *in se*' and crimes which are 'mala *quia prohibita*'. By reason of the division of positive law into *jus gentium* and *jus civile*, crimes are divided, by the classical Roman jurists, into such as are crimes *juris gentium* and such as are crimes *jure civili*. Which divisions of crimes, like the divisions of law wherefrom they are respectively derived, are exactly equivalent.

Now without a clear apprehension of the hypothesis of utility, of the pure hypothesis of a moral sense, and of the modified or mixed hypothesis which is compounded of the others, the distinction of positive law into *natural* and *positive*, with the various derivative distinctions which rest upon that main one, are utterly unintelligible. Assuming the hypothesis of utility, or assuming the pure hypothesis of a moral sense, the distinction of positive law into *natural* and *positive* is senseless. But, assuming the intermediate hypothesis which is compounded of the others, positive law, and also positive morality, is inevitably distinguished into *natural* and *positive*. In other words, if the modified or mixed hypothesis be founded in truth, positive human rules fall into two parcels:

1. Positive human rules which obtain with all mankind; and the conformity of which to Divine commands is, therefore, indicated by the moral sense:
2. Positive human rules which do not obtain universally; and the conformity of which to Divine commands is, therefore, not indicated by that infallible guide.

When I treat of positive law as considered with reference to its *sources*, I shall show completely that the modified or mixed hypothesis is involved by the distinction of positive law into law natural and law positive. I touch upon the topic, at the present point of my Course, to the following purpose: namely, to show that my disquisitions on the hypothesis of utility, on the hypothesis of a moral sense, and on that intermediate hypothesis which is compounded of the others, are necessary steps in a series of discourses occupied with the *rationale* of jurisprudence. It will, indeed, appear, as I advance in my projected Course, that *many* of the distinctions, which the science of jurisprudence presents, cannot be expounded, in a complete and satisfactory manner, without a previous exposition of those seemingly irrelative hypotheses. But the topic upon which I have touched at the present point of my Course shows most succinctly the pertinence of the disquisitions in question.

The foregoing disquisitions on the index to God's commands, closed with an endeavour to clear the theory of utility from two current though gross misconceptions

Having stated the hypothesis of utility, the hypothesis of a moral sense, and the modified or mixed hypothesis which is compounded of the others, I will close my disquisitions on the index to God's commands with an endeavour to clear the hypothesis of utility from two current though gross misconceptions.

The two misconceptions stated

Of the writers who maintain and impugn the theory of utility, three out of four fall into one or the other of the following errors:

1. Some of them confound the *motives* which ought to determine our conduct with the proximate *measure* or *test* to which our conduct should conform and by which our conduct should be tried.
2. Others confound the *theory of general utility* with that *theory or hypothesis concerning the origin of benevolence* which is branded by its ignorant or disingenuous adversaries with the misleading and invidious name of the *selfish system*.

Now these errors are so palpable, that perhaps I ought to conclude with the bare statement, and leave my hearers to supply the corrective. But, let them be never so palpable, they have imposed upon persons of unquestionable penetration, and therefore may impose upon all who will not pause to examine them. Accordingly, I will clear the theory of utility from these gross but current misconceptions as completely as my limits will permit.

I will first examine the error of confounding *motives* to conduct with the proximate *measure* or *test* to which our conduct should conform and by which our conduct should be tried. I will then examine the error of confounding the *theory of utility* with that *theory or hypothesis concerning the origin of benevolence* which is styled the *selfish system*.

The first misconception examined

According to the theory of utility, the measure or test of human conduct is the law set by God to his human creatures. Now some of his commands are revealed, whilst others are unrevealed. Or (changing the phrase) some of his commands are express, whilst others are tacit. The commands which God has revealed we must gather from the terms wherein they are promulged. The commands which he has not revealed we must construe by the principle of utility: by the probable effects of our conduct on that general happiness or good which is the final cause or purpose of the good and wise lawgiver in all his laws and commandments.

Strictly speaking, therefore, utility is not the *measure* to which our conduct should conform, nor is utility the *test* by which our conduct should be tried. It is not in itself the source or spring of our highest or paramount obligations, but it guides us to the source whence these obligations flow. It is merely the *index* to the measure, the *index* to the test. But, since we conform to the measure by following the suggestions of the index, I may say with sufficient, though not with strict, propriety that utility is the measure or test *proximately* or *immediately*. Accordingly, I style the Divine commands the *ultimate* measure or test: but I style the principle of utility, or the general happiness or good, the *proximate* measure to which our conduct should conform, or the *proximate* test by which our conduct should be tried.

Now, though the general good is that proximate *measure*, or though the general good is that proximate *test*, it is not in all, or even in most cases, the *motive* or *inducement* which ought to determine our conduct. If our conduct were always determined by it considered as a *motive* or *inducement*, our conduct would often disagree with it considered as the *standard* or *measure*. If our conduct were always determined by it considered as a *motive* or *inducement*, our conduct would often be blamable, rather than deserving of praise, when tried by it as the *test*.

Though these propositions may sound like paradoxes, they are perfectly just. I should occupy more time than I can give to the disquisition, if I went through the whole of the proofs which would establish them beyond contradiction. But the few hints which I shall now throw out will sufficiently suggest the evidence to those of my hearers who may not have reflected on the subject.

When I speak of the public good, or of the general good, I mean the aggregate enjoyments of the single or individual persons who compose that public or general to which my attention is directed. The good of mankind is the aggregate of the pleasures which are respectively enjoyed by the individuals who constitute the human race. The good of England is the aggregate of the pleasures which fall to the lot of Englishmen considered individually or singly. The good of the public in the town to which I belong is the aggregate of the pleasures which the inhabitants severally enjoy.

'Mankind', 'country', 'public', are concise expressions for a number of individual persons considered collectively or as a whole. In case the good of those persons considered singly or individually were sacrificed to the good of those persons considered collectively or as a whole, the general good would be destroyed by the sacrifice. The sum of the particular enjoyments which constitutes the general good would be sacrificed to the mere name by which that good is denoted.

When it is stated strictly and nakedly, this truth is so plain and palpable that the statement is almost laughable. But experience sufficiently evinces that plain and palpable truths are prone to slip from the memory: that the neglect of plain and palpable truths is the source of most of the errors with which the world is infested. For example, that notion of the public good which was current in the ancient republics supposes a neglect of the truism to which I have called your attention. Agreeably to that notion of the public good, the happiness of the individual citizens is sacrificed without scruple in order that the common weal may wax and prosper. The only substantial interests are the victims of a barren abstraction, of a sounding but empty phrase.

Now (speaking generally) every individual person is the best possible judge of his own interests: of what will affect himself with the greatest pleasures and pains. Compared with his intimate consciousness of his own peculiar interests, his knowledge of the interests of others is vague conjecture.

Consequently, the principle of general utility imperiously demands that he commonly shall attend to his own rather than to the interests of others: that he shall not habitually neglect that which he knows accurately in order that he may habitually pursue that which he knows imperfectly.

This is the arrangement which the principle of general utility manifestly requires. It is also the arrangement which the Author of man's nature manifestly intended. For our self-regarding affections are steadier and stronger than our social: the motives by which we are urged to pursue our peculiar good operate with more constancy, and commonly with more energy, than the motives by which we are solicited to pursue the good of our fellows.

If every individual neglected his own to the end of pursuing and promoting the interests of others, every individual would neglect the objects with which he is intimately acquainted to the end of forwarding objects of which he is comparatively ignorant. Consequently, the interests of every individual would be managed unskilfully. And, since the general good is an aggregate of individual enjoyments, the good of the general or public would diminish with the good of the individuals of whom that general or public constituted or composed.

The principle of general utility does not demand of us that we shall always or habitually intend the general good: though the principle of general utility does demand of us that we shall never pursue our own peculiar good by means which are inconsistent with that paramount object.

For example: the man who delves or spins, delves or spins to put money in his purse, and not with the purpose or thought of promoting the general well-being. But by delving or spinning, he adds to the sum of commodities: and he therefore promotes that general well-being, which is not, and ought not to be, his practical end. General utility is not his motive to action. But his action conforms to utility considered as the standard of conduct: and when tried by utility considered as the test of conduct, his action deserves approbation.

Again: of all pleasures bodily or mental, the pleasures of mutual love, cemented by mutual esteem, are the most enduring and varied. They therefore contribute largely to swell the sum of well-being, or they form an important item in the account of human happiness. And, for that reason, the well-wisher of the general good, or the adherent of the principle of utility, must, in that character, consider them with much complacency. But, though he approves of love because it accords with his principle, he is far from maintaining that the general good ought to be the motive of the lover. It was never contended or conceited by a sound, orthodox utilitarian that the lover should kiss his mistress with an eye to the common weal.

And by this last example, I am naturally conducted to this further consideration.

Even where utility requires that benevolence shall be our motive, it commonly requires that we shall be determined by partial, rather than by general, benevolence: by the love of the narrower circle which is formed of family or relations, rather than by sympathy with the wider circle which is formed of friends or acquaintance; by sympathy with friends or acquaintance, rather than by patriotism; by patriotism, or love of country, rather than by the larger humanity which embraces mankind.

In short, the principle of utility requires that we shall act with the utmost effect, or that we shall so act as to produce the utmost good. And (speaking generally) we act with the utmost effect, or we so act as to produce the utmost good, when our motive or inducement to conduct is the most urgent and steady, when the sphere wherein we act is the most restricted and the most familiar to us, and when the purpose which we directly pursue is the most determinate or precise.

The foregoing general statement must, indeed, be received with numerous limitations. The principle of utility not unfrequently requires that the order at which I have pointed shall be inverted or reversed: that the self–regarding affections shall yield to the love of family, or to sympathy with friends or acquaintance; that the love of family, or sympathy with friends or acquaintance, shall yield to the love of country; that the love of country shall yield to the love of mankind; that the general happiness or good, which is always the test of our conduct, shall also be the motive determining our conduct, or shall also be the practical end to which our conduct is directed.

Goodness and badness of motives

In order further to dissipate the confusion of ideas giving rise to the misconception last examined, I shall here pause to analyse the expression 'good and bad motives', and to show in what sense it represents a sound distinction.

We often say of a man on any given occasion that his motive was good or bad, and in a certain sense we may truly say that some motives are better than others; in as much as some motives are more likely than others to lead to beneficial conduct.

But, in another and more extended sense, no motive is good or bad: since there is no motive which may not by possibility, and which does not occasionally in fact, lead both to beneficial and to mischievous conduct.

Thus in the case which I have already used as an illustration, that of the man who digs or weaves for his own subsistence; the motive is self–regarding, but the action is beneficial. The same motive, the desire of subsistence, may lead to pernicious acts, such as stealing. (Love of reputation, though a self–regarding motive, is a motive generally productive of beneficial acts; and there are persons with whom it is one of the most powerful incentives to acts for the public good. That form of love of reputation called vanity, on the other hand, implying, as it does, that the aim of its possessor is set upon worthless objects, commonly leads to evil, since it leads to a waste of energy which might otherwise have been turned to useful ends. Yet if, as a motive, it be subordinate in the individual to other springs of action, and exist merely as a latent feeling of self–complacency arising out of considerations, however foolish or unsubstantial, it may be harmless, or even useful as tending to promote energy.) Benevolence, on the other hand, and even religion, though certainly unselfish and generally esteemed good motives, may, when narrowed in their aims, or directed by a perverted understanding, lead to actions most pernicious. For instance, the affection for children, and the consequent desire of pushing or advancing them in the world (a species of narrow benevolence), is with many persons more apt to lead to acts contrary to the public good than any purely selfish motive; and the palliation, which the supposed goodness of the motive constitutes in the eyes of the public for the pernicious act, encourages men to do for the sake of their children, actions which they would be ashamed to do for their own direct interest. Even that enlarged benevolence which embraces humanity may lead to actions extremely mischievous, unless guided by a perfectly sound judgment. Few will doubt, for example, that Sand and those other enthusiasts in Germany, who have at different times thought it right to assassinate those persons whom they believed to be tyrants, have acted in a manner highly pernicious as regards the general good. Of the purity (as it is commonly termed) of their motives, I have not the least doubt; that is to say, I am convinced that they acted under the impulse of a most enlarged benevolence; but I have as little doubt that, by this benevolence, they were led to the commission of acts utterly inconsistent with that general good at which they aimed.

But, although every motive may lead to good or bad, some are pre-eminently likely to lead to good; *e.g.* benevolence, love of reputation, religion. Others pre-eminently likely to lead to bad, and little likely to lead to good; *e.g.* the anti-social; antipathy—particular or general. Others, again, are as likely to lead to good as to bad: *e.g.* the self-regarding. They are the origin of most of the steady industry, but also of most of the offences of men.

In this qualified sense, therefore, motives may be divided into such as are good, such as are bad, and such as are neither good nor bad.

If an action is good, that is, conforming to general utility, the motive makes it more laudable. If not, not. But it is only secondarily that the nature of the motive affects the quality of the action.

(That the nature of the motive does affect the quality of the action is evident from this consideration. Acts are never insulated. And as their moral complexion is ultimately tested by their conformity to the law having utility for its index, so is that moral complexion immediately tested by the nature and tendency of the course of conduct of which the acts are samples. Now, the conduct of an individual is (speaking generally) determined partly by the *motives* which are his springs of action, and partly by the *intention*, or the state of his understanding at the instant of action, regarding the effects or tendency of his acts; both being antecedent to the *volition* by which these immediately emerge into act. Human conduct is, in short, determined by the motives which urge, as well as by the intentions which direct. The intention is the aim of the act, of which the motive is the spring.)

It is, therefore, wrong to maintain that the complexion of the action mainly depends on the complexion of the motive. It is equally wrong to maintain that the nature of the motive does not, to a certain degree, determine its complexion.

In this limited sense, therefore, the moral complexion of the action is determined by the motive. If the intention be good, the action is the better for being prompted by a social motive. If the action be bad, it is less bad if prompted by a social one.

It is important that good dispositions should be recognised and approved. But the goodness of the action depends upon its conformity to utility; (and even if judged from the narrow point of view commanded by the individual whose acts are in question, depends upon the state of his understanding as to the effects of the action; that is, upon the intention, no less than upon the motive).

But to adjust the respective claims of the selfish and social motives, of partial sympathy and general benevolence, is a task which belongs to the detail, rather than to the principles, of ethics: a task which I could hardly accomplish in a clear and satisfactory manner unless I visited my hearers with a complete *dissertation* upon ethics, and wandered at unconscionable length from the appropriate purpose of my Course. What I have suggested will suffice to conduct the reflecting to the following conclusions.

1. General utility considered as the measure or test, differs from general utility considered as a motive or inducement.

2. If our conduct were truly adjusted to the principle of utility, our conduct would conform to rules fashioned on the principle of utility, or our conduct would be guided by sentiments associated with such rules. But, this notwithstanding, general utility or the general happiness or good, would not be in all, or even in most cases, our motive to action or forbearance.

The second misconception examined

Having touched generally and briefly on the first of the two misconceptions, I will now advert to the second with the like generality and brevity.

They who fall into this misconception are guilty of two errors:

1. They mistake and distort the hypothesis concerning the origin of benevolence which is styled the *selfish system*.
2. They imagine that that hypothesis, as thus mistaken and distorted, is an essential or necessary ingredient in the *theory of utility*.[1]

I will examine the two errors into which the misconception may be resolved, in the order wherein I have stated them.

One. According to an hypothesis of Hartley and of various other writers, benevolence or sympathy is not an ultimate fact, or is not unsusceptible of analysis or resolution, or is not a simple or inscrutable element of man's being or nature. According to their hypothesis, it emanates from self-love, or from the self-regarding affections, through that familiar process styled 'the association of ideas' to which I have briefly adverted in a preceding portion of my discourse.

Now it follows palpably from the foregoing concise statement that these writers dispute not the *existence* of disinterested benevolence or sympathy: that, assuming the existence of disinterested benevolence or sympathy, they endeavour to trace the feeling, through its supposed generation, to the simpler and ulterior feeling of which they believe it the offspring.

But, palpable as this consequence is, it is fancied by many opponents of the theory of utility, and (what is more remarkable) by some of its adherents also, that these writers dispute the *existence* of disinterested benevolence or sympathy.

According to the hypothesis in question, *as thus mistaken and distorted*, we have no sympathy, properly so called, with the pleasures and pains of others. That which is styled sympathy, or that which is styled benevolence, is provident regard to self. Every good office done by man to man springs from a *calculation* of which self is the object. We perceive that we depend on others for much of our own happiness; and, perceiving that we depend on others for much of our own happiness we do good unto others that others may do it unto us. The seemingly disinterested services that are rendered by men to men are the offspring of the very motives, and are governed by the very principles, which engender and regulate *trade*.[2]

Two. Having thus mistaken and distorted the so-called *selfish system*, many opponents of the *theory of utility*, together with some adherents of the same theory, imagine that the former, as thus mistaken and distorted, is a necessary portion of the latter. And hence it naturally follows that the adherents of the theory of utility are styled by many of its opponents 'selfish, sordid, and coldblooded calculators'.

Now the *theory of ethics* which I style the *theory of utility* has no necessary connection with any *theory of motives*. It has no necessary connection with any theory or hypothesis which concerns the nature or origin of benevolence or sympathy. The theory of utility will hold good, whether benevolence or sympathy be truly a portion of our nature, or be nothing but a mere name for provident regard to self. The theory of utility will hold good, whether benevolence or sympathy be a simple or ultimate fact, or be engendered by the principle of association on the self-regarding affections.

According to the theory of utility the principle of *general* utility is the index to God's commands, and is therefore the proximate measure of all human conduct. We are bound by the awful sanctions with which his commands are armed to adjust our conduct to rules formed on that proximate measure. Though benevolence be nothing but a name for provident regard to self, we are moved by regard to self, when we think of those awful sanctions, to pursue the generally useful and to forbear from the generally pernicious. Accordingly, that is the version of the theory of utility which is rendered by Dr Paley. He supposes that *general* utility is the proximate *test* of conduct: but he supposes that all the *motives* by which our conduct is determined are purely *self-regarding*. And his version of the *theory of utility* is, nevertheless, coherent: though I think that his *theory of motives* is miserably partial and shallow, and that mere regard to self, although it were never so provident, would hardly perform the office of genuine benevolence or sympathy. For if genuine benevolence or sympathy be not a portion of our nature, we have only one inducement to consult the general good: namely, a provident regard to our own welfare or happiness. But if genuine benevolence or sympathy be a portion of our nature, we have two distinct inducements to consult the general good: namely, the same provident regard to our own welfare or happiness, and also a disinterested regard to the welfare or happiness of others. If genuine benevolence or sympathy were not a portion of our nature, our motives to consult the general good would be more defective than they are.[3]

Again: assuming that benevolence or sympathy is truly a portion of our nature, the theory of utility has no connection whatever with any hypothesis or theory which concerns the origin of the motive. Whether benevolence or sympathy be a simple or ultimate fact, or be engendered by the principle of association on the self-regarding affections, it is one of the motives by which our conduct is determined. And, on either of the conflicting suppositions, the principle of utility, and not benevolence or sympathy, is the *measure* or *test* of conduct. For as conduct may be generally useful, though the motive is self-regarding; so may conduct be generally pernicious, though the motive is purely benevolent. Accordingly, in all his expositions of the theory of utility, Mr Bentham assumes or supposes the existence of disinterested sympathy, and scarcely adverts to the hypotheses which regard the origin of the feeling.[4]

Notes

1. *The first of these mistakes is made by Godwin. The second by Paley*
   'From Epicurus and Lucretius down to Paley and Godwin, Mr Bentham is the only writer who has explained this subject with clearness and accuracy. He is not, indeed, the inventor of the theory of utility (for that is as old as the human race), but he is the first of all philosophers who has viewed it from every aspect, and has fitted it for practice.

   'Many of the writers who appear to reject utility do, in fact, embrace it (*e.g.* Cicero, Seneca, Johnson, etc.) (Eudæmonismus). The *honestum* is the *generally* useful. The *utile* is the *generally* pernicious; but which would answer some selfish and sinister purpose.' [*MS Fragment* inserted by R Campbell.]
2. The selfish system, in this its literal import, is flatly inconsistent with obvious facts, and therefore is hardly deserving of serious refutation. We are daily and hourly *conscious* of disinterested benevolence or sympathy, or of wishing the good of others without regard to our own. In the present wretched condition of human society, so unfavourable are the outward circumstances wherein most men are placed, and so bad is the education or training received by most men in their youth, that the benevolence of most men wants the intensity and endurance which are requisite to their own happiness and to the happiness of their fellow-creatures. With most men, benevolence or sympathy is rather a barren emotion than a strong and steady incentive to vigorous and efficient action. Although the feeling or sentiment affects them often enough it is commonly stifled at the birth by antagonist feelings or sentiments. But to deny, with Rochefoucauld or Mandeville, the *existence* of benevolence or sympathy, is rather a wild paradox, hazarded in the wantonness of satire, than the deliberate position of a philosopher examining the springs of conduct.

   And here I may briefly remark that the expression *selfish*, as applied to motives, has a larger and a narrower meaning. Taking the expression *selfish* with its larger meaning, *all* motives are *selfish*. For every motive is a wish: and every wish is a pain which affects a man's *self*, and which urges him to seek relief, by attaining the object wished. Taking the expression *selfish* with its narrower meaning, motives which are *selfish* must be distinguished from motives which are *benevolent*: our wishes for our own good from our wishes for the good of our neighbour, the desires which impel us to pursue our own advantage or benefit from the desires which solicit us to pursue the advantage or benefit of others.

To obviate this ambiguity, with the wretched quibbling which it begets, Mr Bentham has judiciously discarded the dubious expression *selfish*. The motives which solicit us to pursue the advantage or good of others he styles *social*. The motives which impel us to pursue our own advantage or good he styles *self-regarding*.

But, besides the social and self-regarding motives, there are disinterested motives, or disinterested wishes, by which we are impelled or solicited to visit others with evil. These disinterested but malevolent motives, he styles *anti-social*. When I style a motive of the sort a *disinterested* motive, I apply the epithet with the meaning wherein I apply it to a benevolent motive. Speaking with absolute precision, the motive is not disinterested in either case: for, in each of the two cases, the man desires relief from a wish importuning himself. But, excepting the desire of relief which the wish necessarily implies, the wish, in each of the cases, is purely disinterested. The end or object to which it urges the man is the good or evil of another, and not his own advantage. By imputing to human nature disinterested malevolence, Mr Bentham has drawn upon himself the reproaches of certain critics. But in imputing disinterested malevolence to human nature, he is far from being singular. The fact is admitted or assumed by Aristotle and Butler, and by all who have closely examined the springs or motives of conduct. And the fact is easily explained by the all-pervading principle which is styled 'the association of ideas'. Disinterested malevolence or antipathy, like disinterested benevolence or sympathy, is begotten by that principle on the self-regarding affections.

3. *Confusion of Sympathy with Moral Sense*

Sympathy is the pleasure or pain which we feel when another enjoys or suffers. In common language it is fellow-feeling. This is totally different from moral approbation or disapprobation, and instead of always coinciding with moral sentiments (let their origin be what it may), often runs counter to them. As (*e.g.*) that large sympathy with every sentient being, or at least with every human being, which is called humanity or benevolence, inclines us to sympathise with the sufferings of the culprit whose punishment we approve. Like the pains and pleasures which purely regard ourselves, the pains and pleasures of sympathy are not moral sentiments, but feelings or motives which, according to the justness of our moral sentiments, may lead us wrong or right.

This sympathy may be an original instinct, like our appetites, or begotten by association, like diseased curiosity, love of money, etc. (Bishop Butler).

But on neither of these hypotheses is the theory which derives our moral sentiments from utility at all affected.

The theory of utility assumes sympathy, but maintains that our judgments of actions ought to be, and in a great measure are, derived from our perception of the *general* consequences of actions; *i.e.* not their immediate but their remote consequences, supposing them unregulated by Morals and Law; and not only their consequences upon ourselves, but also upon our relations, our friends, our country, our fellow-men with whom, according to the theory, as I understand it, we are held by bonds of sympathy which, though not so strong nor so constant as our mere regard to ourselves, is just as necessary to our own well-being. Sympathy, as well as pure self-love, is not a moral sentiment, but a principle or motive to action: either being liable to disturb our moral judgment. Indeed a narrow sympathy is, in some minds, as tyrannous as the self-love of the most narrow and contracted being that crawls the earth. Maternal love, the passion between the sexes when exalted into Love, the spirit of sect and party, a narrow patriotism—all these are as likely to mislead the judgment or the moral sense as the purely self-regarding affections; which, on the other hand, though often misleading, are, to a great extent, the causes of good, prompting men to all long and obscure effort. [*MS Fragment* inserted by R. Campbell.]

4. But here I would briefly remark that, though the hypothesis of Hartley is no necessary ingredient in the theory of general utility, it is a necessary ingredient (if it be not unfounded) in every sound system of education or training. For the sake of our own happiness, and the happiness of our fellow-creatures, the affection of benevolence or sympathy should be strong and steady as possible: for though, like other motives, it may lead us to pernicious conduct, it is less likely than most of the others to seduce us from the right road. Now if benevolence or sympathy be engendered by the principle of association, the affection may be planted and nurtured by education or training. The truth or falsehood of the hypothesis, together with the process by which the affection is generated, are therefore objects of great practical moment and well deserving of close and minute examination.

LECTURE V

SYNOPSIS OF LECTURE V

Laws proper or properly so called, and laws improper or improperly so called
Analogy and metaphor as used in common parlance, defined
Laws improper are of two kinds:
1. Laws closely analogous to laws proper
2. Laws metaphorical or figurative

Division of laws proper, and of such improper laws as are closely analogous to the proper
Distribution of laws proper, and of such improper laws as are closely analogous to the proper, under three capital classes:
1. The law of God, or the laws of God
2. Positive law, or positive laws
3. Positive morality, rules of positive morality, or positive moral rules

Digression to explain the expressions *positive law* and *positive morality*
Explanation of the following expressions, viz. *science of jurisprudence* and *science of positive morality*; *science of ethics* or *deontology*, *science of legislation* and *science of morals*
Meaning of the epithet good or bad as applied to a human law
Meaning of the epithet good as applied to the law of God
The expression *law of nature*, or *natural law*, has two disparate meanings. It signifies the law of God, or a portion of positive law and positive morality

First: tendency to confound positive law with the science of legislation, and positive morality with deontology. Example from Blackstone
Another example from Blackstone
Paley's definition of civil liberty
Example from the writers on civil law
Second: tendency to confound positive law with positive morality, and both with legislation and deontology. Examples from the Roman jurists
Example from Lord Mansfield
Laws set by men, as private persons, in pursuance of legal rights
The acts and forbearances which, according to the theory of utility, are objects of the law of God; and other acts and forbearances which, according to the same theory, ought to be objects respectively of positive morality and law

TEXT OF LECTURE V

Laws proper or properly so called, and laws improper or improperly so called

The term *law*, or the term *laws*, is applied to the following objects: to laws proper or properly so called, and to laws improper or improperly so called; to objects which have all the essentials of an imperative law or rule; and to objects which are wanting in some of those essentials, but to which the term is unduly extended either by reason of *analogy* or in the way of *metaphor*.

Strictly speaking, *all* improper laws are *analogous* to laws proper: and the term *law*, as applied to *any* of them, is a *metaphorical* or *figurative* expression.

For every metaphor springs from an analogy: and every analogical extension given to a term is a metaphor or figure of speech. The term is extended from the objects which it properly signifies to objects of another nature; to objects not of the class wherein the former are contained, although they are allied to the former by that more distant resemblance which is usually styled *analogy*. But, taking the expressions with the meanings which custom or usage has established, there is a difference between an employment of a term analogically and a metaphor.

Analogy and metaphor as used in common parlance, defined

Analogy is a species of *resemblance*. The word resemblance is here taken in that large sense in which all subjects which have any property in common, are said to resemble. But besides this more extended acceptation according to which resemblance is a genus, and analogy one of the species included therein, there is another and a narrower sense, in which resemblance is opposed to analogy. Two resembling subjects are said to *resemble*, in the narrower meaning of the term, when they both belong to some determinate genus or species expressly or tacitly referred to; when they both have every property which belongs to all the subjects included in the class. Two resembling subjects are said on the contrary to be *analogous* when *one* of them belongs to some class expressly or tacitly referred to, and the *other* does *not*: when one possesses all the properties common to the class and the other only some of them. I choose, for instance, on account of a particular convenience, to range together in one class all animals having feet. When I am speaking with reference to this class, the foot of a lion and the foot of a man would be said to resemble in the narrower as well as in the wider sense of the word. But the foot of a table, though it resembles the foot of a lion and of a man in the more enlarged sense, does not resemble these in the narrower sense, but is only analogous to them. For *these* possess the whole of the qualities belonging universally to the class, while *it* possesses only a part of the same qualities. If I were not tacitly referring to a genus, I might say that all the three objects resemble, but if the genus be referred to, the foot of the lion and the foot of the man resemble, the foot of the table is only analogous to them.

Resemblance is hence an ambiguous term. When two things resemble in the narrower sense, that is, when they both possess all the properties which belong universally to the class, the common name (such as *foot* in the instance above given) is applied to both of them strictly and properly. When they are analogous, that is when the one possesses all, the other only some of the properties which belong universally to the class, the name denotes the one properly, the other improperly or analogically.

It is extremely important to fix our conception with respect to this ambiguity as the words analogy and analogous often recur in the science of jurisprudence, and by the laxity with which they are employed involve it in a scarcely penetrable mist. The nature of unwritten law, and the principles of interpretation or construction, are among the most obscure of all the questions which arise in jurisprudence. This obscurity springs, as is usually the case, from nonsense or jargon; which jargon, on these questions, arises from hence, that men talk profusely of analogy and things analogous, without ascertaining the precise meaning of those terms or taking pains to employ them with any precise meaning. Professor Thibaut of Berlin, in his treatise on the interpretation of the Roman Law, is, as far as I know, the only writer who has seen this perplexity; and notwithstanding my warm respect for that learned and discerning jurist, it seems to me that even he has scarcely solved the difficulty, though he has pointed out the path by which we may arrive at a solution.

A metaphor is the transference of a term from its primitive signification to subjects to which it is applied not in that, but in a secondary sense. An analogy, real or supposed, is always the ground of the transference; hence every metaphor is an analogical application of a term, and every analogical application of a term is a metaphor. But a metaphorical or figurative application is scarcely, in common parlance, synonymous with an analogical application. By a metaphorical or figurative application, we usually mean one in which the analogy is faint, the alliance between the primitive and the derivative signification remote. When the analogy is clear, strong, and close; when the subjects to which the term is deflected lie on the confines of the class properly denoted by it, and have many of the properties common to the class, we hardly say that the name is employed figuratively or metaphorically.

In the language of logic, objects which have all the qualities composing the essence of the class, and all the qualities which are the necessary consequences of those composing the essence, *resemble*. When an object does not possess all the essence of the class, but possesses many of the qualities which compose the essence, or many of those which necessarily result from the essence, the application of the name to that object will be said to be analogical and not a metaphor. The difference between metaphor and analogy is hence a difference of degree and not to be settled precisely by drawing a strict line between them.

Laws improper are of two kinds: 1. Laws closely analogous to laws proper; 2. Laws metaphorical or figurative

Now a broad distinction obtains between laws improperly so called. Some are *closely*, others are *remotely*, analogous to laws proper. The term *law* is extended to some by a decision of the reason or understanding. The term law is extended to others by a turn or caprice of the fancy.

In order that I may mark this distinction briefly and commodiously, I avail myself of the difference, established by custom or usage, between the meanings of the expressions *analogical* and *figurative*. I style laws of the first kind *laws closely analogous to laws proper*. I say that they are called *laws* by an *analogical* extension of the term. I style laws of the second kind *laws metaphorical* or *figurative*. I say that they are called *laws* by a *metaphor* or *figure of speech*.

Division of laws proper, and of such improper laws as are closely analogous to the proper

Now laws proper, with such improper laws as are closely analogous to the proper, are divisible thus.

Of laws properly so called, some are set by God to his human creatures; others are set by men to men.

Of the laws properly so called which are set by men to men, some are set by men as political superiors, or by men, as private persons, in pursuance of legal rights. Others may be described in the following negative manner: they are not set by men as political superiors, nor are they set by men, as private persons, in pursuance of legal rights.

The laws improperly so called, which are closely analogous to the proper, are merely opinions or sentiments held or felt by men in regard to human conduct. As I shall show hereafter, these opinions and sentiments are styled *laws* because they are *analogous* to laws properly so called: because they resemble laws properly so called in *some* of their properties or *some* of their effects or consequences.

Distribution of laws proper, and of such improper laws as are closely analogous to the proper, under three capital classes: 1. The law of God, or the laws of God; 2. Positive law, or positive laws; 3. Positive morality, rules of positive morality, or positive moral rules

Accordingly, I distribute laws proper, with such improper laws as are closely analogous to the proper, under three capital classes.

The first comprises the laws (properly so called) which are set by God to his human creatures. The second comprises the laws (properly so called) which are set by men as political superiors, or by men, as private persons, in pursuance of legal rights.

The third comprises laws of the two following species:

1. The laws (properly so called) which are set by men to men, but not by men as political superiors, nor by men as private persons, in pursuance of legal rights;
2. The laws which are closely analogous to laws proper, but are merely opinions or sentiments held or felt by men in regard to human conduct.

I put laws of these species into a common class, and I mark them with the common name to which I shall advert immediately, for the following reason. No law of either species is a direct or circuitous command of a monarch or sovereign number in the character of political superior. In other words, no law of either species is a direct or circuitous command of a monarch or sovereign number to a person or persons in a state of subjection to its author. Consequently, laws of both species may be aptly opposed to laws of the second capital class. For every law of that second capital class is a direct or circuitous command of a monarch or sovereign number in the character of political superior: that is to say, a direct or circuitous command of a monarch or sovereign number to a person or persons in a state of subjection in its author.

Laws comprised by these three capital classes I mark with the following names.

I name laws of the first class *the law* or *laws of God*, or *the Divine law* or *laws*.

For various reasons which I shall produce immediately, I name laws of the second class *positive law*, or *positive laws*.

For the same reasons, I name laws of the third class *positive morality, rules of positive morality*, or *positive moral rules*.

Digression to explain the expressions positive law *and* positive morality

My reasons for using the two expressions '*positive* law' and '*positive* morality', are the following.

There are two capital classes of human laws. The first comprises the laws (properly so called) which are set by men as political superiors, or by men as private persons, in pursuance of legal rights. The second comprises the laws (proper and improper) which belong to the two species mentioned on the preceding page.

As merely distinguished from the second, the first of those capital classes might be named simply *law*. As merely distinguished from the first, the second of those capital classes might be named simply *morality*. But both must be distinguished from the law of God: and, for the purpose of distinguishing both from the law of God, we must qualify the names *law* and *morality*. Accordingly, I style the first of those capital classes '*positive* law': and I style the second of those capital classes '*positive* morality'. By the common epithet *positive*, I denote that both classes flow from human sources. By the distinctive names *law* and *morality*, I denote the difference between the human sources from which the two classes respectively emanate.

Strictly speaking, every law properly so called is a *positive* law. For it is *put* or set by its individual or collective author, or it exists by the *position* or institution of its individual or collective author.

But, as opposed to the law of nature (meaning the law of God), human law of the first of those capital classes is styled by writers on jurisprudence '*positive* law'. This application of the expression '*positive* law' was manifestly made for the purpose of obviating confusion; confusion of human law of the first of those capital classes with that Divine law which is the measure or test of human.

And, in order to obviate similar confusion, I apply the expression '*positive* morality' to human law of the second capital class. For the name *morality*, when standing unqualified or alone, may signify the law set by God, or human law of that second capital class. If you say that an act or omission violates *morality*, you speak ambiguously. You may mean that it violates the law which I style '*positive* morality', or that it violates the Divine law which is the measure or test of the former.

Again: the human laws or rules which I style '*positive* morality', I mark with that expression for the following additional reason.

I have said that the name *morality*, when standing unqualified or alone, may signify positive morality or may signify the law of God. But the name *morality*, when standing unqualified or alone, is perplexed with a further ambiguity. It may import indifferently either of the two following senses:

1. The name *morality*, when standing unqualified or alone, may signify positive morality which is good or worthy of approbation, or positive morality as it would be if it were good or worthy of approbation. In other words, the name *morality*, when standing unqualified or alone, may signify positive morality which agrees with its measure or test, or positive morality as it would be if it agreed with its measure or test.
2. The name *morality*, when standing unqualified or alone, may signify the human laws, which I style positive morality, as considered without regard to their goodness or badness. For example, such laws of the class as are peculiar to a given age, or such laws of the class as are peculiar to a given nation, we style the *morality* of that given age or nation whether we think them good or deem them bad. Or, in case we mean to intimate that we approve or disapprove of them, we name them the *morality* of that given age or nation and we qualify that name with the epithet *good* or *bad*.

Now, by the name '*positive* morality', I mean the human laws which I mark with that expression, as considered without regard to their goodness or badness. Whether human laws be worthy of praise or blame, or whether they accord or not with their measure or test, they are 'rules of *positive* morality', in the sense which I give to the expression, if they belong to either of the two species lastly mentioned on p. 94. But, in consequence of that ambiguity which I have now attempted to explain, I could hardly express my meaning with passable distinctness by the unqualified name *morality*.

Explanation of the following expressions: viz. science of jurisprudence *and* science of positive morality; science of ethics or deontology, science of legislation *and* science of morals

From the expression *positive law* and the expression *positive morality*, I pass to certain expressions with which they are closely connected.

The *science of jurisprudence* (or, simply and briefly, *jurisprudence*) is concerned with positive laws, or with laws strictly so called, as considered without regard to their goodness or badness.

Positive morality, as considered without regard to its goodness or badness, *might* be the subject of a science closely analogous to jurisprudence. I say '*might* be' since it is only in one of its branches (namely, the law of nations or international law) that positive morality, as considered without regard to its goodness or badness, has been treated by writers in a scientific or systematic manner. For the science of positive morality, as considered without regard to its goodness or badness, current or established language, will hardly afford us a name. The name *morals*, or *science of morals*, would denote it ambiguously: the name *morals*, or *science of morals*, being commonly applied (as I shall show immediately) to a department of ethics or deontology. But, since the science of jurisprudence is not unfrequently styled 'the science of *positive* law', the science in question might be styled analogically 'the science of *positive* morality'. The department of the science in question which relates to international law, has actually been styled by Von Martens, a recent writer of celebrity, '*positives* oder *practisches* Völkerrecht': that is to say, '*positive* international law' or '*practical* international law'. Had he named that department of the science '*positive* international *morality*', the name would have hit its import with perfect precision.

The science of ethics (or, in the language of Mr Bentham, *the science of deontology*) may be defined in the following manner: it affects to determine the test of positive law and morality, or it affects to determine the principles whereon they must be fashioned in order that they may merit approbation. In other words, it affects to expound them as they should be; or it affects to expound them as they ought to be; or it affects to expound them as they would be if they were good or worthy of praise; or it affects to expound them as they would be if they conformed to an assumed measure.

The science of ethics (or, simply and briefly, ethics) consists of two departments: one relating specially to positive law, the other relating specially to positive morality. The department which relates specially to positive law is commonly styled *the science of legislation*, or, simply and briefly, *legislation*. The department which relates specially to positive morality is commonly styled *the science of morals*, or, simply and briefly, *morals*.

Meaning of the epithet good *or* bad *as applied to a human law*

The foregoing attempt to define the science of ethics naturally leads me to offer the following explanatory remark.

When we say that a human law is good or bad, or is worthy of praise or blame, or is what it should be or what it should not be, or is what it ought to be or what it ought not to be, we mean (unless we intimate our mere liking or aversion) this: namely, that the law agrees with or differs from a something to which we tacitly refer it as to a measure or test.

For example, according to either of the hypotheses which I stated in preceding lectures, a human law is good or bad as it agrees or does not agree with the law of God: that is to say, with the law of God as indicated by the principle of utility, or with the law of God as indicated by the moral sense. To the adherent of the theory of utility, a human law is good if it be generally useful, and a human law is bad if it be generally pernicious. For, in *his* opinion, it is consonant or not with the law of God inasmuch as it is consonant or not with the principle of general utility. To the adherent of the hypothesis of a moral sense, a human law is good if he likes it he knows not why, and a human law is bad if he hates it he knows not wherefore. For, in *his* opinion, that his inexplicable feeling of liking or aversion shows that the human law pleases or offends the Deity.

To the atheist, a human law is good if it be generally useful, and a human law is bad if it be generally pernicious. For the principle of general utility would serve as a measure or test, although it were not an index to an ulterior measure or test. But if he call the law a good one without believing it useful, or if he call a law a bad one without believing it pernicious, the atheist simply intimates his mere liking or aversion. For, unless it be thought an index to the law set by the Deity, an inexplicable feeling of approbation or disapprobation can hardly be considered a measure or test. And, in the opinion of the atheist, there is no law of God which his inexplicable feeling can point at.

To the believer in a supposed revelation, a human law is good or bad as it agrees with or differs from the terms wherein the revelation is expressed.

In short, the goodness or badness of a human law is a phrase of relative and varying import. A law which is good to one man is bad to another, in case they tacitly refer it to different and adverse tests.

Meaning of the epithet good *as applied to the law of God*

The Divine laws may be styled good, in the sense with which the atheist may apply the epithet to human. We may style them good, or worthy of praise, inasmuch as they agree with utility considered as an ultimate test. And this is the only meaning with which we can apply the epithet to the laws of God. Unless we refer them to utility considered as an ultimate test, we have no test by which we can try them. To say that they are good because they are set by the Deity is to say that they are good as measured or tried by themselves. But to say this is to talk absurdly: for every object which is measured, or every object which is brought to a test, is compared with a given object other than itself. If the laws set by the Deity were not generally useful, or if they did not promote the general happiness of his creatures, or if their great Author were not wise and benevolent, they would not be good or worthy of praise, but were devilish and worthy of execration.

Before I conclude the present digression I must submit this further remark to the attention of the reader.

The expression law of nature, *or* natural law, *has two disparate meanings. It signifies the law of God, or a portion of positive law and positive morality*

I have intimated in the course of this digression that the phrase *law of nature*, or the phrase *natural law*, often signifies the law of God.

Natural law as thus understood, and the *natural law* which I mentioned in my fourth lecture, are disparate expressions. The *natural law* which I there mentioned is a portion of positive law and positive morality. It consists of the human rules, legal and moral, which have obtained at all times and obtained at all places.

According to the compound hypothesis which I mentioned in my fourth lecture, these human rules, legal and moral, have been fashioned on the law of God as indicated by the *moral sense*. Or, adopting the language of the classical Roman jurists, these human rules, legal and moral, have been fashioned on the Divine law as known by *natural reason*.

But, besides the human rules which have obtained with all mankind, there are human rules, legal and moral, which have been limited to peculiar times or limited to peculiar places.

Now, according to the compound hypothesis which I mentioned in my fourth lecture, these last have not been fashioned on the law of God, or have been fashioned on the law of God as conjectured by the light of utility.

Being fashioned on the law of God as known by an infallible guide, human rules of the first class are styled *the law of nature*: for they are not of human position purely or simply, but are laws of God or Nature clothed with human sanctions. As obtaining at all times and obtaining at all places, they are styled by the classical jurists *jus gentium*, or *jus omnium gentium*.

But human rules of the second class are styled *positive*. For, not being fashioned on the law of God, or being fashioned on the law of God as merely conjectured by utility, they, certainly or probably, are of purely human position. They are not laws of God or Nature clothed with human sanctions.

As I stated in my fourth lecture, and shall show completely hereafter, the distinction of human rules into natural and positive involves the compound hypothesis which I mentioned in that discourse.

The connection of the present (the fifth) lecture with the first, second, third, fourth, and sixth

Positive laws, the appropriate matter of jurisprudence, are related in the way of resemblance, or by a close or remote analogy, to the following objects:

1. In the way of resemblance, they are related to the laws of God.

2. In the way of resemblance, they are related to those rules of positive morality which are laws properly so called.
3. By a close or strong analogy, they are related to those rules of positive morality which are merely opinions or sentiments held or felt by men in regard to human conduct.
4. By a remote or slender analogy, they are related to laws merely metaphorical, or laws merely figurative.

To distinguish positive laws from the objects now enumerated is the purpose of the present attempt to determine the province of jurisprudence.

In pursuance of the purpose to which I have now adverted, I stated, in my first lecture, the essentials of a *law* or *rule* (taken with the largest signification which can be given to the term *properly*).

In my second, third, and fourth lectures, I stated the marks or characters by which the laws of God are distinguished from other laws. And, stating those marks or characters, I explained the nature of the index to his unrevealed laws, or I explained and examined the hypotheses which regard the nature of that index. I made this explanation at a length which may seem disproportionate, but which I have deemed necessary because these laws, and the index by which they are known, are the standard or measure to which all other laws should conform and the standard measure or test by which they should be tried.

But before I can complete the purpose to which I have adverted above, I must examine or discuss especially the following principal topics (and must touch upon other topics of secondary or subordinate importance):

1. I must examine the marks or characters by which positive laws are distinguished from other laws.
2. I must examine the distinguishing marks of those positive moral rules which are laws properly so called.
3. I must examine the distinguishing marks of those positive moral rules which are styled *laws* or *rules* by an analogical extension of the term.
4. I must examine the distinguishing marks of laws merely metaphorical, or laws merely figurative.

In order to give an explanation of the marks which distinguish positive laws, I must analyse the expression *sovereignty*, the correlative expression *subjection*, and the inseparably connected expression *independent political society*. For the essential difference of a positive law (or the difference that severs it from a law which is not a positive law) may be stated thus. Every positive law, or every law simply and strictly so called, is set by a sovereign person, or a sovereign body of persons, to a member or members of the independent political society wherein that person or body is sovereign or supreme. Or (changing the expression) it is set by a monarch, or sovereign number, to a person or persons in a state of subjection to its author.

But my analysis of those expressions occupies so large a space that in case I placed it in the lecture which I am now delivering, the lecture which I am now delivering would run to insufferable length.

The purpose mentioned above will, therefore, be completed in the following order.

Excluding from my present discourse my analysis of those expressions, I shall complete, in my present discourse, the purpose mentioned above, so far as I can complete it consistently with that exclusion. In my present discourse I shall examine or discuss especially the following principal topics: namely, the distinguishing marks of those positive moral rules which are laws properly so called; the distinguishing marks of those positive moral rules which are styled *laws* or *rules* by an analogical extension of the term; the distinguishing marks of the laws which are styled *laws* by a metaphor.

I shall complete, in my sixth lecture, the purpose mentioned above, by explaining the marks or characters which distinguish positive laws, or laws strictly so called: an explanation involving an analysis of the capital expression *sovereignty*, the correlative expression *subjection*, and the inseparably connected expression *independent political society*.

Having shown the connection of my present discourse with foregoing and following lectures, I now examine or discuss its appropriate topics or subjects.

The essentials of a law properly so called, together with certain consequences which those essentials import

In my first lecture, I endeavoured to resolve a *law* (taken with the largest signification which can be given to the term *properly*) into the necessary or essential elements of which it is composed.

Now those essentials of a law proper, together with certain consequences which those essentials import, may be stated briefly in the following manner:

1. Laws properly so called are a species of *commands*. But, being a *command*, every law properly so called flows from a *determinate* source, or emanates from a *determinate* author. In other words, the author from whom it proceeds is a *determinate* rational being, or a *determinate* body or aggregate of rational beings. For whenever a *command* is expressed or intimated, one party signifies a wish that another shall do or forbear: and the latter is obnoxious to an evil which the former intends to inflict in case the wish be disregarded. But every *signification* of a wish made by a single individual, or made by a

body of individuals *as a body or collective whole*, supposes that the individual or body is *certain* or *determinate*. And every *intention* or *purpose* held by a single individual, or held by a body of individuals *as a body or collective whole*, involves the same supposition.

2. Every sanction properly so called is an eventual evil *annexed to a command*. Any eventual evil may operate as a *motive* to conduct: but, unless the conduct be commanded and the evil be annexed to the command purposely to enforce obedience, the evil is not a *sanction* in the proper acceptation of the term.
3. Every duty properly so called supposes a *command* by which it is created. For every sanction properly so called is an eventual evil *annexed to a command*. And duty properly so called is obnoxiousness to evils of the kind.

The laws of God, and positive laws, are laws properly so called

Now it follows from these premises, that the laws of God, and positive laws, are laws proper, or laws properly so called.

The laws of God are laws proper, inasmuch as they are *commands* express or tacit, and therefore emanate from a *certain* source.

Positive laws, or laws strictly so called, are established directly or immediately by authors of three kinds: by monarchs or sovereign bodies as supreme political superiors; by men in a state of subjection as subordinate political superiors; by subjects, as private persons, in pursuance of legal rights. But every positive law, or every law strictly so called, is a direct or circuitous command of a monarch or sovereign number in the character of political superior: that is to say, a direct or circuitous command of a monarch or sovereign number to a person or persons in a state of subjection to its author. And being a *command* (and therefore flowing from a *determinate* source), every positive law is a law proper, or a law properly so called.

The generic character of positive moral rules

Besides the human laws which I style positive law, there are human laws which I style positive morality, rules of positive morality, or positive moral rules.

The generic character of laws of the class may be stated briefly in the following negative manner: no law belonging to the class is a direct or circuitous command of a monarch or sovereign number in the character of political superior. In other words, no law belonging to the class is a direct or circuitous command of a monarch or sovereign number to a person or persons in a state of subjection to its author.

Of positive moral rules, some are laws proper, but others are laws improper. The positive moral rules, which are laws properly so called, are commands

But of positive moral rules, some are laws proper, or laws properly so called: others are laws improper, or laws improperly so called. Some have all the essentials of an *imperative* law or rule: others are deficient in some of those essentials and are styled *laws* or *rules* by an analogical extension of the term.

The positive moral rules, which are laws properly so called, are distinguished from other laws by the union of two marks:

1. They are imperative laws or rules set by men to men.
2. They are not set by men as political superiors, nor are they set by men as private persons, in pursuance of legal rights.

Inasmuch as they bear the latter of these two marks, they are not commands of sovereigns in the character of political superiors. Consequently, they are not positive laws: they are not clothed with legal sanctions, nor do they oblige legally the persons to whom they are set. But being *commands* (and therefore being established by *determinate* individuals or bodies), they are laws properly so called: they are armed with sanctions, and impose duties, in the proper acceptation of the terms.

It will appear from the following distinctions that positive moral rules which are laws properly so called may be reduced to three kinds.

Of positive moral rules which are laws properly so called, some are established by men who are not subjects, or are not in a state of subjection: meaning by 'subjects', or by 'men in a state of subjection', men in a state of subjection to a monarch or sovereign number. Of positive moral rules which are laws properly so called, and are not established by men in a state of subjection, some are established by men living in the negative state which is styled a state of nature or a state of anarchy: that is to say, by men who are *not* in the state which is styled a state of government, or are *not* members, sovereign or subject, of any political society. Of positive moral rules which are laws properly so called, and are not established by men in a state of subjection, others are established by sovereign individuals or bodies but are not established by sovereigns in the character of political superiors. Or a positive moral rule of this kind may be described in the following manner: it is set by a monarch or sovereign number but not to a person or persons in a state of subjection to its author.

Of laws properly so called which are set by subjects, some are set by subjects as subordinate political superiors. But of laws properly so called which are set by subjects, others are set by subjects as private persons: meaning by 'private persons' subjects not in the class of subordinate political superiors, or subordinate political superiors not considered as such. Laws set by subjects as subordinate political superiors are positive laws: they are clothed with legal sanctions and impose legal duties. They are set by sovereigns or states in the character of political superiors, although they are set by sovereigns circuitously or remotely. Although they are made directly by subject or subordinate authors, they are made through legal rights granted by sovereigns or states and held by those subject authors as mere trustees for the granters. Of laws set by subjects as private persons, some are not established by sovereign or supreme authority. And these are rules of positive morality: they are not clothed with legal sanctions, nor do they oblige legally the parties to whom they are set. But of laws set by subjects as private persons, others are set or established in pursuance of legal rights residing in the subject authors. And these are positive laws or laws strictly so called. Although they are made directly by subject authors, they are made in pursuance of rights granted or conferred by sovereigns in the character of political superiors: they legally oblige the parties to whom they are set, or are clothed with legal sanctions. They are commands of sovereigns as political superiors, although they are set by sovereigns circuitously or remotely.[1]

It appears from the foregoing distinctions that positive moral rules which are laws properly so called are of three kinds:

1. Those which are set by men living in a state of nature.
2. Those which are set by sovereigns, but not by sovereigns as political superiors.
3. Those which are set by subjects as private persons and are not set by the subject authors in pursuance of legal rights.

To cite an example of rules of the first kind were superfluous labour. A man living in a state of nature may impose an imperative law: though, since the man *is* in a state of nature, he cannot impose the law in the character of sovereign, and cannot impose the law in pursuance of a legal right. And the law being *imperative* (and therefore proceeding from a *determinate* source) is a law properly so called: though, for want of a sovereign author proximate or remote, it is not a positive law but a rule of positive morality.

An imperative law set by a sovereign to a sovereign, or by one supreme government to another supreme government, is an example of rules of the second kind. Since no supreme government is in a state of subjection to another, an imperative law set by a sovereign to a sovereign is not set by its author in the character of political superior. Nor is it set by its author in pursuance of a legal right: for every legal right is conferred by a supreme government and is conferred on a person or persons in a state of subjection to the granter. Consequently, an imperative law set by a sovereign to a sovereign is not a positive law or a law strictly so called. But being *imperative* (and therefore proceeding from a *determinate* source), it amounts to a law in the proper signification of the term, although it is purely or simply a rule of positive morality.

If they be set by subjects as private persons, and be not set by their authors in pursuance of legal rights, the laws following are examples of rules of the third kind: namely, imperative laws set by parents to children; imperative laws set by masters to servants; imperative laws set by lenders to borrowers; imperative laws set by patrons to parasites. Being *imperative* (and therefore proceeding from *determinate* sources), the laws foregoing are laws properly so called: though, if they be set by subjects as private persons, and be not set by their authors in pursuance of legal rights, they are not positive laws but rules of positive morality.

Again: a club or society of men, signifying its collective pleasure by a vote of its assembled members, passes or makes a law to be kept by its members severally under pain of exclusion from its meetings. Now if it be made by subjects as private persons, and be not made by its authors in pursuance of a legal right, the law voted and passed by the assembled members of the club is a further example of rules of the third kind. If it be made by subjects as private persons, and be not made by its authors in pursuance of a legal right, it is not a positive law or a law strictly so called. But being an *imperative* law (and the body by which it is set being therefore *determinate*), it may be styled a *law* or *rule* with absolute precision or propriety, although it is purely or simply a rule of positive morality.

The positive moral rules, which are laws improperly so called, are laws set or imposed by general opinion

The positive moral rules which are laws improperly so called, *are laws set* or *imposed by general opinion*: that is to say, by the general opinion of any class or any society of persons. For example, some are set or imposed by the general opinion of persons who are members of a profession or calling; others, by that of persons who inhabit a town or province; others, by that of a larger society formed of various nations.

A few species of the laws which are set by general opinion have gotten appropriate names. For example, there are laws or rules imposed upon gentlemen by opinions current amongst gentlemen. And these are usually styled *the rules of honour, or the laws* or *law of honour*. There are laws or rules imposed upon people of fashion by opinions current in the fashionable world. And these are usually styled *the law set by fashion*. There are laws which regard the conduct of independent political societies in their various relations to one another: or, rather, there are laws which regard the conduct of sovereigns or supreme governments in their various relations to one another. And laws or rules of this species, which are imposed upon nations or sovereigns by opinions current amongst nations, are usually styled *the law of nations* or *international law*.

A law set or imposed by general opinion, is merely the opinion *or* sentiment *of an* indeterminate *body of persons in regard to a kind of conduct*

Now a law set or imposed by general opinion is a law improperly so called. It is styled a *law* or *rule* by an analogical extension of the term. When we speak of a law set by general opinion, we denote, by that expression, the following fact: some *indeterminate* body or *uncertain* aggregate of persons regards a kind of conduct with a sentiment of aversion or liking: or (changing the expression) that indeterminate body opines unfavourably or favourably of a given kind of conduct. In *consequence* of that sentiment, or in *consequence* of that opinion, it is likely that they or some of them will be displeased with a party who shall pursue or not pursue conduct of that kind. And, in *consequence* of that displeasure, it is likely that *some* party (*what* party being undetermined) will visit the party provoking it with some evil or another.

The body by whose opinion the law is said to be set does not *command*; expressly or tacitly, that conduct of the given kind shall be forborne or pursued. For, since it is not a body precisely determined or certain, it cannot, *as a body*, express or intimate a wish. *As a body*, it cannot *signify* a wish by oral or written words, or by positive or negative deportment. The so-called *law* or *rule* which its opinion is said to impose is merely the *sentiment* which it feels, or is merely the *opinion* which it holds, in regard to a kind of conduct.

A determinate member of the body, who opines or feels with the body, may doubtless be moved or impelled, by that very opinion or sentiment, to *command* that conduct of the kind shall be forborne or pursued. But the command expressed or intimated by that determinate party is not a law or rule imposed by general opinion. It is a law properly so called, set by a determinate author. For example, the so-called law of nations consists of opinions or sentiments current among nations generally. It therefore is not law properly so called. But one supreme government may doubtless *command* another to forbear from a kind of conduct which the law of nations condemns. And, though it is fashioned on law which is law improperly so called, this command is a law in the proper signification of the term. Speaking precisely, the command is a rule of positive morality set by a determinate author. For, as no supreme government is in a state of subjection to another, the government commanding does not command in its character of political superior. If the government receiving the command were in a state of subjection to the other, the command, though fashioned on the law of nations, would amount to a positive law.

The foregoing description of a law set by general opinion imports the following consequences: that the party who will enforce it against any future transgressor is never determinate and assignable. The party who actually enforces it against an actual transgressor is, of necessity, certain. In other words, if an actual transgressor be harmed in consequence of the breach of the law, and in consequence of that displeasure which the breach of the law has provoked, he receives the harm from a party who, of necessity, is certain. But that certain party is not the executor of a *command* proceeding from the uncertain body. He has not been authorised by that uncertain body to enforce that so-called law which its opinion is said to establish. He is not in the position of a minister of justice appointed by the sovereign or state to execute commands which it issues. He harms the actual offender against the so-called law or (to speak in analogical language) he applies the sanction annexed to it, of his own spontaneous movement. Consequently, though a party who actually enforces it is, of necessity, certain, the party who will enforce it against any future offender is never determinate and assignable.

A brief statement of the analogy between a law proper and a law set or imposed by general opinion

It follows from the foregoing reasons that a so-called law set by general opinion is not a law in the proper signification of the term. It also follows from the same reasons that it is not armed with a sanction, and does not impose a duty, in the proper acceptation of the expressions. For a sanction properly so called is an evil annexed to a command. And duty properly so called is an obnoxiousness to evils of the kind.

But a so-called law set by general opinion is closely analogous to a law in the proper signification of the term. And, by consequence, the so-called sanction with which the former is armed, and the so-called duty which the former imposes, are closely analogous to a sanction and a duty in the proper acceptation of the expressions.

The analogy between a law in the proper signification of the term and a so-called law set by general opinion, may be stated briefly in the following manner:

1. In the case of a law properly so called, the determinate individual or body by whom the law is established wishes that conduct of a kind shall be forborne or pursued. In the case of a law imposed by general opinion, a wish that conduct of a kind shall be forborne or pursued is felt by the uncertain body whose general opinion imposes it.
2. If a party obliged by the law proper shall not comply with the wish of the determinate individual or body, he probably will suffer, in *consequence* of his not complying, the evil or inconvenience annexed to the law as a sanction. If a party obnoxious to their displeasure shall not comply with the wish of the uncertain body of persons, he probably will suffer, in *consequence* of his not complying, some evil or inconvenience from some party or another.

3. By the sanction annexed to the law proper, the parties obliged are inclined to act or forbear agreeably to its injunctions or prohibitions. By the evil which probably will follow the displeasure of the uncertain body, the parties obnoxious are inclined to act or forbear agreeably to the sentiment or opinion which is styled analogically a law.
4. In consequence of the law properly so called, the conduct of the parties obliged has a steadiness, constancy, or uniformity, which, without the existence of the law, their conduct would probably want. In consequence of the sentiment or opinion which is styled analogically a law, the conduct of the parties obnoxious has a steadiness, constancy, or uniformity which, without the existence of that sentiment in the uncertain body of persons, their conduct would hardly present. For they who are obnoxious to the sanction which arms the law proper, commonly do or forbear from the acts which the law enjoins or forbids; whilst they who are obnoxious to the evil which will probably follow the displeasure of the uncertain body of persons, commonly do or forbear from the acts which the body approves or dislikes. Many of the applications of the term *law* which are merely metaphorical or figurative were probably suggested (as I shall show hereafter) by that uniformity of conduct which is consequent on a law proper.

Distinction between a determinate *and an* indeterminate *body of single or individual persons*

In the foregoing analysis of a law set by general opinion, the meaning of the expression '*indeterminate* body of persons' is indicated rather than explained. To complete my analysis of a law set by general opinion (and to abridge that analysis of sovereignty which I shall place in my sixth lecture) I will here insert a concise exposition of the following pregnant distinction: namely, the distinction between a *determinate* and an *indeterminate* body of single or individual persons. If my exposition of the distinction shall appear obscure and crabbed, my hearers (I hope) will recollect that the distinction could hardly be expounded in lucid and flowing expressions.

I will first describe the distinction in general or abstract terms, and will then exemplify and illustrate the general or abstract description.

If a body of persons be determinate, *all* the persons who compose it are determined and assignable, or *every* person who belongs to it is determined and may be indicated.

But determinate bodies are of two kinds. A determinate body of one of those kinds is distinguished by the following marks:

1. The body is composed of persons determined specifically or individually, or

determined by characters or descriptions respectively appropriate to themselves.

2. Though every individual member must of necessity answer to many generic descriptions, every individual member is a member of the determinate body, not by reason of his answering to any generic description but by reason of his bearing his specific or appropriate character.

A determinate body of the other of those kinds is distinguished by the following marks:

1. It comprises *all* the persons who belong to a given class, or who belong respectively to two or more of such classes. In other words, *every* person who answers to a given generic description, or to any of two or more given generic descriptions, is also a member of the determinate body.
2. Though every individual member is of necessity determined by a specific or appropriate character, every individual member is a member of the determinate body, not by reason of his bearing his specific or appropriate character, but by reason of his answering to the given generic description.

If a body be indeterminate, *all* the persons who compose it are not determined and assignable. Or (changing the expression) *every* person who belongs to it is not determined, and, therefore, cannot be indicated. For an indeterminate body consists of *some* of the persons who belong to another and larger aggregate. But *how many of those persons* are members of the indeterminate body, or which of those persons in particular are members of the indeterminate body, is not and cannot be known completely and exactly.

For example, the trading firm or partnership of A B and C is a determinate body of the kind first described above. Every member of the firm is determined specifically, or by a character or description peculiar or appropriate to himself. And every member of the firm belongs to the determinate body, not by reason of his answering to any generic description, but by reason of his bearing his specific or appropriate character. It is as being that very individual person that A B or C is a limb of the partnership.

The British Parliament for the time being is a determinate body of the kind lastly described above. It comprises the *only* person who answers for the time being to the generic description of king. It comprises *every* person belonging to the class of peers who are entitled for the time being to vote in the upper house. It comprises *every* person belonging to the class of commoners who for the time being represent the commons in parliament. And, though every member of the British Parliament is of necessity determined by a specific or appropriate character, he is not a member of the parliament by reason of his bearing that character, but by reason of his answering to the given generic description. It is not as being the individual George, but as being the individual who answers to the generic description of king, that George is king of Britain and Ireland, and a limb of the determinate body which is sovereign or supreme therein. It is not as being the individual Grey, or as being the individual Peel, that Grey is a member of the upper house, or Peel a member of the lower. Grey is a member of the upper house, as belonging to the class of peers entitled to vote therein. Peel is a member of the lower house, as answering the generic description 'representative of the commons in parliament'. The generic characters of the persons who compose the British Parliament are here described generally, and, therefore, inaccurately. To describe those generic characters minutely and accurately were to render a complete description of the intricate and perplexed system which is styled the British Constitution. A maxim of that Constitution may illustrate the subject of the present paragraph. The meaning of the maxim, 'the king never dies', may, I believe, be rendered in the following manner. Though an actual occupant of the kingly office is human, mortal, and transient, the duration of the office itself has no possible limit which the British Constitution can contemplate. And on the death of an actual occupant, the office instantly devolves to that individual person who bears the generic character which entitles to take the crown: to that individual person who is then heir to the crown, according to the generic description contained in the Act of Settlement.

To exemplify the foregoing description of an indeterminate body I will revert to the nature of a law set by general opinion. Where a so called law is set by *general* opinion, *most* of the persons who belong to a determinate body or class opine or feel alike in regard to a kind of conduct. But the number of that majority, or the several individuals who compose it, cannot be fixed or assigned with perfect fullness or accuracy. For example, a law set or imposed by the *general* opinion of a nation, by the *general* opinion of a legislative assembly, by the *general* opinion of a profession, or by the general opinion of a club, is an opinion or sentiment, relating to conduct of a kind, which is held or felt by *most* of those who belong to that certain body. But how many of that body, or which of that body in particular, hold or feel that given opinion or sentiment is not and cannot be known completely and correctly. Consequently, that majority of the certain body forms a body uncertain. Or (changing the expression) the body which is formed by that majority is an indeterminate portion of a determinate body or aggregate. Generally speaking, therefore, an indeterminate body is an indeterminate portion of a body determinate or certain. But a body or class of persons may also be indeterminate because it consists of persons of a vague generic character. For example, the body or class of gentlemen consists of individual persons whose generic character of gentleman cannot be described precisely. Whether a given man were a genuine gentleman or not is a question which different men might answer in different ways. An indeterminate body may therefore be indeterminate after a twofold manner. It may consist of an uncertain portion of an uncertain body or class. For example, a law set or imposed by the *general* opinion of gentlemen is an opinion or sentiment of *most* of those who are commonly deemed gentlemanly. But what proportion of the class holds the opinion in question, or what proportion of the class feels the sentiment in question, is not less indeterminate than the generic character of gentlemen. The body by whose opinion the so called law is set, is therefore, an uncertain portion of an uncertain body or aggregate. And here I may briefly remark that a certain portion of a certain body is itself a body determinate. For example, the persons who answer the generic description 'representative of the commons in parliament', are a certain portion of the persons who answer the generic description 'commoner of the United Kingdom'. A select committee of the representative body, or any portion of the body happening to form a house, is a certain or determined portion of the representatives of the commons in parliament. And, in any of these or similar cases, the certain portion of the certain body is itself a body determinate.

A determinate body of persons is capable of *corporate* conduct, or is capable, *as a body*, of positive or negative deportment. Whether it consists of persons determined by specific characters, or of persons determined or defined by a character or characters generic, every person who belongs to it is determined and may be indicated. In the first case, every person who belongs to it may be indicated by his specific character. In the second case, every person who belongs to it is also knowable: for *every* person who answers to the given generic description, or who answers to any of the given generic descriptions, is therefore a member of the body. Consequently, the entire body, or any proportion of its members, is capable, *as a body*, of positive or negative deportment: as, for example, of meeting at determinate times and places; of issuing expressly or tacitly a law or other command; of choosing and deputing representatives to perform its intentions or wishes; of receiving obedience from others, or from any of its own members.

But an indeterminate body is incapable of *corporate* conduct, or is incapable, *as a body*, of positive or negative deportment. An indeterminate body is incapable of corporate conduct, inasmuch as the several persons of whom it consists cannot be known and indicated completely and correctly. In case a portion of its members act or forbear in concert, that given portion of its members is, by that very concert, a determinate or certain body. For example, a law set or imposed by the *general* opinion of barristers condemns the sordid practice of hugging or caressing attorneys. And as those whose opinion or sentiment sets the so called law are an indeterminate part of the determinate body of barristers, they form a body uncertain and incapable of corporate conduct. But in case a number or portion of that uncertain body assembled and passed a resolution to check the practice of hugging, that number or portion of that uncertain body would be, by the very act, a certain body or aggregate. It would form a determinate body consisting of the determined individuals who assembled and passed the resolution. A law imposed by general opinion may be the cause of a law in the proper acceptation of the term. But the law properly so called, which is the consequent or effect, utterly differs from the so called law which is the antecedent or cause. The one is an opinion or sentiment of an uncertain body of persons; of a body essentially incapable of joint or corporate conduct. The other is set or established by the positive or negative deportment of a certain individual or aggregate.

For the purpose of rendering my exposition as little intricate as possible, I have supposed that a body of persons, forming a body determinate, either consists of persons determined by specific characters, or of persons determined or defined by a generic description or descriptions. But a body of persons, forming a body determinate, may consist of persons determined by specific or appropriate characters, and also of persons determined by a character or characters generic. Let us suppose, for example, that the individual Oliver Cromwell was sovereign or supreme in England: or that the individual Cromwell, and the individuals Ireton and Fleetwood, formed a triumvirate which was sovereign in that country. Let us suppose, moreover, that Cromwell, or the triumvirs, convened a house of commons elected in the ancient manner: and that Cromwell, or the triumvirs, yielded a part in the sovereignty to this representative body. Now the sovereign or supreme body formed by Cromwell and the house, or the sovereign and supreme body formed by the triumvirs and the house, would have consisted of a person or persons determined or defined specifically, and of persons determined or defined by a generic character or description. The members of the house of commons would have been members of the sovereign body, as answering the generic description 'representatives of the commons in parliament'. But it is as being the very individual Cromwell, or as being the very individuals Cromwell, Ireton, and Fleetwood, that he or they would have formed a limb of the sovereign or supreme body. It is not as answering to a given generic description, or as acquiring a part in the sovereignty by a given generic mode, that he or they would have shared the sovereignty with the body representing the people. A body of persons, forming a body determinate, may also consist of persons determined or defined specifically, and determined or defined moreover by a character or characters generic. A select committee of a body representing a people or nation consists of individual persons named or appointed specifically to sit on that given committee. But those specific individuals could not be members of the committee unless they answered the generic description 'representative of the people or nation'.

It follows from the exposition immediately preceding that the one or the number which is sovereign in an independent political society is a *determinate* individual person or a *determinate* body of persons. If the sovereign one or number were not determinate or certain, it could not command expressly or tacitly, and could not be an object of obedience to the subject members of the community. Inasmuch as this principle is amply explained by the exposition immediately preceding, I shall refer to it in my sixth lecture, as to a principle sufficiently known. The intricate and difficult analysis which I shall place in that discourse will thus be somewhat facilitated, and not inconsiderably abridged.

As closely connected with the matter of the exposition immediately preceding, the following remark concerning supreme government may be put commodiously in the present place. In order that a supreme government may possess much stability, and that the society wherein it is supreme may enjoy much tranquillity, the persons who take the sovereignty in the way of succession must take or acquire by a given generic mode, or by given generic modes. Or (changing the expression) they must take by reason of their answering to a given generic description, or by reason of their respectively answering to given generic descriptions. For example, the Roman Emperors or Princes (who were virtually monarchs or autocrators) did not succeed to the sovereignty of the Roman Empire or World by a given generic title: by a mode of acquisition given or preordained, and susceptible of generic description. It was neither as lineal descendant of Julius Cæsar or Augustus, nor by the testament or other disposition of the last possessor of the throne, nor by the appointment or nomination of the Roman people or senate, nor by the election of a determinate body formed of the military class, nor by any mode of acquisition generic and preordained, that every successive Emperor, or every successive Prince, acquired the virtual sovereignty of the Roman Empire or World. Every successive Emperor acquired by a mode of acquisition which was purely anomalous or accidental: which had not been predetermined by any law or custom, or by any positive law or rule of positive morality. Every actual occupant of the Imperial office or dignity (whatever may have been the manner wherein he had gotten possession) was obeyed, for the time, by the bulk of the military class; was acknowledged, of course, by the impotent and trembling senate; and received submission, of course, from the inert and helpless mass which inhabited the city and provinces. By reason of this irregularity in the succession to the virtual sovereignty, the demise of an Emperor was not uncommonly followed by a shorter or longer dissolution of the general supreme government. Since no one could claim to succeed by a given generic title, or as answering for the time being to a given generic description, a contest for the prostrate sovereignty almost inevitably arose between the more influential of the actual military chiefs. And till one of the military candidates had vanquished and crushed his rivals, and had forced with an armed hand his way to the vacant throne, the generality or bulk of the inhabitants in the Roman Empire or World could hardly render obedience to one and the same superior. By reason also of this irregularity in the succession to the Imperial office, the general and habitual obedience to an actual occupant of the office was always extremely precarious. For, since he was not occupant by a given generic title, or by reason of his having answered to a given generic description, the title of any rebel, who might anyhow eject him, would not have been less legitimate or less constitutional than his own. Or (speaking with greater precision) there was no mode of acquiring the office which could be styled legitimate, or which could be styled constitutional: which was susceptible of generic description, and which had been predetermined by positive law or morality. There was not, in the Roman World, any determinate person whom positive law or morality had pointed out to its inhabitants as the exclusively appropriate object of general and habitual obedience. The reasoning which applies in the case of a monarchy will also apply, with few variations, in the case of a government by a number. Unless the members of the supreme body held their respective stations by titles generic and fixed, the given supreme government must be extremely unstable, and the given society wherein it is supreme must often be torn by contests for the possession of shares in the sovereignty.

Laws set by general *opinion, or opinions or sentiments of* indeterminate *bodies, are the only opinions or sentiments that have gotten the name of* laws. *But an opinion or sentiment held or felt by an* individual, *or by all the members or a* certain aggregate, *may be as closely analogous to a law proper as the opinion or sentiment of an indeterminate body*

Before I close my analysis of those laws improperly so called which are closely analogous to laws in the proper acceptation of the term, I must advert to a seeming caprice of current or established language.

A law set or imposed by *general* opinion is an opinion or sentiment, regarding conduct of a kind, which is held or felt by an *indeterminate body*: that is to say, an indeterminate portion of a certain or uncertain aggregate.

Now a like opinion or sentiment held or felt by an *individual*, or held or felt *universally* by the members of a *body determinate*, may be as closely analogous to a law proper as a so-called law set by *general* opinion. It may bear an analogy to a law in the proper acceptation of the term, exactly or nearly resembling the analogy to a law proper which is borne by an opinion or sentiment of an *indeterminate body*. An opinion, for example, of a patron, in regard to conduct of a kind, may be a law or rule to his own dependent or dependants, just as a like opinion of an indeterminate body is a law or rule to all who might suffer by provoking its displeasure. And whether a like opinion be held by an uncertain aggregate, or be held by *every* member of a precisely determined body, its analogy to a law proper is exactly or nearly the same.

But when we speak of a law set or imposed by opinion, we always or commonly mean (I rather incline to believe) a law set or imposed by *general* opinion: that is to say, an opinion or sentiment, regarding conduct of a kind, which is held or felt by an uncertain body or class. The term *law*, or *law set by opinion*, is never or rarely applied to a like opinion or sentiment of a precisely determined party: that is to say, a like opinion or sentiment held or felt by an individual, or held or felt universally by the members of a certain aggregate.

This seeming caprice of current or established language probably arose from the following causes.

An opinion, regarding conduct, which is held by an individual person, or which is held universally by a *small* determinate body, is commonly followed by consequences of comparatively trifling importance. The circle of the persons to whom its influence reaches, or whose desires or conduct it affects or determines, is rarely extensive. The analogy which such opinions bear to laws proper has, therefore, attracted little attention and has, therefore, not gotten them the name of *laws*. An opinion held universally by a *large* determinate body is not less largely influential, or is more largely influential, than an opinion of an uncertain portion of the same certain aggregate. But since the determinate body is large or numerous, an opinion held by *all* its members can hardly be distinguished from an opinion held by *most* of its members. An opinion held *universally* by the members of the body determinate is, therefore, equivalent in practice to a general opinion of the body and is, therefore, classed with the laws which *general* opinion imposes.

Deferring to this seeming caprice of current or established language, I have forborne from ranking sentiments of precisely determined parties with the laws improperly so called which are closely analogous to the proper. I have restricted that description to sentiments, regarding conduct, of uncertain bodies or classes. My foregoing analysis or exposition of laws of that description is, therefore, an analysis of laws set by *general* opinion.

If the description ought to embrace (as, I think, it certainly ought) opinions, regarding conduct, of precisely determined parties, my foregoing analysis or exposition will still be correct substantially. With a few slight and obvious changes, my foregoing analysis of a law set by *general* opinion will serve as an analysis of a law set by *any* opinion: of a law set by the opinion of an indeterminate body, and of a law set by the opinion of a precisely determined party.

For the character or essential difference of a law imposed by opinion is this: that the law is not a *command*, issued expressly or tacitly, but is merely an *opinion* or *sentiment*, relating to conduct of a kind, which is held or felt by an uncertain body, or by a determinate party. A wish that conduct of the kind shall be pursued or forborne is not *signified*, expressly or tacitly, by that uncertain body, or that determinate party: nor does that body or party *intend* to inflict an evil upon any whose conduct may deviate from the given opinion or sentiment. The opinion or sentiment is merely an opinion or sentiment, although it subjects a transgressor to the chance of a consequent evil, and may even lead to a command regarding conduct of the kind.

Between the opinion or sentiment of the indeterminate body, and the opinion or sentiment of the precisely determined party, there is merely the following difference: the precisely determined party is *capable* of issuing a command in pursuance of the opinion or sentiment. But the uncertain body is not. For, being essentially incapable of joint or corporate conduct, it cannot, as a body, signify a wish or desire, and cannot, as a body, hold an intention or purpose.

The foregoing distribution of laws proper, and of such improper laws as are closely analogous to the proper, briefly recapitulated

It appears from the expositions in the preceding portion of my discourse that laws properly so called, with such improper laws as are closely analogous to the proper, are of three capital classes:

1. The law of God, or the laws of God.
2. Positive law, or positive laws.
3. Positive morality, rules of positive morality, or positive moral rules.

It also appears from the same expositions that positive moral rules are of two species:

1. Those positive moral rules which are express or tacit commands, and which are therefore laws in the proper acceptation of the term.
2. Those laws improperly so called (but closely analogous to laws in the proper acceptation of the term) which are set by general opinion, or are set by opinion: which are set by opinions of uncertain bodies; or by opinions of uncertain bodies, and opinions of determinate parties.

The sanctions, proper and improper, by which those laws are respectively enforced; the duties, proper and improper, which those laws respectively impose; and the rights, proper and improper, which those laws respectively confer

The sanctions annexed to the laws of God may be styled *religious*. The sanctions annexed to positive laws may be styled, emphatically, *legal*: for the laws to which they are annexed are styled, simply and emphatically, *laws* or *law*. Or, as every positive law supposes a πόλις or *civitas*, or supposes a society political and independent, the epithet *political* may be applied to the sanctions by which such laws are enforced. Of the sanctions which enforce compliance with positive moral rules, some are sanctions properly so called, and others are styled *sanctions* by an analogical extension of the term: that is to say, some are annexed to rules which are laws imperative and proper, and others enforce the rules which are laws set by opinion. Since rules of either species may be styled positive morality, the sanctions which enforce compliance with rules of either species may be styled *moral* sanctions. Or (changing the expression) we may say of rules of either species that they are sanctioned or enforced *morally*.[2]

The duties imposed by the laws of God may be styled *religious*. The duties imposed by positive laws may be styled, emphatically, *legal*: or, like the laws by which they are imposed, they may be said to be sanctioned *legally*. Of the duties imposed by positive moral rules, some are duties properly so called, and others are styled *duties* by an analogical extension of the term: that is to say, some are creatures of rules which are laws imperative and proper, and others are creatures of the rules which are laws set by opinion. Like the sanctions proper and improper by which they are respectively enforced, these duties proper and improper may be styled *moral*. Or we may say of the duties, as of the rules of which they are imposed, that they are sanctioned or enforced *morally*.[3]

Every right supposes a duty incumbent on a party or parties other than the party entitled. Through the imposition of that corresponding duty, the right was conferred. Through the continuance of that corresponding duty, the right continues to exist. If that corresponding duty be the creature of a law imperative, the right is a right properly so called. If that corresponding duty be the creature of a law improper, the right is styled a *right* by an analogical extension of the term. Consequently, a right existing through a duty imposed by the law of God, or a right existing through a duty imposed by positive law, is a right properly so called. Where the duty is the creature of a positive moral rule, the nature of the corresponding right depends upon the nature of the rule. If the rule imposing the duty be a law imperative and proper, the right is a right properly so called. If the rule imposing the duty be a law set by opinion, the right is styled a *right* through an analogical extension of the term. Rights conferred by the law of God, or rights existing through duties imposed by the law of God, may be styled *Divine*. Rights conferred by positive law, or rights existing through duties imposed by positive law, may be styled, emphatically, *legal*. Or it may be said of rights conferred by positive law, that they are sanctioned or protected *legally*. The rights proper and improper which are conferred by positive morality may be styled *moral*. Or it may be said of rights conferred by positive morality that they are sanctioned or protected *morally*.

The law of God, positive law, and positive morality sometimes coincide, *sometimes do* not *coincide, and sometimes* conflict

The body or aggregate of laws which may be styled the law of God, the body or aggregate of laws which may be styled positive law, and the body or aggregate of laws which may be styled positive morality, sometimes *coincide*, sometimes do *not* coincide, and sometimes *conflict*.

One of these bodies of laws *coincides* with another when acts, which are enjoined or forbidden by the former, are also enjoined or are also forbidden by the latter. For example, the killing which is styled *murder* is forbidden by the positive law of every political society: it is also forbidden by a so called law which the general opinion of the society has set or imposed: it is also forbidden by the law of God as known through the principle of utility. The murderer commits a crime, or he violates a positive law: he commits a conventional immorality, or he violates a so called law which general opinion has established; he commits a sin, or he violates the law of God. He is obnoxious to punishment, or other evil, to be inflicted by sovereign authority: he is obnoxious to the hate and the spontaneous ill-offices of the generality or bulk of the society: he is obnoxious to evil or pain to be suffered here or hereafter by the immediate appointment of the Deity.

One of these bodies of laws does *not* coincide with another when acts, which are enjoined or forbidden by the former, are not enjoined or are not forbidden by the latter. For example, though smuggling is forbidden by positive law, and (speaking generally) is not less pernicious than theft, it is not forbidden by the opinions or sentiments of the ignorant or unreflecting. Where the impost or tax is itself of pernicious tendency, smuggling is hardly forbidden by the opinions or sentiments of any: and it is therefore practised by any without the slightest shame, or without the slightest fear of incurring general censure. Such, for instance, is the case where the impost or tax is laid upon the foreign commodity, not for the useful purpose of raising a public revenue, but for the absurd and mischievous purpose of protecting a domestic manufacture. Offences against the game laws are also in point: for they are not offences against positive morality, although they are forbidden by positive law. A gentleman is not dishonoured, or generally shunned by gentlemen, though he shoots without a qualification. A peasant who wires a hare escapes the censure of peasants, though the squires, as doing justiceship, send him to the prison and the treadmill.

One of these bodies of laws *conflicts* with another when acts, which are enjoined or forbidden by the former, are forbidden or enjoined by the latter. For example, in most of the nations of modern Europe the practice of duelling is forbidden by positive law. It is also at variance with the law which is received in most of those nations as having been set by the Deity in the way of express revelation. But in spite of positive law, and in spite of his religious convictions, a man of the class of gentlemen may be forced by the law of honour to give or to take a challenge. If he forebore from giving, or if he declined a challenge, he might incur the general contempt of gentlemen or men of honour, and might meet with slights and insults sufficient to embitter his existence. The negative *legal* duty which certainly is incumbent upon him, and the negative *religious* duty to which he believes himself subject, are therefore mastered and controlled by that positive *moral* duty which arises from the so called law set by the opinion of his class.

The simple and obvious considerations to which I have now adverted are often overlooked by legislators. If they fancy a practice pernicious, or hate it they know not why, they proceed, without further thought, to forbid it by positive law. They forget that positive law may be superfluous or impotent, and therefore may lead to nothing but purely gratuitous vexation. They forget that the moral or the religious sentiments of the community may already suppress the practice as completely as it can be suppressed: or that, if the practice is favoured by those moral or religious sentiments, the strongest possible fear which legal pains can inspire may be mastered by a stronger fear of other and conflicting sanctions.[4]

In consequence of the frequent coincidence of positive law and morality, and of positive law and the law of God, the true nature and fountain of positive law is often absurdly mistaken by writers upon jurisprudence. Where positive law has been fashioned on positive morality, or where positive law has been fashioned on the law of God, they forget that the copy is the creature of the sovereign, and impute it to the author of the model.

For example: customary laws are positive laws fashioned by judicial legislation upon pre-existing customs. Now, till they become the grounds of judicial decisions upon cases, and are clothed with legal sanctions by the sovereign one or number, the customs are merely rules set by opinions of the governed, and sanctioned or enforced morally. Though, when they become the reasons of judicial decisions upon cases, and are clothed with legal sanctions by the sovereign one or number, the customs are rules of positive law as well as of positive morality. But, because the customs were observed by the governed before they were clothed with sanctions by the sovereign one or number, it is fancied that customary laws exist as *positive laws* by the institution of the private persons with whom the customs originated. Admitting the conceit, and reasoning by analogy, we ought to consider the sovereign the author of the positive morality which is often a consequence of positive law. Where a positive law, not fashioned on a custom, is favourably received by the governed, and enforced by their opinions or sentiments, we must deem the so called law, set by those opinions or sentiments, a law imperative and proper of the supreme political superior.

Again: the portion of positive law which is parcel of the *law of nature* (or, in the language of the classical jurists, which is parcel of the *jus gentium*) is often supposed to emanate, even as positive law, from a Divine or Natural source. But (admitting the distinction of positive law into law natural and law positive) it is manifest that law natural, considered as a portion of positive, is the creature of human sovereigns, and not of the Divine monarch. To say that it emanates, as positive law, from a Divine or Natural source is to confound positive law with law whereon it is fashioned, or with law whereunto it conforms.

The foregoing distribution of laws proper, and of such improper laws as are closely analogous to the proper, tallies, in the main, with a division of laws which is given incidentally by Locke in his Essay on Human Understanding

The foregoing distribution of laws proper, and of such improper laws as are closely analogous to the proper, tallies, in the main, with a division of laws which is given incidentally by Locke in his *Essay on Human Understanding*. And since this division of laws, or of the sources of duties or obligations, is recommended by the great authority which the writer has justly acquired, I gladly append it to my own division or analysis. The passage of his essay in which the division occurs is part of an inquiry into the nature of *relation*, and is therefore concerned indirectly with the nature and kinds of *law*. With the exclusion of all that is foreign to the nature and kinds of law, with the exclusion of a few expressions which are obviously redundant, and with the correction of a few expressions which are somewhat obscure, the passage containing the divisions may be rendered in the words following:[5]

> The conformity or disagreement men's voluntary actions have to a rule to which they are referred, and by which they are judged of, is a sort of relation which may be called *moral relation*.
>
> Human actions, when with their various ends, objects, manners, and circumstances, they are framed into distinct complex ideas, are, as has been shown, so many *mixed modes*, a great part whereof have names annexed to them. Thus, supposing gratitude to be a readiness to acknowledge and return kindness received, or *polygamy* to be the having more wives than one at once, when we frame those notions thus in our minds, we have there so many determined ideas of mixed modes.
>
> But this is not all that concerns our actions. It is not enough to have determined ideas of them, and to know what names belong to such and such combinations of ideas. We have a further and greater concernment. And that is, to know whether such actions are morally good or bad.
>
> Good or evil is nothing but pleasure or pain, or that which occasions or procures pleasure or pain to us. *Moral good or evil*, then, is only the conformity or disagreement of our voluntary actions to some law, whereby

good or evil is drawn on us by the will and power of the law-maker: which good or evil, pleasure or pain, attending our observance or breach of the law, by the decree of the law-maker, is that we call reward or punishment.

Of these moral rules or laws, to which men generally refer, and by which they judge of the rectitude or pravity of their actions, there seem to me to be three sorts, with their three different enforcements, or rewards and punishments. For since it would be utterly in vain to suppose a rule set to the free actions of man, without annexing to it some enforcement of good and evil to determine his will, we must, wherever we suppose a law, suppose also some reward or punishment annexed to that law. It would be in vain for one intelligent being to set a rule to the actions of another, if he had it not in his power to reward the compliance with, and punish deviation from his rule, by some good and evil that is not the natural product and consequence of the action itself: for that being a natural convenience or inconvenience, would operate of itself without a law. This, if I mistake not, is the true nature of all *law* properly so called.

The laws that men generally refer their actions to, to judge of their rectitude or obliquity, seem to me to be these three:

1. The *Divine* law.
2. The *civil* law.
3. The law of *opinion* or *reputation*, if I may so call it.

By the relation they bear to the first of these, men judge whether their actions are sins or duties: by the second, whether they be criminal or innocent: and by the third, whether they be virtues or vices.

By the *Divine* law, I mean that law which God hath set to the actions of men, whether promulgated to them by the light of nature, or the voice of revelation. This is the only true touchstone of *moral rectitude*. And by comparing them to this law, it is that men judge of the most considerable *moral good* or *evil* of their actions: that is, whether as *duties* or *sins*, they are like to procure them happiness or misery from the hands of the Almighty.

The *civil* law, the rule set by the commonwealth to the actions of those who belong to it, is a rule to which men refer their actions, to judge whether they be *criminal* or no. This law nobody overlooks, the rewards and punishments that enforce it being ready at hand, and suitable to the power that makes it: which is the force of the commonwealth, engaged to protect the lives, liberties and possessions of those who live according to its law, and has power to take away life, liberty or goods from him who disobeys.

The law of *opinion* or *reputation* is another law that men generally refer their actions to, to judge of their rectitude or obliquity.

Virtue and *vice* are names pretended, and supposed everywhere to stand for actions in their own nature right or wrong: and as far as they really are so applied, they so far are coincident with the Divine law above mentioned. But yet, whatever is pretended, this is visible, that these names *virtue* and *vice*, in the particular instances of their application through the several nations and societies of men in the world, are constantly attributed to such actions only as in each country and society are in reputation or discredit. Nor is it to be thought strange, that men everywhere should give the name of *virtue* to those actions which amongst them are judged praiseworthy, and call that *vice* which they account blameable; since they would condemn themselves, if they should think anything *right*, to which they allowed not commendation; anything *wrong*, which they let pass without blame.

Thus the measure of what is everywhere called and esteemed *virtue* and *vice*, is this approbation or dislike, praise or blame, which by a secret and tacit consent establishes itself in the several societies, tribes, and clubs of men in the world; whereby several actions come to find credit or disgrace amongst them, according to the judgment, maxims, or fashions of that place. For though men uniting into politick societies have resigned up to the publick the disposing of all their force, so that they cannot employ it against any fellow citizens any further than the law of the country directs, yet they retain still the power of thinking well or ill, approving or disapproving of the actions of those whom they live amongst and converse with: and by this approbation and dislike, they establish amongst themselves what they will call *virtue* and *vice*.

That this is the common *measure of virtue and vice* will appear to any one who considers, that, though that passes for *vice* in one country, which is counted *virtue* (or, at least, not *vice*) in another, yet everywhere *virtue* and praise, *vice* and blame go together. *Virtue* is everywhere that which is thought praiseworthy; and nothing but that which has the allowance of public esteem is called *virtue*. *Virtue* and praise are so united, that they are often called by the same name. 'Sunt sua prœmia laudi', says Virgil. And, says Cicero, 'nihil habet natura præstantius, quam *honestatem*, quam *laudem*, quam *dignitatem*, quam *decus*': all which, he tells you, are names for the same thing. Such is the language of the heathen philosophers, who well understood wherein the notions of *virtue* and *vice* consisted.

But though, by the different temper, education, fashion, maxims, or interest of different sorts of men, it fell out, that what was thought praiseworthy in one place, escaped not censure in another, and so in different societies *virtues* and *vices* were changed, yet, as to the main, they for the most part kept the same everywhere. For since nothing can be more natural than to encourage with esteem and reputation that wherein everyone finds his advantage, and to blame and discountenance the contrary, it is no wonder that esteem and discredit, virtue and vice, should in a great measure everywhere correspond with the unchangeable rule of right and wrong which the law of God hath established: there being nothing that so directly and visibly secures and advances the general good of mankind in this world as obedience to the law He has set them, and nothing that breeds such mischiefs and confusion as the neglect of it. And therefore men, without renouncing all sense and reason, and their own interest, could not generally mistake in placing their commendation or blame on that side which really deserved it not. Nay, even those men, whose practice was otherwise, failed not to give their approbation right: few being depraved to that degree, as not to condemn, at least in others, the faults they themselves were guilty of. Whereby, even in the corruption of manners, the law of God, which ought to be the rule of virtue and vice, was pretty well observed.

If any one shall imagine that I have forgotten my own notion of a law, when I make the law, whereby men judge of *virtue* and *vice*, to be nothing but the consent of private men who have not authority to make a law; especially wanting that which is so necessary and essential to a law, a power to enforce it: I think, I may say, that he who imagines commendation and disgrace not to be strong motives on men to accommodate themselves to the opinions and rules of those with whom they converse, seems little skilled in the nature or history of mankind, the greatest part whereof he shall find to govern themselves chiefly, if not solely, by this law of fashion, and so they do that which keeps them in reputation with their company, little regard the law of God or the magistrate. The penalties that attend the breach of God's law, some, nay, perhaps most men seldom seriously reflect on; and amongst those that do, many, whilst they break the law, entertain thoughts of future reconciliation, and making their peace for such breaches. And as to the punishments due from the law of the commonwealth, they frequently flatter themselves with the hope of impunity. But no man escapes the punishment of their censure and dislike, who offends against the fashion and opinion of the company he keeps, and would recommend himself to. Nor is there one of ten thousand, who is stiff and insensible enough to bear up under the constant dislike and condemnation of his own club. He must be of a strange and unusual constitution, who can content himself to live in constant disgrace and disrepute with his own particular society. Solitude many men have sought and been reconciled to: but nobody that has the least thought or sense of a man about him, can live in society under the constant dislike and ill opinion of his familiars, and those he converses with. This is a burthen too heavy for human sufferance: and he must be made up of irreconcilable contradictions, who can take pleasure in company, and yet be insensible of contempt and disgrace from his companions.

The law of God, the law of politick societies, and the law of fashion or private censure, are, then, the three rules to which men variously compare their actions. And it is from their conformity or disagreement to one of these rules, that they judge of their rectitude or obliquity, and name them good or bad.

Whether we take the rule, to which, as to a touchstone, we bring our voluntary actions, from the fashion of the country, or from the will of a law-maker, the mind is easily able to observe the relation any action hath to it, and to judge whether the action agrees or disagrees with the rule. And thus the mind hath a notion of *moral goodness or evil*: which is either conformity or not conformity of any action to that rule. If I find an action to agree or disagree with the esteem of the country I have been bred in, and to be held by most men there worthy of praise or blame, I call the action virtuous or vicious. If I have the will of a supreme invisible law-maker for my rule, then, as I suppose the action commanded or forbidden by God, I call it good or evil, duty or sin. And if I compare it to the civil law, the rule made by the legislative power of the country, I call it lawful or unlawful, no crime or a crime. So that whencesoever we take the rule of actions, or by what standard soever we frame in our minds the ideas of virtues or vices, their rectitude or obliquity consists in their agreement or disagreement with the patterns prescribed by some law.

Before I quit this argument, I would observe that, in the relations which I call *moral relations*, I have a true notion of relation, by comparing the action with the rule, whether the rule be true or false. For if I measure any thing by a supposed yard, I know whether the thing I measure be longer or shorter than that supposed yard, though the yard I measure by be not exactly the standard. Measuring an action by a wrong rule, I shall judge amiss of its moral rectitude: but I shall not mistake the relation which the action bears to the rule whereunto I compare it.

Essay concerning Human Understanding. Book II, Chap. XXVIII.

Laws metaphorical or figurative. The common and negative nature of laws of the class

The analogy borne to a law proper by a law which opinion imposes, lies mainly in the following point of resemblance. In the case of a law set by opinion, as well as in the case of a law properly so called, a rational being or beings are obnoxious to contingent evil, in the event of their not complying with a known or presumed desire of another being or beings of a like nature. If, in either of the two cases, the contingent evil is suffered, it is suffered by a rational being, through a rational being: and it is suffered by a rational being, through a rational being, in consequence of the suffering party having disregarded a desire of a rational being or beings. The analogy, therefore, by which the laws are related mainly lies in the resemblance of the improper sanction and duty to the sanction and duty properly so called. The contingent evil in prospect which enforces the law improper, and the present obnoxiousness to that contingent evil, may be likened to the genuine sanction which enforces the law proper, and the genuine duty or obligation which the law proper imposes. The analogy between a law in the proper acceptation of the term, and a law improperly so called which opinion sets or imposes, is, therefore, strong or close. The defect which excludes the latter from the rank of a law proper merely consists in this: that the wish or desire of its authors has not been duly *signified*, and that they have no formed *intention* of inflicting evil or pain upon those who may break or transgress it.

But, beside the laws improper which are set or imposed by opinion, there are laws improperly so called which are related to laws proper by slender or remote analogies. And, since they have gotten the name of *laws* from their slender or remote analogies to laws properly so called, I style them laws metaphorical, or laws merely metaphorical.

The metaphorical applications of the term *law* are numerous and different. The analogies by which they are suggested, or by which metaphorical laws are related to laws proper, will, therefore, hardly admit of a common and positive description. But laws metaphorical, though numerous and different, have the following common and negative nature. No property or character of any metaphorical law can be likened to a sanction or a duty. Consequently, every metaphorical law wants that point of resemblance which mainly constitutes the analogy between a law proper and a law set by opinion.

The common and negative nature of laws metaphorical or figurative, shown by examples

To show that figurative laws want that point of resemblance, and are therefore remotely analogous to laws properly so called, I will touch slightly and briefly upon a few of the numberless cases in which the term *law* is extended and applied by a metaphor.

The most frequent and remarkable of those metaphorical applications is suggested by that uniformity, or that stability of conduct, which is one of the ordinary consequences of a law proper. By reason of the sanction working on their wills or desires, the parties obliged by a law proper commonly adjust their conduct to the pattern which the law prescribes. Consequently, wherever we observe a uniform order of events, or a uniform order of coexisting phænomena, we are prone to impute that order to a *law* set by its author, though the case presents us with nothing that can be likened to a sanction or a duty.

For example: we say that the movements of lifeless bodies are determined by certain *laws*: though, since the bodies are lifeless and have no desires or aversions, they cannot be touched by aught which in the least resembles a sanction, and cannot be subject to aught which in the least resembles an obligation. We mean that they move in certain uniform modes, and that they move in those uniform modes through the pleasure and appointment of God: just as parties obliged behave in a uniform manner through the pleasure and appointment of the party who imposes the law and the duty. Again: we say that certain actions of the lower and irrational animals are determined by certain *laws*: though, since they cannot understand the purpose and provisions of a law, it is impossible that sanctions should effectually move them to obedience, or that their conduct should be guided by a regard to duties or obligations. We mean that they act in certain uniform modes, either in consequence of instincts (or causes which we cannot explain), or else in consequence of hints which they catch from experience and observation: and that, since their uniformity of action is an effect of the Divine pleasure, it closely resembles the uniformity of conduct which is wrought by the authors of laws in those who are obnoxious to the sanctions.[6] In short, whenever we talk of *laws* governing the irrational world, the metaphorical application of the term *law* is suggested by this double analogy:

1. The successive and synchronous phænomena composing the irrational world, happen and exist, for the most part, in uniform series: which uniformity of succession and coexistence resembles the uniformity of conduct produced by an imperative law.
2. That uniformity of succession and coexistence, like the uniformity of conduct produced by an imperative law, springs from the will and intention of an intelligent and rational author.

When an atheist speaks of *laws* governing the irrational world, the metaphorical application is suggested by an analogy still more slender and remote than that which I have now analysed. He means that the uniformity of succession and coexistence resembles the uniformity of conduct produced by an imperative rule. If, to draw the analogy closer, he ascribes those laws to an author, he personifies a verbal abstraction, and makes it play the legislator. He attributes the uniformity of succession and coexistence to *laws* set by *nature*: meaning, by *nature*, the world itself; or, perhaps, that very uniformity which he imputes to nature's commands.

Many metaphorical applications of the term *law* or *rule* are suggested by the analogy following. An imperative law or rule guides the conduct of the obliged, or is a *norma*, model, or pattern, to which their conduct conforms. A proposed guide of human conduct, or a model or pattern offered to human imitation, is, therefore, frequently styled a *law* or *rule* of conduct, although there be not in the case a shadow of a sanction or a duty.

For example: to every law properly so called there are two distinct parties: a party by whom it is established, and a party to whom it is set. But, this notwithstanding, we often speak of a law set by a man to himself: meaning that he intends to pursue some given course of conduct as exactly as he would pursue it if he were bound to pursue it by a law. An intention of pursuing exactly some given course of conduct is the only law or rule which a man can set to himself. The binding virtue of a law lies in the sanction annexed to it. But in the case of a so called law set by a man to himself, he is not constrained to observe it by aught that resembles a sanction. For though he may fairly purpose to inflict a pain on himself, if his conduct shall depart from the guide which he intends it shall follow, the infliction of the conditional pain depends upon his own will. Again: when we talk of *rules* of art, the metaphorical application of the term *rules* is suggested by the analogy in question. By a *rule* of art, we mean a prescription or pattern which is offered to practitioners of an art, and which they are advised to observe when performing some given process. There is not the semblance of a sanction, nor is there the shadow of a duty. But the offered prescription or pattern may guide the conduct of practitioners, as a rule imperative and proper guides the conduct of the obliged.[7]

Laws metaphorical and figurative are often blended and confounded with laws imperative and proper

The preceding disquisition on figurative laws is not so superfluous as some of my hearers may deem it. Figurative laws are not unfrequently mistaken for laws imperative and proper. Nay, attempts have actually been made, and by writers of the highest celebrity, to explain and illustrate the nature of laws imperative and proper by allusions to so called laws which are merely such through a metaphor. Of these most gross and scarcely credible errors, various cases will be mentioned in future stages of my Course. For the present, the following examples will amply demonstrate that the errors are not impossible.

In an excerpt from Ulpian placed at the beginning of the Pandects, and also inserted by Justinian in the second title of his Institutes, a fancied *jus naturale*, common to all animals, is thus distinguished from the *jus naturale* or *gentium* to which I have adverted above.

> *Jus naturale* est, quod natura omnia animalia docuit: nam jus istud non humani generis proprium, sed omnium animalium, quæ in terra, quæ in mari

> nascuntur, avium quoque commune est. Hinc descendit maris atque feminæ conjunctio, quam nos matrimonium appellanus; hinc liberorum procreatio, hinc educatio: videmus etenim cetera quoque animalia, feras etiam, istius juris peritia censeri. *Jus gentium* est, quo gentes humanæ utuntur. Quod a *naturali* recedere, inde facile intelligere licet; quia illud omnibus animalibus, hoc solis hominibus inter se commune est.

The *jus naturale* which Ulpian here describes, and which he here distinguishes from the *jus naturale* or *gentium*, is a name for the instincts of animals. More especially, it denotes that instinctive appetite which leads them to propagate their kinds, with that instinctive sympathy which inclines parent animals to nourish and educate their young. Now the instincts of animals are related to laws by the slender or remote analogy which I have already endeavoured to explain. They incline the animals to act in certain uniform modes, and they are given to the animals for that purpose by an intelligent and rational Author. But these metaphorical laws which govern the lower animals, and which govern (though less despotically) the human species itself, should not have been blended and confounded, by a grave writer upon jurisprudence, with laws properly so called. It is true that the instincts of the animal man, like many of his affections which are not instinctive, are amongst the causes of laws in the proper acceptation of the term. More especially, the laws regarding the relation of husband and wife, and the laws regarding the relation of parent and child, are mainly caused by the instincts which Ulpian particularly points at. And that, it is likely, was the reason which determined this legal oracle to class the instincts of animals with laws imperative and proper. But nothing can be more absurd than the ranking with laws themselves the causes which lead to their existence. And if human instincts are laws because they are causes of laws, there is scarcely a faculty or affection belonging to the human mind, and scarcely a class of objects presented by the outward world, that must not be esteemed a law and an appropriate subject of jurisprudence. I must, however, remark, that the *jus quod natura omnia animalia docuit* is a conceit peculiar to Ulpian: and that this most foolish conceit, though inserted in Justinian's compilations, has no perceptible influence on the detail of the Roman law. The *jus naturale* of the classical jurists generally, and the *jus naturale* occurring generally in the Pandects, is equivalent to the *natural law* of modern writers upon jurisprudence, and is synonymous with the *jus gentium*, or the *jus naturale et gentium*, which I have tried to explain concisely at the end of a preceding note. It means those positive laws and those rules of positive morality which are not peculiar or appropriate to any nation or age, but obtain, or are thought to obtain, in all nations and ages: and which, by reason of their obtaining in all nations and ages, are supposed to be formed or fashioned on the law of God or Nature as known by the moral sense.

> Omnes populi [*says Gaius*] qui legibus et moribus reguntur, partim suo proprio, partim communi omnium hominum jure utuntur. Nam quod quisque populus ipse sibi jus constituit, id ipsius proprium est, vocaturque jus civile; quasi jus proprium ipsius civitatis. Quod vero naturalis ratio inter omnes homines constituit, id aput omnes populos peræque custoditur, vocaturque jus gentium; quasi quo jure omnes gentes utuntur.

The universal *leges et mores* here described by Gaius, and distinguished from the *leges et mores* peculiar to a particular nation, are styled indifferently, by most of the classical jurists, *jus gentium*, *jus naturale*, or *jus naturale et gentium*. And the law of nature, as thus understood, is not intrinsically absurd. For as some of the dictates of utility are always and everywhere the same, and are also so plain and glaring that they hardly admit of mistake, there are legal and moral rules which are nearly or quite *universal*, and the expediency of which must be seen by merely *natural* reason, or by reason without the lights of extensive experience and observation. The distinction of law and morality into natural and positive is a needless and futile subtility: but still the distinction is founded on a real and manifest difference. The *jus naturale* or *gentium* would be liable to little objection if it were not supposed to be the offspring of a moral instinct or sense, or of innate practical principles. But, since it is closely allied (as I shall show hereafter[8]) to that misleading and pernicious jargon, it ought to be expelled, with the *natural law* of the moderns, from the sciences of jurisprudence and morality.

The following passage is the first sentence in Montesquieu's *Spirit of Laws*:

> Les lois, dans la signification la plus étendue, sont les rapports nécessaires qui dérivent de la nature des choses: et dans ce sens tous les êtres ont leurs lois: la Divinité a ses lois; le monde matériel a ses lois; les intelligences supérieures à l'homme ont leurs lois; les bêtes ont leurs lois; l'homme a ses lois.

Now objects widely different, though bearing a common name, are here blended and confounded. Of the laws which govern the conduct of intelligent and rational creatures, some are laws imperative and proper, and others are closely analogous to laws of that description. But the so called laws which govern the material world, with the so called laws which govern the lower animals, are merely laws by a metaphor. And the so called laws which govern or determine the Deity are clearly in the same predicament. If his actions were governed or determined by laws imperative and proper, he would be in a state of dependence on another and superior being. When we say that the actions of the Deity are governed or determined by laws, we mean that they conform to intentions which the Deity himself has conceived, and which he pursues or observes with inflexible steadiness or constancy. To mix these figurative laws with laws imperative and proper is to obscure, and not to elucidate, the nature or essence of the latter. The beginning of the passage is worthy of the sequel. We are told that laws are the necessary relations which flow from the nature of things. But what, I would crave, are relations? What, I would also crave, is the nature of things? And how do the necessary relations which flow from the nature of things differ from those relations which originate in other sources? The terms of the definition are incomparably more obscure than the term which it affects to expound.

If you read the disquisition in Blackstone on the nature of laws in general, or the fustian description of law in Hooker's *Ecclesiastical Polity*, you will find the same confusion of laws imperative and proper with laws which are merely such by a glaring perversion of the term. The cases of this confusion are, indeed, so numerous that they would fill a considerable volume.

Physical or natural sanctions

From the confusion of laws metaphorical with laws imperative and proper, I turn to a mistake, somewhat similar, which, I presume to think, has been committed by Mr Bentham.

Sanctions proper and improper are of three capital classes: the sanctions properly so called which are annexed to the laws of God; the sanctions properly so called which are annexed to positive laws; the sanctions properly so called; and the sanctions closely analogous to sanctions properly so called, which respectively enforce compliance with positive moral rules. But to sanctions religious, legal, and moral, this great philosopher and jurist adds a class of sanctions which he styles *physical* or *natural*.

When he styles these sanctions *physical*, he does not intend to intimate that they are distinguished from other sanctions by the mode wherein they operate: he does not intend to intimate that these are the only sanctions which affect the suffering parties through physical or material means. Any sanction of any class may reach the suffering party through means of that description. If a man were smitten with blindness by the immediate appointment of the Deity, and in consequence of a sin he had committed against the Divine law, he would suffer a religious sanction through his physical or bodily organs. The thief who is hanged or imprisoned by virtue of a judicial command suffers a legal sanction through physical or material means. If a man of the class of gentlemen violates the law of honour, and happens to be shot in a duel arising from his moral delinquency, he suffers a moral sanction in a physical or material form.

The meaning annexed by Mr Bentham to the expression 'physical sanction', may, I believe, be rendered in the following manner: a physical sanction is an evil brought upon the suffering party by an act or omission of his own. But, though it is brought upon the sufferer by an act or omission of his own, it is not brought upon the sufferer through any Divine law, or through any positive law, or rule of positive morality. For example: if your house be destroyed by fire through your neglecting to put out a light, you bring upon yourself, by your negligent omission, a *physical* or *natural* sanction: supposing, I mean, that your omission is not to be deemed a sin, and that the consequent destruction of your house is not to be deemed a punishment inflicted by the hand of the Deity. In short, though a physical sanction is an evil falling on a rational being, and brought on a rational being by an act or omission of his own, it is neither brought on the sufferer through a law imperative and proper, nor through an analogous law set or imposed by opinion. In case I borrowed the just, though tautological, language of Locke, I should describe a physical sanction in such some terms as the following: 'It is an evil *naturally* produced by the conduct whereon it is consequent: and, being *naturally* produced by the conduct whereon it is consequent, it reaches the suffering party *without the intervention of a law.*'

Such physical or natural evils are related by the following analogy to sanctions properly so called.

1. When they are actually suffered, they are suffered by rational beings through acts or omissions of their own.
2. Before they are actually suffered, or whilst they exist in prospect, they affect the wills or desires of the parties obnoxious to them as sanctions properly so called affect the wills of the obliged. The parties are urged to the acts which may avert the evils from their heads, or the parties are deterred from the acts which may bring the evils upon them.

But in spite of the specious analogy at which I have now pointed, I dislike, for various reasons, the application of the term *sanction* to these physical or natural evils. Of those reasons I will briefly mention the following:

1. Although these evils are suffered by intelligent rational beings, and by intelligent rational beings through acts or omissions of their own, they are not suffered as consequences of their not complying with desires of intelligent rational beings. The acts or omissions whereon these evils are consequent can hardly be likened to breaches of duties, or to violations of imperative laws. The analogy borne by these evils to sanctions properly so called is nearly as remote as the analogy borne by laws metaphorical to laws imperative and proper.
2. By the term *sanction*, as it is now restricted, the evils enforcing compliance with laws imperative and proper, or with the closely analogous laws which opinion sets or imposes, are distinguished from other evils briefly and commodiously. If the term were commonly extended to these physical or

natural evils, this advantage would be lost. The term would then comprehend every possible evil which a man may bring upon himself by his own voluntary conduct. The term would then comprehend every contingent evil which can work on the will or desires as a motive to action or forbearance.

In strictness, declaratory law, laws repealing laws, and laws of imperfect obligation (in the sense of the Roman jurists), ought to be classed respectively with laws, metaphorical or figurative, and rules of positive morality

I close my disquisitions on figurative laws, and on those metaphorical sanctions which Mr Bentham denominates *physical*, with the following connected remarks.

Declaratory laws, laws repealing laws, and laws of imperfect obligation (in the sense of the Roman jurists) are merely analogous to laws in the proper acceptation of the term. Like laws imperative and proper, declaratory laws, laws repealing laws, and laws of imperfect obligation (in the sense of the Roman jurists) are signs of pleasure or desire proceeding from law-makers. A law of imperfect obligation (in the sense of the Roman jurists) is also allied to an imperative law by the following point of resemblance. Like a law imperative and proper, it is offered as a *norma*, or guide of conduct, although it is not armed with a legal or political sanction.

Declaratory laws, and laws repealing laws, ought in strictness to be classed with laws metaphorical or figurative: for the analogy by which they are related to laws imperative and proper is extremely slender or remote. Laws of imperfect obligation (in the sense of the Roman jurists) are laws set or imposed by the opinions of the law-makers, and ought in strictness to be classed with rules of positive morality. But though laws of these three species are merely analogous to laws in the proper acceptation of the term, they are closely connected with positive laws, and are appropriate subjects of jurisprudence. Consequently I treat them as improper laws of anomalous or eccentric sorts, and exclude them from the classes of laws to which in strictness they belong.

Note: on the prevailing tendency to confound what is with what ought to be law or morality, that is, first, to confound positive law with the science of legislation, and positive morality with deontology; and secondly, to confound positive law with positive morality, and both with legislation and deontology. (See p. 119.)

First: tendency to confound positive law with the science of legislation, and positive morality with deontology. Example from Blackstone

The existence of law is one thing; its merit or demerit is another. Whether it be or be not is one enquiry; whether it be or be not conformable to an assumed standard is a different enquiry. A law, which actually exists, is a law, though we happen to dislike it, or though it vary from the text by which we regulate our approbation and disapprobation. This truth, when formally announced as an abstract proposition, is so simple and glaring that it seems idle to insist upon it. But simple and glaring as it is, when enunciated in abstract expressions the enumeration of the instances in which it has been forgotten would fill a volume.

Sir William Blackstone, for example, says in his *Commentaries* that the laws of God are superior in obligation to all other laws; that no human laws should be suffered to contradict them; that human laws are of no validity if contrary to them; and that all valid laws derive their force from that Divine original.

Now, he *may* mean that all human laws ought to conform to the Divine laws. If this be his meaning, I assent to it without hesitation. The evils which we are exposed to suffer from the hands of God as a consequence of disobeying His commands are the greatest evils to which we are obnoxious; the obligations which they impose are consequently paramount to those imposed by any other laws, and if human commands conflict with the Divine law, we ought to disobey the command which is enforced by the less powerful sanction; this is implied in the term *ought*: the proposition is identical, and therefore perfectly indisputable—it is in our interest to choose the smaller and more uncertain evil, in preference to the greater and surer. If this be Blackstone's meaning, I assent to his proposition, and have only to object to it that it tells us just nothing. Perhaps, again, he means that human lawgivers are themselves obliged by the Divine laws to fashion the laws which they impose by that ultimate standard, because if they do not, God will punish them. To this also I entirely assent: for if the index to the law of God be the principle of utility, that law embraces the whole of our voluntary actions in so far as motives applied from without are required to give them a direction conformable to the general happiness.

But the meaning of this passage of Blackstone, if it has a meaning, seems rather to be this: that no human law which conflicts with the Divine law is obligatory or binding; in other words, that no human law which conflicts with the Divine law *is a law*, for a law without an obligation is a contradiction in terms. I suppose this to be his meaning, because when we say of any transaction that it is invalid or void, we mean that it is not binding: as, for example, if it be a contract, we mean that the political law will not lend its sanction to enforce the contract.

Now, to say that human laws which conflict with the Divine law are not binding, that is to say, are not laws, is to talk stark nonsense. The most pernicious laws, and therefore those which are most opposed to the will of God, have been and are continually enforced as laws by judicial tribunals. Suppose an act innocuous, or positively beneficial, be prohibited by the sovereign under the penalty of death; if I commit this act, I shall be tried and condemned, and if I object to the sentence, that it is contrary to the law of God, who has commanded that human lawgivers shall not prohibit acts which have no evil consequences, the Court of Justice will demonstrate the inconclusiveness of my reasoning by hanging me up, in pursuance of the law of which I have impugned the validity. An exception, demurrer, or plea founded on the law of God was never heard in a Court of Justice, from the creation of the world down to the present moment.

But this abuse of language is not merely puerile, it is mischievous. When it is said that a law ought to be disobeyed, what is meant is that we are urged to disobey it by motives more cogent and compulsory than those by which it is itself sanctioned. If the laws of God are certain, the motives which they hold out to disobey any human command which is at variance with them are paramount to all others. But the laws of God are not always certain. All divines, at least all reasonable divines, admit that no scheme of duties perfectly complete and unambiguous was ever imparted to us by revelation. As an index to the Divine will, utility is obviously insufficient. What appears pernicious to one person may appear beneficial to another. And as for the moral sense, innate practical principles, conscience, they are merely convenient cloaks for ignorance or sinister interest: they mean either that I hate the law to which I object and cannot tell why, or that I hate the law, and that the cause of my hatred is one which I find it incommodious to avow. If I say openly, I hate the law, *ergo*, it is not binding and ought to be disobeyed, no one will listen to me; but by calling my hate my conscience or my moral sense, I urge the same argument in another and more plausible form: I seem to assign a reason for my dislike, when in truth I have only given it a sounding and specious name. In times of civil discord the mischief of this detestable abuse of language is apparent. In quiet times the dictates of utility are fortunately so obvious that the anarchical doctrine sleeps, and men habitually admit the validity of laws which they dislike. To prove by pertinent reasons that a law is pernicious is highly useful, because such process may lead to the abrogation of the pernicious law. To incite the public to resistance by determinate views of *utility* may be useful, for resistance, grounded on clear and definite prospects of good, is sometimes beneficial. But to proclaim generally that all laws which are pernicious or contrary to the will of God are void and not to be tolerated is to preach anarchy, hostile and perilous as much to wise and benign rule as to stupid and galling tyranny.

Another example from Blackstone

In another passage of his *Commentaries*, Blackstone enters into an argument to prove that a master cannot have a right to the labour of his slave. Had he contented himself with expressing his *disapprobation*, a very well-grounded one certainly, of the institution of slavery, no objection could have been made to his so expressing himself. But to dispute the existence or the possibility of the right is to talk absurdly. For in every age, and in almost every nation, the right has been given by positive law, whilst that pernicious disposition of positive law has been backed by the positive morality of the free or master classes.

Paley's definition of civil liberty

Paley's admired definition of civil liberty appears to me to be obnoxious to the very same objection: it is a definition of civil liberty as it ought to be. 'Civil liberty', he says, 'is the not being restrained by any law but which conduces in a greater degree to the public welfare'; and this is distinguished from *natural* liberty, which is the not being restrained at all. But when liberty is not exactly synonymous with right, it means, and can mean nothing else, but exemption from restraint or obligation, and is therefore altogether incompatible with law, the very idea of which implies restraint and obligation. But restraint is restraint although it be useful, and liberty is liberty though it may be pernicious. You may, if you please, call a useful restraint *liberty*, and refuse the name liberty to exemption from restraint when restraint is for the public advantage. But by this abuse of language you throw not a ray of light upon the nature of political liberty; you only add to the ambiguity and indistinctness in which it is already involved. I shall have to define and analyse the notion of liberty hereafter, on account of its intimate connection with right, obligation, and sanction.

Example from the writers on international law

Grotius, Puffendorf, and the other writers on the so called law of nations, have fallen into a similar confusion of ideas: they have confounded positive international morality, or the rules which actually obtain among civilised nations in their mutual intercourse, with their own vague conceptions of international morality as it *ought to be*, with that indeterminate something which they conceived it would be, if it conformed to that indeterminate something which they call the law of nature. Professor Von Martens, of Göttingen, who died only a few years ago[9] is actually the first of the writers on the law of nations who has seized this distinction with a firm grasp, the first who has distinguished the rules which ought to be received in the intercourse of nations, or which would be received if they conformed to an assumed standard of whatever kind, from those which *are* so received, endeavoured to collect from the practice of civilised communities what are the rules actually recognised and acted upon by them, and gave to these rules the name of positive international law.

Second: tendency to confound positive law with positive morality, and both with legislation and deontology. Examples from the Roman jurists

I have given several instances in which law and morality as they ought to be are confounded with the law and morality which actually exist. I shall next mention some examples in which positive law is confounded with positive morality, and both with the science of legislation and deontology.

Those who know the writings of the Roman lawyers only by hearsay are accustomed to admire their philosophy. Now this, in my estimation, is the only part of their writings which deserves contempt. Their extraordinary merit is evinced, not in general speculation, but as expositors of the Roman law. They have seized its general principles with great clearness and penetration, have applied these principles with admirable logic to the explanation of details, and have thus reduced this positive system of law to a compact and coherent whole. But the philosophy which they borrowed from the Greeks, or which, after the examples of the Greeks, they themselves fashioned, is naught. Their attempts to define jurisprudence and to determine the province of the jurisconsult are absolutely pitiable, and it is hardly conceivable how men of such admirable discernment should have displayed such contemptible imbecility.

At the commencement of the *Digest* is a passage attempting to define jurisprudence. I shall first present you with this passage in a free translation, and afterwards in the original. 'Jurisprudence', says this definition, 'is the knowledge of things divine and human; the science which teaches men to discern the just from the unjust.' 'Jurisprudentia est divinarum atque humanarum rerum notitia, justi atque injusti scientia.' In the excerpt from Ulpian, which is placed at the beginning of the *Digest*, it is attempted to define the office or province of the jurisconsult:

> Law derives its name from justice, *justitia*, and is the science or skill in the good and the equitable. Law being the creature of justice, we the jurisconsults may be considered as her priests, for justice is the goddess whom we worship, and to whose service we are devoted. Justice and equity are our vocation; we teach men to know the difference between the just and the unjust, the lawful and the unlawful; we strive to reclaim them from vice, not only by the terrors of punishment, but also by the blandishment of rewards; herein, unless we flatter ourselves, aspiring to sound and real philosophy, and not like some whom we could mention, contenting ourselves with vain and empty pretension.

> Juri operam daturum prius nosse oportet, unde nomen juris descendat. Est autem a justitia appellatum; nam, ut eleganter Celsus definit, jus est ars boni et æqui. Cujus merito quis nos sacerdotes appellet; justitiam namque

> colimus, et boni et æqui notitiam profitemur, æquum ab iniquo separantes, licitum ab illicita discernentes, bonos non solum metu pœnarum verum etiam prœmiorum quoque exhortatione efficere cupientes, veram, nisi fallor, philosophiam, non simulatam affectantes.

Were I to present you with all the criticisms which these two passages suggest, I should detain you a full hour. I shall content myself with one observation on the scope and purpose of them both. That is, that they affect to define jurisprudence, or what comes exactly to the same thing, the office or province of the jurisconsult. Now jurisprudence, if it is anything, is the science of law, or at most the science of law combined with the art of applying it; but what is here given as a definition of it embraces not only law, but positive morality, and even the test to which both these are to be referred. It therefore comprises the science of legislation and deontology. Further, it affirms that law is the creature of justice, which is as much as to say that it is the child of its own offspring. For when by *just* we mean anything but to express our own approbation, we mean something which *accords with some given law*. True, we speak of law and justice, or of law and equity, as opposed to each other, but when we do so, we mean to express mere dislike of the law, or to intimate that it conflicts with another law, the law of God, which is its standard. According to this, every pernicious law is unjust. But, in truth, law is itself the standard of justice. What deviates from any law is unjust with reference to that law, though it may be just with reference to another law of superior authority. The terms just and unjust imply a standard, and conformity to that standard and a deviation from it; else they signify mere dislike, which it would be far better to signify by a grunt or a groan than by a mischievous and detestable abuse of articulate language. But justice is commonly erected into an entity, and spoken of as a legislator, in which character it is supposed to prescribe the law, conformity to which it should denote. The veriest dolt who is placed in a jury box, the merest old woman who happens to be raised to the bench, will talk finely of equity or justice—the justice of the case, the equity of the case, the imperious demands of justice, the plain dictates of equity. He forgets that he is there to enforce *the law of the land*, else he does not administer that justice or that equity with which alone he is immediately concerned.

Example from Lord Mansfield

This is well known to have been a strong tendency of Lord Mansfield—a strange obliquity in so great a man. I will give an instance. By the English law, a promise to give something or to do something for the benefit of another is not binding without what is called a consideration; that is, a motive assigned for the promise, which motive must be of a particular kind. Lord Mansfield, however, overruled the distinct provisions of the law by ruling that moral obligation was a sufficient consideration. Now, moral obligation is an obligation imposed by opinion, or an obligation imposed by God: that is, moral obligation is anything which we choose to call so, for the precepts of positive morality are infinitely varying, and the will of God, whether indicated by utility or by a moral sense, is equally a matter of dispute. This decision of Lord Mansfield, which assumes that the judge is to enforce morality, enables the judge to enforce just whatever he pleases.

I must here observe that I am not objecting to Lord Mansfield for assuming the office of a legislator. I by no means disapprove of what Mr Bentham has chosen to call by the disrespectful, and therefore, as I conceive, injudicious, name of judge-made law. For I consider it injudicious to call by any name indicative of disrespect what appears to me highly beneficial and even absolutely necessary. I cannot understand how any person who has considered the subject can suppose that society could possibly have gone on if judges had not legislated, or that there is any danger whatever in allowing them that power which they have in fact exercised, to make up for the negligence or the incapacity of the avowed legislator. That part of the law of every country which was made by judges has been far better made than that part which consists of statutes enacted by the legislative. Notwithstanding my great admiration for Mr Bentham, I cannot but think that, instead of blaming judges for having legislated, he should blame them for the timid, narrow, and piecemeal manner in which they have legislated, and for legislating under cover of vague and indeterminate phrases, such as Lord Mansfield employed in the above example, and which would be censurable in any legislator.

Notes

1. *Laws set by men, as private persons, in pursuance of legal rights*

   A law set by a subject as a private person, but in pursuance of a legal right residing in the subject author, is either a positive law purely or simply, or is compounded of a positive law and a rule of positive morality. Or (changing the expression) it is either a positive law purely or simply, or it is a positive law as viewed from one aspect, and a rule of positive morality as viewed from another.

   The person who makes the law in pursuance of the legal right is either legally bound to make the law, or he is not. In the first case, the law is a positive law purely or simply. In the second case, the law is compounded of a positive law and a positive moral rule.

   For example, a guardian may have a right over his pupil or ward, which he is legally bound to exercise, for the benefit of the pupil or ward, in a given or specified manner. In other words, a guardian may be clothed with a right, over his pupil or ward, in trust to exercise the same, for the benefit of the pupil or ward, in a given or specified manner. Now if, in pursuance of his right, and agreeably to his duty or trust, he sets a law or rule to the pupil or ward, the law is a positive law purely or simply. It is properly a law which the state sets to the ward through its minister or instrument, the guardian. It is not made by the guardian of his own spontaneous movement, or is made in pursuance of a duty which the state has imposed upon him. The position of the guardian is closely analogous to the position of subordinate political superiors who hold their delegated powers of direct or judicial legislation as mere trustees for the sovereign granters.

Again: the master has legal rights over or against his slave, which are conferred by the state upon the master for his own benefit. And, since they are conferred upon him for his own benefit, he is not legally bound to exercise or use them. Now if, in pursuance of these rights, he sets a law to his slave, the law is compounded of a positive law and a positive moral rule. Being made by sovereign authority, and clothed by the sovereign with sanctions, the law made by the master is properly a positive law. But, since it is made by the master of his own spontaneous movement, or is not made by the master in pursuance of a legal duty, it is properly a rule of positive morality, as well as a positive law. Though the law set by the master is set circuitously by the sovereign, it is set or established by the sovereign at the pleasure of the subject author. The master is not the instrument of the sovereign or state, but the sovereign or state is rather the instrument of the master.

Before I dismiss the subject of the present note, I must make two remarks.

One. Of laws made by men as private persons, some are frequently styled 'laws *autonomic*'. Or it is frequently said of some of those laws, that they are made through an αὐτονομία residing in the subject authors. Now laws *autonomic*, or *autonomical*, are laws made by subjects, as private persons, in pursuance of legal rights: that is to say, in pursuance of legal rights which they are free to exercise or not, or in pursuance of legal rights which are not saddled with trusts. A law of the kind is styled *autonomic* because it is made by its author of his own spontaneous disposition, or not in pursuance of a duty imposed upon him by the state.

It is clear, however, that the term *autonomic* is not exclusively applicable to laws of the kind in question. The term will apply to every law which is not made by its author in pursuance of a legal duty. It will apply, for instance, to every law which is made immediately or directly by a monarch or sovereign number: independence of legal duty being of the essence of sovereignty.

Two. Laws which are positive law as viewed from one aspect, but which are positive morality as viewed from another, I place simply or absolutely in the first of those capital classes. If, affecting exquisite precision, I placed them in each of those classes, I could hardly indicate the boundary by which those classes are severed without resorting to expressions of repulsive complexity and length.

2. The term *morality*, *moral*, or *morally*, is often opposed tacitly to *immorality*, *immoral*, or *immorally*, and imports that the object to which it is applied or referred is approved of by the speaker or writer. But by the term *morality*, I merely denote the human rules which I style 'positive morality'. And by the terms '*moral* sanctions', 'rules sanctioned *morally*', '*moral* duties or rights', and 'duties or rights sanctioned *morally*', I merely mean that the rules to which the sanctions are annexed, or by which the duties or rights are imposed or conferred, are positive moral rules:

rules bearing the generic character which I have stated and explained above. If I mean to praise or blame a positive human rule, or a duty or right which the rule imposes or confers, I style it consonant to the law of God, or contrary to the law of God. Or (what, in effect, is the same thing) I style it generally useful, or generally pernicious.

3. Here I may briefly observe that, in order to a complete determination of the appropriate province of jurisprudence, it is necessary to explain the import of the term *right*. For, as I have stated already, numerous positive laws proceed directly from subjects through *rights* conferred upon the authors by supreme political superiors. And, for various other reasons which will appear in my sixth lecture, the appropriate province of jurisprudence cannot be defined completely unless an explanation of the term *right* constitute a part of the definition. But, in order to an explanation of right *in abstract* (or in order to an explanation of the nature which is common to *all* rights), I must previously explain the differences of the principal kinds of rights, with the meaning of various terms which the term *right* implies. And as that previous explanation cannot be given with effect till positive law is distinguished from the objects to which it is related, it follows that an explanation of the expression *right* cannot enter into the attempt to determine the province of jurisprudence.

At every step which he takes on his long and scabrous road, a difficulty similar to that which I have now endeavoured to suggest encounters the expositor of the science. As every department of the science is implicated with every other, any detached exposition of a single and separate department is inevitably a fragment more or less imperfect.

4. *The acts and forbearances which, according to the theory of utility, are objects of the law of God; and other acts and forbearances which, according to the same theory, ought to be objects respectively of positive morality and law*

There are classes of useful acts which it were useless to enjoin, and classes of mischievous acts which it were useless to forbid: for we are sufficiently prone to the useful, and sufficiently averse from the mischievous acts, without the incentives and restraints applied by religious sanctions, or by sanctions legal or moral. And, assuming that general utility is the index to the Divine commands, we may fairly infer that acts of such classes are not enjoined or forbidden by the law of God; that he no more enjoins or forbids acts of the classes in question, than he enjoins or forbids such acts as are generally pernicious or useful.

There are also classes of acts, generally useful or pernicious, which demand the incentives or restraints applied by religious sanctions or by sanctions legal or moral. Without the incentives and restraints applied by religious sanctions, or applied by sanctions legal or moral, we are not sufficiently prone to those which are generally useful, and are not sufficiently averse from those which are generally pernicious. And, assuming that general utility is the index to the Divine commands, all these classes of useful, and all these classes of pernicious acts, are enjoined and forbidden respectively by the law of God.

Being enjoined or being forbidden by the Deity, all these classes of useful, and all these classes of pernicious acts, ought to be enjoined or forbidden by positive morality: that is to say, by the positive morality which consists of opinions or sentiments. But, this notwithstanding, some of these classes of acts ought not to be enjoined or forbidden by positive law. Some of these classes of acts ought not to be enjoined or forbidden even by the positive morality which consists of imperative rules.

Every act or forbearance that ought to be an object of positive law, ought to be an object of the positive morality which consists of opinions or sentiments. Every act or forbearance that ought to be an object of the latter is an object of the law of God as construed by the principle of utility. But the circle embraced by the law of God, and which may be embraced to advantage by positive morality, is larger than the circle which can be embraced to advantage by positive law. Inasmuch as the two circles have one and the same centre, the whole of the region comprised by the latter is also comprised by the former. But the whole of the region comprised by the former is not comprised by the latter.

To distinguish the acts and forbearances that ought to be objects of law from those that ought to be abandoned to the exclusive cognisance of morality is, perhaps, the hardest of the problems which the science of ethics presents. The only existing approach to a solution of the problem may be found in the writings of Mr Bentham who, in most of the departments of the two great branches of ethics, has accomplished more for the advancement of the science than all his predecessors put together. See, in particular, his *Principles of Morals and Legislation*, ch. xvii.

5. Locke's division or analysis is far from being complete, and the language in which it is stated is often extremely unapt. It must, however, be remembered that the nature of *relation* generally (and not the nature of *law*, with its principal kinds) is the appropriate object of his inquiry. Allowing for the defects, which, therefore, were nearly inevitable, his analysis is strikingly accurate. It evinces that matchless power of precise and just thinking, with that religious regard for general utility and truth, which marked the incomparable man who emancipated human reason from the yoke of mystery and jargon. And from this, his incidental excursion into the field of law and morality, and from other passages of his essay wherein he touches upon them, we may infer the important services which he would have rendered to the science of ethics if, complying with the instances of Molyneux, he had examined the subject exactly.
6. Speaking with absolute precision, the lower animals, or the animals inferior to man, are not destitute of reason. Since their conduct is partly determined by conclusions drawn from experience, they observe, compare, abstract, and infer. But the intelligence of the lower animals is so extremely limited that, adopting the current expression, I style them *irrational*. Some of the more sagacious are so far from being irrational that they understand and observe laws set to them by human masters. But these laws being few and of little importance, I throw them, for the sake of simplicity, out of my account. I say universally of the lower animals that they cannot understand a law, or guide their conduct by duty.
7. Supposed difference between law and rule. [MS note inserted by R. Campbell.]
8. Lecture xxxii *post*.
9. This, it will be remembered, was spoken in the year 1830 or 1831.

LECTURE VI

SYNOPSIS OF LECTURE VI

The connection of the sixth lecture with the first, second, third, fourth, and fifth

The distinguishing marks of sovereignty and independent political society

The relation of sovereignty and subjection

Strictly speaking, the sovereign portion of the society, and not the society itself, is independent, sovereign, or supreme

In order that a given society may form a society political and independent, the two distinguishing marks which are mentioned above must unite

A society independent but natural

Society formed by the intercourse of independent political societies

A society political but subordinate

A society not political, but forming a limb or member of a society political and independent

The definition of the abstract term *independent political society* (including the definition of the correlative term *sovereignty*) cannot be rendered in expressions of perfectly precise import, and is therefore a fallible test of specific or particular cases

In order that an independent society may form a society political, it must not fall short of a *number* which cannot be fixed with precision, but which may be called considerable, or not extremely minute

Certain of the definitions of the term *sovereignty*, and of the implied or correlative term *independent political society*, which have been given by writers of celebrity

The ensuing portion of the present lecture is concerned with the following topics:

1. The forms of supreme government;
2. The limits of sovereign power;
3. The origin of government, or the origin of political society

The forms of supreme government

Every supreme government is a *monarchy* (properly so called), or an *aristocracy* (in the generic meaning of the expression). In other words, it is a government of *one*, or a government of a *number*

Of such distinctions between aristocracies as are founded on differences between the proportions which the number of the sovereign body may bear to the number of the community

Of such distinctions between aristocracies as are founded on differences between the modes wherein the sovereign number may share the sovereign powers

Of such aristocracies as are styled *limited monarchies*

Of the exercise of sovereign powers by a monarch or sovereign body, through political subordinates or delegates representing their sovereign author

Of the distinction of sovereign, and other political powers, into such as are *legislative*, and such as are *executive* or *administrative*

The true natures of the communities or governments which are styled by writers on positive international law *half sovereign states*

The nature of a *composite state* or a *supreme federal government*: with the nature of a *system of confederated states*, or a *permanent confederacy of supreme governments*

The limits of sovereign power

The essential difference of a positive law

It follows from the essential difference of a positive law, and from the nature of sovereignty and independent political society, that the power of a monarch properly so called, or the power of a sovereign number in its collegiate and sovereign capacity, is incapable of *legal* limitation

Attempts of sovereigns to oblige themselves, or to oblige the successors to their sovereign powers

The meanings of the epithet *unconstitutional*, as it is contradistinguished to the epithet *illegal*, and as it is applied to conduct of a monarch, or to conduct of a sovereign number in its collegiate and sovereign capacity

Considered severally, the members of a sovereign body are in a state of subjection to the body, and may therefore be legally bound, even as members of the body, by laws of which it is the author

The nature of political or civil liberty, together with the supposed difference between free and despotic governments

Why it has been doubted that the power of a sovereign is incapable of legal limitation

TEXT OF LECTURE VI

The connection of the sixth lecture with the first, second, third, fourth, and fifth

Positive laws, the appropriate matter of jurisprudence, are related in the way of resemblance, or by a close or remote analogy, to the following objects:

1. In the way of resemblance, they are related to the laws of God.
2. In the way of resemblance, they are related to those rules of positive morality which are laws properly so called.
3. By a close or strong analogy, they are related to those rules of positive morality which are merely opinions or sentiments held or felt by men in regard to human conduct.
4. By a remote or slender analogy, they are related to laws merely metaphorical, or laws merely figurative.

To distinguish positive laws from the objects now enumerated is the purpose of the present attempt to determine the province of jurisprudence.

In pursuance of the purpose to which I have now adverted, I stated, in my first lecture, the essentials of a *law* or *rule* (taken with the largest signification which can be given to the term *properly*).

In my second, third, and fourth lectures, I stated the marks or characters by which the laws of God are distinguished from other laws. And, stating those marks or characters, I explained the nature of the index to his unrevealed laws, or I explained and examined the hypothesis which regard the nature of that index.

In my fifth lecture, I examined or discussed especially the following principal topics (and I touched upon other topics of secondary or subordinate importance). I examined the distinguishing marks of those positive moral rules which are laws properly so called: I examined the distinguishing marks of those positive moral rules which are styled *laws* or *rules* by an analogical extension of the term: and I examined the distinguishing marks of the laws merely metaphorical, or laws merely figurative.

I shall finish, in the present lecture, the purpose mentioned above, by explaining the marks or characters which distinguish positive laws, or laws strictly so called. And, in order to an explanation of the marks which distinguish positive laws, I shall analyse the expression *sovereignty*, the correlative expression *subjection*, and the inseparably connected expression *independent political society*. With the ends or final causes for which governments *ought* to exist, or with their different degrees of fitness to attain or approach those ends, I have no concern. I examine the notions of *sovereignty* and *independent political society* in order that I may finish the purpose to which I have adverted above: in order that I may distinguish completely the appropriate province of jurisprudence from the regions which lie upon its confines and by which it is encircled. It is necessary that I should examine those notions in order that I may finish that purpose. For the essential difference of a positive law (or the difference that severs it from a law which is not a positive law) may be stated thus. Every positive law, or every law simply and strictly so called, is set by a sovereign person, or a sovereign body of persons, to a member or members of the independent political society wherein that person or body is sovereign or supreme. Or (changing the expression) it is set by a monarch, or sovereign number, to a person or persons in a state of subjection to its author. Even though it sprung directly from another fountain or source, it is a positive law, or a law strictly so called, by the institution of that present sovereign in the character of political superior. Or (borrowing the language of Hobbes) 'the legislator is he, not by whose authority the law was first made, but by whose authority it continues to be a law'.

Having stated the topic or subject appropriate to my present discourse, I proceed to distinguish sovereignty from other superiority or might, and to distinguish society political and independent from society of other descriptions.

The distinguishing marks of sovereignty and independent political society

The superiority which is styled sovereignty, and the independent political society which sovereignty implies, is distinguished from other superiority, and from other society, by the following marks or characters:

1. The *bulk* of the given society are in a *habit* of obedience or submission to a *determinate* and *common* superior: let that common superior be a certain individual person, or a certain body or aggregate of individual persons.
2. That certain individual, or that certain body of individuals, is *not* in a habit of obedience to a determinate human superior.

Laws (improperly so called) which opinion sets or imposes may permanently affect the conduct of that certain individual or body. To express or tacit commands of other determinate parties, that certain individual or body may yield occasional submission. But there is no determinate person, or determinate aggregate of persons, to whose commands, express or tacit, that certain individual or body renders habitual obedience.

Or the notions of sovereignty and independent political society may be expressed concisely thus. If a *determinate* human superior, not in a habit of obedience to a like superior, receive *habitual* obedience from the *bulk* of a given society, that determinate superior is sovereign in that society, and the society (including the superior) is a society political and independent.

The relation of sovereignty and subjection

To that determinate superior, the other members of the society are *subject*: or on that determinate superior, the other members of the society are *dependent*. The position of its other members towards that determinate superior is a *state of subjection*, or *a state of dependence*. The mutual relation which subsists between that superior and them may be styled *the relation of sovereign and subject*, or *the relation of sovereignty and subjection*.

Strictly speaking, the sovereign portion of the society, and not the society itself, is independent, sovereign, or supreme

Hence it follows that it is only through an ellipsis, or an abridged form of expression, that the *society* is styled *independent*. The party truly independent (independent, that is to say, of a determinate human superior) is not the society, but the sovereign portion of the society: that certain member of the society, or that certain body of its members, to whose commands, expressed or intimated, the generality or bulk of its members render habitual obedience. Upon that certain person, or certain body of persons, the other members of the society are *dependent*: or to that certain person, or certain body of persons, the other members of the society are *subject*. By 'an independent political society', or 'an independent and sovereign nation', we mean a political society consisting of a sovereign and subjects, as opposed to a political society which is merely subordinate: that is to say, which is merely a limb or member of another political society, and which therefore consists entirely of persons in a state of subjection.

In order that a given society may form a society political and independent, the two distinguishing marks which are mentioned above must unite

In order that a given society may form a society political and independent, the two distinguishing marks which I have mentioned above must unite. The *generality* of the given society must be in the *habit* of obedience to a *determinate* and *common* superior: whilst that determinate person, or determinate body of persons, must *not* be habitually obedient to a determinate person or body. It is the union of that positive, with this negative mark, which renders that certain superior sovereign or supreme, and which renders that given society (including that certain superior) a society political and independent.

To show that the union of those marks renders a given society a society political and independent, I call your attention to the following positions and examples.

One. In order that a given society may form a society political, the generality or bulk of its members must be in a *habit* of obedience to a determinate and common superior.

In case the generality of its members obey a determinate superior, but the obedience be rare or transient and not habitual or permanent, the relation of sovereignty and subjection is not created thereby between that certain superior and the members of that given society. In other words, that determinate superior and the members of that given society do not become thereby an independent political society. Whether that given society be political and independent or not, it is not an independent political society whereof that certain superior is the sovereign portion.

For example: in 1815 the allied armies occupied France; and so long as the allied armies occupied France, the commands of the allied sovereigns were obeyed by the French government, and, through the French government, by the French people generally. But since the commands and the obedience were comparatively rare and transient, they were not sufficient to constitute the relation of sovereignty and subjection between the allied sovereigns and the members of the invaded nation. In spite of those commands, and in spite of that obedience, the French government was sovereign or independent. Or in spite of those commands, and in spite of that obedience, the French government and its subjects were an independent political society whereof the allied sovereigns were not the sovereign portion.

Now if the French nation, before the obedience to those sovereigns, had been an independent society in a state of nature or anarchy, it would not have been changed by the obedience into a society political. And it would not have been changed by the obedience into a society political, because the obedience was not habitual. For, inasmuch as the obedience was not habitual, it was not changed by the obedience from a society political and independent, into a society political but subordinate. A given society, therefore, is not a society political, unless the generality of its members be in a *habit* of obedience to a determinate and common superior.

Again: a feeble state holds its independence precariously, or at the will of the powerful states to whose aggressions it is obnoxious. And since it is obnoxious to their aggressions, it and the bulk of its subjects render obedience to commands which they occasionally express or intimate. Such, for instance, is the position of the Saxon government and its subjects in respect of the conspiring sovereigns who form the Holy Alliance. But since the commands and the obedience are comparatively few and rare, they are not sufficient to constitute the relation of sovereignty and subjection between the powerful states and the feeble state with its subjects. In spite of those commands, and in spite of that obedience, the feeble state is sovereign or independent. Or in spite of those commands, and in spite of that obedience, the feeble state and its subjects are an independent political society whereof the powerful states are not the sovereign portion. Although the powerful states are permanently *superior*, and although the feeble state is permanently *inferior*, there is neither a *habit* of command on the part of the former, nor a *habit* of obedience on the part of the latter. Although the latter is unable to defend and maintain its independence, the latter is independent of the former in fact or practice.

From the example now adduced, as from the example adduced before, we may draw the following inference: that a given society is not a society political, unless the generality of its members be in a *habit* of obedience to a determinate and common superior. By the obedience to the powerful states, the feeble state and its subjects are not changed from an independent into a subordinate political society. And they are not changed by the obedience into a subordinate political society because the obedience is not habitual. Consequently, if they were a natural society (setting that obedience aside), they would not be changed by that obedience into a society political.

Two. In order that a given society may form a society political, habitual obedience must be rendered, by the *generality* or *bulk* of its members, to a determinate and *common* superior. In other words, habitual obedience must be rendered, by the *generality* or *bulk* of its members, to *one and the same* determinate person, or determinate body of persons.

Unless habitual obedience be rendered by the bulk of its members, and be rendered by the bulk of its members to *one and the same* superior, the given society is either in a state of nature, or is split into two or more independent political societies.

For example: in case a given society be torn by intestine war, and in case the conflicting parties be nearly balanced, the given society is in one of the two positions which I have now supposed. As there is no common superior to which the bulk of its members render habitual obedience, it is not a political society single or undivided. If the bulk of each of the parties be in a habit of obedience to its head, the given society is broken into two or more societies, which, perhaps, may be styled independent political societies. If the bulk of each of the parties be not in that habit of obedience, the given society is simply or absolutely in a state of nature or anarchy. It is either resolved or broken into its individual elements, or into numerous societies of an extremely limited size: of a size so extremely limited that they could hardly be styled societies independent and *political*. For, as I shall show hereafter, a given independent society would hardly be styled *political* in case it fell short of a *number* which cannot be fixed with precision, but which may be called considerable, or not extremely minute.

Three. In order that a given society may form a society political, the generality or bulk of its members must habitually obey a superior *determinate* as well as common.

On this position I shall not insist here. For I have shown sufficiently in my fifth lecture that no indeterminate party can command expressly or tacitly, or can receive obedience or submission: that no indeterminate body is capable of corporate conduct, or is capable, as a body, of positive or negative deportment.

Four. It appears from what has preceded that, in order that a given society may form a society political, the bulk of its members must be in a habit of obedience to a certain and common superior. But, in order that the given society may form a society political and independent, that certain superior must *not* be habitually obedient to a determinate human superior.

The given society may form a society political and independent, although that certain superior be habitually affected by laws which opinion sets or imposes. The given society may form a society political and independent, although that certain superior render occasional submission to commands of determinate parties. But the society is not independent, although it may be political, in case that certain superior habitually obey the commands of a certain person or body.

Let us suppose, for example, that a viceroy obeys habitually the author of his delegated powers. And, to render the example complete, let us suppose that the viceroy receives habitual obedience from the generality or bulk of the persons who inhabit his province. Now though he commands habitually within the limits of his province, and receives habitual obedience from the generality or bulk of its inhabitants, the viceroy is not sovereign within the limits of his province, nor are he and its inhabitants an independent political society. The viceroy, and (through the viceroy) the generality or bulk of its inhabitants, are habitually obedient or submissive to the sovereign of a larger society. He and the inhabitants of his province are therefore in a state of subjection to the sovereign of that larger society. He and the inhabitants of his province are a society political but subordinate, or form a political society which is merely a limb of another.

A society independent but natural

A natural society, a society in a state of nature, or a society independent but natural is composed of persons who are connected by mutual intercourse, but are not members, sovereign or subject, of any society political. None of the persons who compose it lives in the positive state which is styled a state of subjection: or all the persons who compose it live in the negative state which is styled a state of independence.

Society formed by the intercourse of independent political societies

Considered as entire communities, and considered in respect of one another, independent political societies live, it is commonly said, in a state of nature. And considered as entire communities, and as connected by mutual intercourse, independent political societies form, it is commonly said, a natural society. These expressions, however, are not perfectly apposite. Since all the members of each of the related societies are members of a society political, none of the related societies is strictly in a state of nature: nor can the larger society formed by their mutual intercourse be styled strictly a natural society. Speaking strictly, the several members of the several related societies are placed in the following positions. The sovereign and subject members of each of the related societies form a society political: but the sovereign portion of each of the related societies lives in the negative condition which is styled a state of independence.

Society formed by the intercourse of independent political societies is the province of international law, or of the law obtaining between nations. For (adopting a current expression) international law, or the law obtaining between nations, is conversant about the conduct of independent political societies considered as entire communities: *circa negotia et causas gentium integrarum*. Speaking with greater precision, international law, or the law obtaining between nations, regards the conduct of sovereigns considered as related to one another.

And hence it inevitably follows that the law obtaining between nations is not positive law: for every positive law is set by a given sovereign to a person or persons in a state of subjection to its author. As I have already intimated, the law obtaining between nations is law (improperly so called) set by general opinion. The duties which it imposes are enforced by moral sanctions: by fear on the part of nations, or by fear on the part of sovereigns, of provoking general hostility, and incurring its probable evils, in case they shall violate maxims generally received and respected.

A society political but subordinate

A society political but subordinate is merely a limb or member of a society political and independent. All the persons who compose it, including the person or body which is its immediate chief, live in a state of subjection to one and the same sovereign.

A society not political, but forming a limb or member of a society political and independent

Besides societies political and independent, societies independent but natural, society formed by the intercourse of independent political societies, and societies political but subordinate, there are societies which will not quadrate with any of those descriptions. Though, like a society political but subordinate, it forms a limb or member of a society political and independent, a society of the class in question is not a political society. Although it consists of members living in a state of subjection, it consists of subjects considered as private persons. A society consisting of parents and children, living in a state of subjection, and considered in those characters, may serve as an example.

To distinguish societies political but subordinate from societies not political but consisting of subject members, is to distinguish the rights and duties of subordinate political superiors from the rights and duties of subjects considered as private persons. And before I can draw that distinction, I must analyse many expressions of large and intricate meaning which belong to the detail of jurisprudence. But an explanation of that distinction is not required by my present purpose. To the accomplishment of my present purpose, it is merely incumbent upon me to determine the notion of sovereignty, with the inseparably connected notion of independent political society. For every positive law, or every law simply and strictly so called, is set directly or circuitously by a monarch or sovereign number to a person or persons in a state of subjection to its author.

The definition of the abstract term independent political society *(including the definition of the correlative term* sovereignty*) cannot be rendered in expressions of perfectly precise import, and is therefore a fallible test of specific or particular cases*

The definition of the abstract term *independent political society* (including the definition of the correlative term *sovereignty*) cannot be rendered in expressions of perfectly precise import, and is therefore a fallible test of specific or particular cases. The least imperfect definition which the abstract term will take would hardly enable us to fix the class of every possible society. It would hardly enable us to determine of every *independent* society whether it were *political* or *natural*. It would hardly enable us to determine of every *political* society whether it were *independent* or *subordinate*.

In order that a given society may form a society political and independent, the positive and negative marks which I have mentioned above must unite. The *generality* or *bulk* of its members must be in a habit of obedience to a *certain* and *common* superior: whilst that certain person, or certain body of persons, must not be habitually obedient to a certain person or body.

But, in order that the *bulk* of its members may render obedience to a *common* superior, *how many* of its members, or *what proportion* of its members, must render obedience to *one and the same* superior? And, assuming that the bulk of its members render obedience to a common superior, *how often* must they render it, and *how long* must they render it, in order that that obedience may be *habitual*? Now since these questions cannot be answered precisely, the positive mark of sovereignty and independent political society is a fallible test of specific or particular cases. It would not enable us to determine of every *independent* society whether it were *political* or *natural*.

In the cases of independent society which lie, as it were, at the extremes, we should apply that positive test without a moment's difficulty, and should fix the class of the society without a moment's hesitation. In some of those cases, so large a proportion of the members obey the same superior, and the obedience of that proportion is so frequent and continued, that, without a moment's difficulty and without a moment's hesitation, we should pronounce the society *political*: that, without a moment's difficulty and without a moment's hesitation, we should say the *generality* of its members were in a *habit* of obedience or submission to a certain and *common* superior. Such, for example, is the ordinary state of England, and of every independent society somewhat advanced in civilisation. In other of those cases, obedience to the same superior is rendered by so few of the members, or general obedience to the same is so unfrequent and broken, that, without a moment's difficulty and without a moment's hesitation, we should pronounce the society *natural*: that, without a moment's difficulty and without a moment's hesitation, we should say the *generality* of its members were *not* in a *habit* of obedience to a certain and *common* superior. Such, for example, is the state of the independent and savage societies which subsist by hunting or fishing in the woods or on the coasts of New Holland.

But in the cases of independent society which lie between the extremes, we should hardly find it possible to fix with absolute certainty the class of the given community. We should hardly find it possible to determine with absolute certainty whether the generality of its members did or did not obey one and the same superior. Or we should hardly find it possible to determine with absolute certainty whether the general obedience to one and the same superior was or was not habitual. For example: during the height of the conflict between Charles the First and the Parliament, the English nation was broken into two distinct societies: each of which societies may perhaps be styled political, and may certainly be styled independent. After the conflict had subsided, those distinct societies were in their turn dissolved; and the nation was reunited, under the common government of the Parliament, into one independent and political community. But at what juncture precisely, after the conflict had subsided, was a common government completely re-established? Or at what juncture precisely, after the conflict had subsided, were those distinct societies completely dissolved, and the nation completely reunited into one political community? When had so many of the nation rendered obedience to the Parliament, and when had the general obedience become so frequent and lasting, that the bulk of the nation were *habitually* obedient to the body which affected sovereignty? And after the conflict had subsided, and until that juncture had arrived, what was the class of the society which was formed by the English people? These are questions which it were impossible to answer with certainty, although the facts of the case were precisely known.

The positive mark of sovereignty and independent political society is therefore a fallible test. It would not enable us to determine of every *independent* society whether it were *political* or *natural*.

The negative mark of sovereignty and independent political society is also an uncertain measure. It would not enable us to determine of every political society whether it were *independent* or *subordinate*. Given a determinate and common superior, and also that the bulk of the society habitually obey that superior, is that common superior free from a habit of obedience to a determinate person or body? Is that common superior sovereign and independent, or is that common superior a superior in a state of subjection?

In numerous cases of political society, it were impossible to answer this question with absolute certainty. For example: although the Holy Alliance dictates to the Saxon government, the commands which it gives, and the submission which it receives, are comparatively few and rare. Consequently, the Saxon government is sovereign or supreme, and the Saxon government and its subjects are an independent political society, notwithstanding its submission to the Holy Alliance. But, in case the commands and submission were somewhat more numerous and frequent, we might find it impossible to determine certainly the class of the Saxon community. We might find it impossible to determine certainly where the sovereignty resided: whether the Saxon government were a government supreme and independent; or were in a *habit* of obedience, and therefore in a state of subjection, to the allied or conspiring monarchs.

The definition or general notion of independent political society is therefore vague or uncertain. Applying it to specific or particular cases, we should often encounter the difficulties which I have laboured to explain.

The difficulties which I have laboured to explain often embarrass the application of those positive moral rules which are styled international law.

For example: when did the revolted colony, which is now the Mexican nation, ascend from the condition of an insurgent province to that of an independent community? When did the body of colonists, who affected sovereignty in Mexico, change the character of rebel leaders for that of a supreme government? Or (adopting the current language about governments *de jure* and *de facto*) when did the body of colonists, who affected sovereignty in Mexico, become sovereign *in fact*? And (applying international law to the specific or particular case) when did international law authorise neutral nations to admit the independence of Mexico with the sovereignty of the Mexican government?

Now the questions suggested above are equivalent to this: when had the inhabitants of Mexico obeyed that body so generally, and when had that general obedience become so frequent and lasting, that the *bulk* of the inhabitants of Mexico were *habitually* disobedient to Spain, and probably would not resume their discarded habit of submission?

Or the questions suggested above are equivalent to this: when had the inhabitants of Mexico obeyed that body so generally, and when had that general obedience become so frequent and lasting, that the inhabitants of Mexico were independent of Spain in practice, and were likely to remain permanently in that state of practical independence?

At that juncture exactly (let it have arrived when it may) neutral nations were authorised, by the morality which obtains between nations, to admit the independence of Mexico with the sovereignty of the Mexican government. But, by reason of the perplexing difficulties which I have laboured to explain, it was impossible for neutral nations to hit that juncture with precision, and to hold the balance of justice between Spain and her revolted colony with a perfectly even hand.

This difficulty presents itself under numerous forms in international law: indeed almost the only difficult and embarrassing questions in that science arise out of it. And as I shall often have occasion to show, law strictly so called is not free from like difficulties. What can be more indefinite, for instance, than the expressions, *reasonable* time, *reasonable* notice, *reasonable* diligence? Than the line of demarcation which distinguishes libel and fair criticism; than that which constitutes a violation of copyright; than that degree of mental aberration which constitutes idiocy or lunacy? In all these cases, the difficulty is of the same nature with that which adheres to the phrases sovereignty and independent society; it arises from the vagueness or indefiniteness of the terms in which the definition or rule is inevitably conceived. And this, I suppose, is what people were driving at when they have agitated the very absurd enquiry whether questions of this kind are questions of law or of fact. The truth is that they are questions neither of law nor of fact. The fact may be perfectly ascertained, and so may the law, as far as it is capable of being ascertained. The rule is known, and so is the given species, as the Roman jurists term it; the difficulty is in bringing the species under the rule; in determining not what the law is, or what the fact is, but whether the given law is applicable to the given fact.

I have tacitly supposed, during the preceding analysis, that every independent society forming a society political possesses the essential property which I will now describe.

In order that an independent society may form a society political, it must not fall short of a number *which cannot be fixed with precision, but which may be called considerable, or not extremely minute*

In order that an independent society may form a society political, it must not fall short of a *number* which cannot be fixed with precision, but which may be called considerable, or not extremely minute. A given independent society, whose number may be called inconsiderable, is commonly esteemed a *natural*, and not a *political* society, although the generality of its members be habitually obedient or submissive to a certain and common superior.

Let us suppose, for example, that a single family of savages lives in absolute estrangement from every other community. And let us suppose that the father, the chief of this insulated family, receives habitual obedience from the mother and children. Now, since it is not a limb of another and larger community, the society formed by the parents and children is clearly an independent society. And, since the rest of its members habitually obey its chief, this independent society would form a society political, in case the number of its members were not extremely minute. But, since the number of its members is extremely minute, it would (I believe) be esteemed a society in a state of nature: that is to say, a society consisting of persons not in a state of subjection. Without an application of the terms which would somewhat smack of the ridiculous, we could hardly style the society a society *political* and independent, the imperative father and chief a *monarch* or *sovereign*, or the obedient mother and children *subjects*. 'La puissance politique' (says Montesquieu) 'comprend nécessairement l'union de plusieurs familles.'

Again: let us suppose a society which may be styled independent, or which is not a limb of another and larger community. Let us suppose that the number of its members is not extremely minute. And let us suppose it in the savage condition, or in the extremely barbarous condition which closely approaches the savage.

Inasmuch as the given society lives in the savage condition, or in the extremely barbarous condition which closely approaches the savage, the generality or bulk of its members is not in a habit of obedience to one and the same superior. For the purpose of attacking an external enemy, or for the purpose of repelling an attack made by an external enemy, the generality or bulk of its members, who are capable of bearing arms, submits to one leader or to one body of leaders. But so soon as that exigency passes, this transient submission ceases; and the society reverts to the state which may be deemed its ordinary state. The bulk of each of the families which compose the given society renders habitual obedience to its own peculiar chief: but those domestic societies are themselves independent societies, or are not united or compacted into one political society by general and habitual obedience to a certain and common superior. And, as the bulk of the given society is not in a habit of obedience to one and the same superior, there is no law (simply or strictly so styled) which can be called the law of that given society or community. The so called laws which are common to the bulk of the community are purely and properly customary laws: that is to say, laws which are set or imposed by the general opinion of the community, but which are not enforced by legal or political sanctions. The state which I have briefly delineated is the ordinary state of the savage and independent societies which live by hunting or fishing in the woods or on the coasts of New Holland. It is also the ordinary state of the savage and independent societies which range in the forests or plains of the North American continent. It was also the ordinary state of many of the German nations whose manners are described by Tacitus.

Now, since the bulk of its members is not in a habit of obedience to one and the same superior, the given independent society would (I believe) be esteemed a society in a state of nature: that is to say, a society consisting of persons not in a state of subjection. But such it could not be esteemed, unless the term *political* were restricted to independent societies whose numbers are not inconsiderable. Supposing that the term *political* applied to independent societies whose numbers are extremely minute, each of the independent families which constitute the given society would form of itself a political community: for the bulk of each of those families renders habitual obedience to its own peculiar chief. And, seeing that each of those families would form of itself an independent political community, the given independent society could hardly be styled with strictness a natural society. Speaking strictly, that given society would form a congeries of independent political communities. Or, seeing that a few of its members might not be members also of those independent families, it would form a congeries of independent political communities mingled with a few individuals living in a state of nature. Unless the term *political* were restricted to independent societies whose numbers are not inconsiderable, few of the many societies which are commonly esteemed natural could be styled natural societies with perfect precision and propriety.

For the reasons which I have now produced, and for reasons which I pass in silence, we must, I believe, arrive at the following conclusion: a given independent society, whose number may be called inconsiderable, is commonly esteemed a *natural*, and not a *political* society, although the generality of its members be habitually obedient or submissive to a certain and common superior.

And arriving at that conclusion, we must proceed to this further conclusion. In order that an independent society may form a society political, it must not fall short of a *number* which may be called considerable.

The lowest possible number which will satisfy that vague condition cannot be fixed precisely. But, looking at many of the communities which commonly are considered and treated as independent political societies, we must infer that an independent society may form a society political, although the number of its members exceed not a few thousands, or exceed not a few hundreds. The ancient Grison Confederacy (like the ancient Swiss Confederacy with which the Grison was connected) was rather an alliance or union of independent political societies than one independent community under a common sovereign. Now the number of the largest of the societies which were independent members of the ancient Grison Confederacy hardly exceeded a few thousands. And the number of the smallest of those numerous confederated nations hardly exceeded a few hundreds.

The definition of the terms *sovereignty* and *independent political society* is, therefore, embarrassed by the difficulty following, as well as by the difficulties which I have stated in a foregoing department of my discourse. In order that an independent society may form a society political, it must not fall short of a *number* which may be called considerable. And the lowest possible number which will satisfy that vague condition cannot be fixed precisely.

But here I must briefly remark that, though the essential property which I have now described is an essential or necessary property of *independent* political society, it is not an essential property of *subordinate* political society. If the independent society, of which it is a limb or member, be a political and not a natural society, a subordinate society may form a society political, although the number of its members might be called extremely minute. For example: a society incorporated by the state for political or public purposes is a society or body politic; and it continues to bear the character of a society or body politic, although its number be reduced, by deaths or other causes, to that of a small family or small domestic community.

Certain of the definitions of the term sovereignty, *and of the implied or correlative term* independent political society, *which have been given by writers of celebrity*

Having tried to determine the notion of sovereignty, with the implied or correlative notion of independent political society, I will produce and briefly examine a few of the definitions of those notions which have been given by writers of celebrity.

Distinguishing *political* from *natural* society, Mr Bentham, in his *Fragment on Government*, thus defines the former: 'When a number of persons (whom we may style *subjects*) are supposed to be in the *habit* of paying *obedience* to a person, or an assemblage of persons, of a known and certain description (whom we may call *governor* or *governors*), such persons altogether (*subjects* and *governors*) are said to be in a state of *political* society.' And in order to exclude from his definition such a society as the single family conceived of above, he adds a second essential of political society, namely that the society should be capable of indefinite duration. Considered as a definition of *independent* political society, this definition is inadequate or defective. In order that a given society may form a society political and independent, the superior habitually obeyed by the bulk or generality of its members must not be habitually obedient to a certain individual or body: which negative character or essential of independent political society Mr Bentham has forgotten to notice. And, since the definition in question is an inadequate or defective definition of independent political society, it is also an inadequate or defective definition of political society in general. Before we can define political society, or can distinguish political society from society not political, we must determine the nature of those societies which are at once political and independent. For a political society which is not independent is a member or constituent parcel of a political society which is. Or (changing the expression) the powers or rights of subordinate political superiors are merely emanations of sovereignty. They are merely particles of sovereignty committed by sovereigns to subjects.

According to the definition of independent political society which is stated or supposed by Hobbes in his excellent treatises on government, a society is not a society political and independent unless it can maintain its independence, against attacks from without, by its own intrinsic or unaided strength. But if power to maintain its independence by its own intrinsic strength be a character or essential property of an independent political society, the name will scarcely apply to any existing society, or to any of the past societies which occur in the history of mankind. The weaker of such actual societies as are deemed political and independent owe their precarious independence to positive international morality, and to the mutual fears or jealousies of stronger communities. The most powerful of such actual societies as are deemed political and independent could hardly maintain its independence, by its own intrinsic strength, against an extensive conspiracy of other independent nations. Any political society is (I conceive) independent if it be not dependent in fact or practice: if the party habitually obeyed by the bulk or generality of its members be not in a habit of obedience to a determinate individual or body.

In his great treatise on international law, Grotius defines sovereignty in the following manner. '*Summa potestas civilis* illa dicitur, cujus actus alterius juri non subsunt, ita ut alterius voluntatis humanæ arbitrio irriti possint reddi. Alterius cum dico, ipsum excludo, qui summa potestate utitur; cui voluntatem mutare licet.' Which definition is thus rendered by his translator and commentator Barbeyrac. '*La puissance souveraine* est celle dont les actes sont indépendans de tout autre pouvoir supérieur, en sorte qu'ils ne peuvent être annullez par aucune autre volonté humaine. Je dis, *par aucune autre volonté humaine*; car il faut excepter ici le souverain luimême, à qui il est libre de changer de volonté.' Now in order that an individual or body may be sovereign in a given society, two essentials must unite. The generality of the given society must render habitual obedience to that certain individual or body: whilst that individual or body must not be habitually obedient to a determinate human superior. In order to an adequate conception of the nature of international morality, as in order to an adequate conception of the nature of positive law, the former as well as the latter of those two essentials of sovereignty must be noted or taken into account. But, this notwithstanding, the former and positive essential of sovereign or supreme power is not inserted by Grotius in that, his formal definition. And the latter and negative essential is stated inaccurately. Sovereign power (according to Grotius) is perfectly or completely independent of other human power inasmuch that its acts cannot be annulled by any human will other than its own. But if perfect or complete independence be of the essence of sovereign power, there is not in fact the human power to which the epithet *sovereign* will apply with propriety. Every government, let it be never so powerful, renders occasional obedience to commands of other governments. Every government defers frequently to those opinions and sentiments which are styled international law. And every government defers habitually to the opinions and sentiments of its own subjects. If it were not in a habit of obedience to the commands of a determinate party, a government has all the independence which a government can possibly enjoy.

According to Von Martens of Göttingen (the writer on positive international law already referred to), 'a sovereign government is a government which *ought* not to receive commands from any external or foreign government'. Of the conclusive and obvious objections to this definition of sovereignty the following are only a few.

1. If the definition in question will apply to sovereign governments, it will also apply to subordinate. If a sovereign ought to be free from the commands of foreign governments, so ought every government which is merely the creature of a sovereign, and which holds its powers or rights as a mere trustee for its author.
2. Whether a given government be or be not supreme is rather a question of fact than a question of international law. A government reduced to subjection is actually a subordinate government, although the state of subjection wherein it is actually held be repugnant to the positive morality which obtains between nations or sovereigns. Though, according to that morality, it *ought* to be sovereign or independent, it is subordinate or dependent in practice.
3. It cannot be affirmed absolutely of a sovereign or independent government that it *ought* not to receive commands from foreign or external governments. The intermeddling of independent governments with other independent governments is often repugnant to the morality which actually obtains between nations. But according to that morality which actually obtains between nations (and to that international morality which general utility commends), no independent government ought to be freed completely from the supervision and control of its fellows.
4. In this definition by Von Martens (as in that which is given by Grotius) there is not the shadow of an allusion to the positive character of sovereignty. The definition points at the relations which are borne by sovereigns to sovereigns: but it omits the relations, not less essential, which are borne by sovereigns to their own subjects.

The ensuing portion of the present lecture is concerned with the following topics: 1. The forms of supreme government; 2. The limits of sovereign power; 3. The origin of government, or the origin of political society

I have now endeavoured to determine the general notion of sovereignty, including the general notion of independent political society. But in order that I may further elucidate the nature or essence of sovereignty, and of the independent political society which sovereignty implies, I will call the attention of my hearers to a few concise remarks upon the following subjects or topics.

1. The various shapes which sovereignty may assume, or the various possible forms of supreme government.
2. The real and imaginary limits which bound the power of sovereigns, and by which the power of sovereigns is supposed to be bounded.
3. The origin of government, with the origin of political society: or the causes of the habitual obedience which is rendered by the bulk of subjects, and from which the power of sovereigns to compel and restrain the refractory is entirely or mainly derived.

The forms of supreme government

An independent political society is divisible into two portions: namely, the portion of its members which is sovereign or supreme, and the portion of its members which is merely subject. The sovereignty can hardly reside in *all* the members of a society: for it can hardly happen that some of those members shall not be naturally incompetent to exercise sovereign powers. In most actual societies, the sovereign powers are engrossed by a single member of the whole, or are shared exclusively by a very few of its members: and even in the actual societies whose governments are esteemed popular, the sovereign number is a slender portion of the entire political community. An independent political society governed by itself, or governed by a sovereign body consisting of the whole community, is not impossible: but the existence of such societies is so extremely improbable that, with this passing notice, I throw them out of my account.[1]

Every supreme government is a monarchy *(properly so called), or an* aristocracy *(in the generic meaning of the expression). In other words, it is a government of* one, *or a government of a* number

Every society political and independent is therefore divisible into two portions: namely, the portion of its members which is sovereign or supreme, and the portion of its members which is merely subject. In case that sovereign portion consists of a single member, the supreme government is properly a *monarchy*, or the sovereign is properly a *monarch*. In case that sovereign portion consist of a number of members, the supreme government may be styled an *aristocracy* (in the generic meaning of the expression). And here I may briefly remark that a monarchy or government of one, and an aristocracy or government of a number, are essentially and broadly distinguished by the following important difference. In the case of a monarchy or government of one, the sovereign portion of the community is simply or purely sovereign. In the case of an aristocracy or government of a number, that sovereign portion is sovereign as viewed from one aspect, but is also subject as viewed from another. In the case of an aristocracy or government of a number, the sovereign number is an aggregate of individuals, and, commonly, of smaller aggregates composed by those individuals. Now, considered collectively, or considered in its corporate character, that sovereign number is sovereign and independent. But, considered severally, the individuals and smaller aggregates composing that sovereign number are subject to the supreme body of which they are component parts.

In every society, therefore, which may be styled political and independent, *one* of the individual members engrosses the sovereign powers, or the sovereign powers are shared by a *number* of the individual members less than the number of the individuals composing the entire community. Changing the phrase, every supreme government is a *monarchy* (properly so called), or an *aristocracy* (in the generic meaning of the expression).[2]

Of such distinctions between aristocracies as are founded on differences between the proportions which the number of the sovereign body may bear to the number of the community

Governments which may be styled aristocracies (in the generic meaning of the expression) are not unfrequently distinguished into the three following forms: namely, *oligarchies*, *aristocracies* (in the specific meaning of the name), and *democracies*. If the proportion of the sovereign number to the number of the entire community be deemed extremely small, the supreme government is styled an *oligarchy*. If the proportion be deemed small, but not extremely small, the supreme government is styled an *aristocracy* (in the specific meaning of the name). If the proportion be deemed large, the supreme government is styled *popular*, or is styled a *democracy*. But these three forms of aristocracy (in the generic meaning of the expression) can hardly be distinguished with precision, or even with a distant approach to it. A government which one man shall deem an oligarchy will appear to another a liberal aristocracy: whilst a government which one man shall deem an aristocracy will appear to another a narrow oligarchy. A government which one man shall deem a democracy will appear to another a government of a few: whilst a government which one man shall deem an aristocracy will appear to another a government of many. The proportion, moreover, of the sovereign number to the number of the entire community may stand, it is manifest, at any point in a long series of minute degrees.

The distinctions between aristocracies to which I have now adverted are founded on differences between the proportions which the number of the sovereign body may bear to the number of the community.

Of such distinctions between aristocracies as are founded on differences between the modes wherein the sovereign number may share the sovereign powers

Other distinctions between aristocracies are founded on differences between the modes wherein the sovereign number may share the sovereign powers.

For though the sovereign number may be a homogeneous body, or a body of individual persons whose political characters are similar, it is commonly a mixed or heterogeneous body, or a body of individual persons whose political characters are different. The sovereign number, for example, may consist of an oligarchical or narrower, and a democratical or larger, body; of a single individual person styled an emperor or king, and a body oligarchical, or a body democratical; or of a single individual person bearing one of those names, and a body of the former description, with another of the last mentioned kind. And in any of these cases, or of numberless similar cases, the various constituent members of the heterogeneous and sovereign body may share the sovereign powers in any of infinite modes.

Of such aristocracies as are styled limited monarchies

The infinite forms of aristocracy which result from those infinite modes have not been divided systematically into kinds and sorts, or have not been distinguished systematically by generic and specific names. But some of those infinite forms have been distinguished broadly from the rest, and have been marked with the common name of *limited monarchies*.

Now (as I have intimated above, and shall show more fully hereafter), the difference between monarchies or governments of one, and aristocracies or governments of a number, is of all the differences between governments the most precise or definite, and, in regard to the pregnant distinction between positive law and morality, incomparably the most important. And, since this capital difference between governments of one and a number is involved in some obscurity through the name of *limited monarchy*, I will offer a few remarks upon the various forms of aristocracy to which that name is applied.

In all or most of the governments which are styled limited monarchies, a single individual shares the sovereign powers with an aggregate or aggregates of individuals: the share of that single individual, be it greater or less, surpassing or exceeding the share of any of the other individuals who are also constituent members of the supreme and heterogeneous body. And by that pre-eminence of share in the sovereign or supreme powers, and (perhaps) by precedence in rank or other honorary marks, that single individual is distinguished, more or less conspicuously, from any of the other individuals with whom he partakes in the sovereignty.

But in spite of that pre-eminence, and in spite of that precedence, that foremost individual member of the mixed or heterogeneous aristocracy is not a monarch in the proper acceptation of the term: nor is the mixed aristocracy of which he is the foremost member a monarchy properly so called. Unlike a monarch in the proper acceptation of the term, that single individual is not a sovereign, but is one of a sovereign number. Unlike a monarch properly so called, that single individual, considered singly, lives in a state of subjection. Considered singly, he is subject to the sovereign body of which he is merely a limb.

Limited monarchy, therefore, is not monarchy. It is one or another of those infinite forms of aristocracy which result from the infinite modes wherein the sovereign number may share the sovereign powers. And, like any other of those infinite forms, it belongs to one or another of those three forms of aristocracy which I have noticed in a preceding paragraph. If the number of the sovereign body (the so called monarch included) bear to the number of the community an extremely small proportion, the so called monarchy is an oligarchy. If the same proportion be small, but not extremely small, the so called limited monarchy is an aristocratical government (in the specific meaning of the name). If the same proportion be large, the so called limited monarchy is a democratical or popular government, or a government of many.[3]

As meaning monarchical power limited by positive law, the name *limited monarchy* involves a contradiction in terms. For a monarch properly so called is sovereign or supreme; and, as I shall show hereafter, sovereign or supreme power is incapable of legal limitation, whether it reside in an individual or in a number of individuals. It is true that the power of an aristocracy, styled a *limited monarchy*, is limited by positive morality and also by the law of God. But, the power of every government being limited by those restraints, the name limited monarchy, as pointing to those restraints, is not a whit more applicable to such aristocracies as are marked with it, than to monarchies properly so called. And as the name is absurd or inappropriate, so is its application capricious. Although it is applied to some of the aristocracies wherein a single individual has the pre-eminence mentioned above, it is also withheld from others to which it is equally applicable. Its application, indeed, is commonly determined by a purely immaterial circumstance: by the nature of the title, or the nature of the name of office, which that foremost member of the mixed aristocracy happens to bear. If he happen to bear a title which commonly is borne by monarchs in the proper acceptation of the term, the supreme government whereof he is a member is usually styled a limited monarchy. Otherwise, the supreme government whereof he is a member is usually marked with a different name. For example: the title of Βασιλεύς *rex*, or *king*, is commonly borne by monarchs in the proper acceptation of the term: and since our own king happens to bear that title, our own mixed aristocracy of king, lords, and commons, is usually styled a limited monarchy. If his share in the sovereign powers were exactly what it is now, but he were called protector, president, or stadtholder, the mixed aristocracy of which he is a member would probably be styled a republic. And for such verbal differences between forms of supreme government has the peace of mankind been frequently troubled by ignorant and headlong fanatics.[4]

To the foregoing brief analysis of the forms of supreme government, I append a short examination of the four following topics: for they are far more intimately connected with the subject of that analysis than with any of the other subjects which the scope of my lecture embraces.

1. The exercise of sovereign powers, by a monarch or sovereign body, through political subordinates or delegates representing their sovereign author.
2. The distinction of sovereign and other political powers, into such as are *legislative*, and such as are *executive* or *administrative*.
3. The true natures of the communities or governments which are styled by writers on positive international law *half-sovereign states*.
4. The nature of a *composite state*, or a *supreme federal government*: with the nature of a *system of confederated states*, or a *permanent confederacy of supreme governments*.

Of the exercise of sovereign powers by a monarch or sovereign body, through political subordinates or delegates representing their sovereign author

In an independent political society of the smallest possible magnitude, inhabiting a territory of the smallest possible extent, and living under a monarchy or an extremely narrow oligarchy, all the supreme powers brought into exercise (save those committed to subjects as private persons) might possibly be exercised directly by the monarch or supreme body. But by every actual sovereign (whether the sovereign be one individual, or a number or aggregate of individuals), some of those powers are exercised through political subordinates or delegates representing their sovereign author. This exercise of sovereign powers through political subordinates or delegates is rendered absolutely necessary, in every actual society, by innumerable causes. For example, if the number of the society be large, or if its territory be large although its number be small, the quantity of work to be done in the way of political government is more than can be done by the sovereign without the assistance of ministers. If the society be governed by a popular body, there is some of the business of government which cannot be done by the sovereign without the intervention of representatives; for there is some of the business of government to which the body is incompetent by reason of its own bulk; and some of the business of government the body is prevented from performing by the private avocations of its members. If the society be governed by a popular body whose members live dispersedly throughout an extensive territory, the sovereign body is constrained by the wide dispersion of its members to exercise through representatives some of its sovereign powers.

In most or many of the societies whose supreme governments are monarchical, or whose supreme governments are oligarchical, or whose supreme governments are aristocratical (in the specific meaning of the name), many of the sovereign powers are exercised by the sovereign directly, or the sovereign performs directly much of the business of government.

Many of the sovereign powers are exercised by the sovereign directly, or the sovereign performs directly much of the business of government, even in some of the societies whose supreme governments are popular. For example: in all or most of the democracies of ancient Greece and Italy, the sovereign people or number, formally assembled, exercised directly many of its sovereign powers. And in some of the Swiss Cantons whose supreme governments are popular, the sovereign portion of the citizens, regularly convened, performs directly much of the business of government.

But in many of the societies whose supreme governments are popular, the sovereign or supreme body (or any numerous body forming a component part of it) exercises through representatives, whom it elects and appoints, the whole, or nearly the whole, of its sovereign or supreme powers. In our own country, for example, one component part of the sovereign or supreme body is the numerous body of *the commons* (in the strict signification of the name): that is to say, such of the commons (in the large acceptation of the term) as share the sovereignty with the king and the peers, and elect the members of the commons' house. Now the commons exercise through representatives the whole of their sovereign powers; or they exercise through representatives the whole of their sovereign powers, except their sovereign power of electing and appointing representatives to represent them in the British Parliament. So that if the commons were sovereign without the king and the peers, not a single sovereign power, save that which I have now specified, would be exercised by the sovereign directly.

Where a sovereign body (or any smaller body forming a component part of it) exercises through representatives the whole of its sovereign powers, it may delegate those its powers to those its representatives, in either of two modes.

1. It may delegate those its powers to those its representatives, subject to a trust or trusts.
2. It may delegate those its powers to those its representatives, absolutely or unconditionally: insomuch that the representative body, during the period for which it is elected and appointed, occupies completely the place of the electoral; or insomuch that the former, during the period for which it is elected and appointed, is invested completely with the sovereign character of the latter.

For example: the commons delegate their powers to the members of the commons' house, in the second of the above mentioned modes. During the period for which those members are elected, or during the parliament of which those members are a limb, the sovereignty is possessed by the king and the peers, with the members of the commons' house, and not by the king and the peers, with the delegating body of the commons: though when that period expires, or when that parliament is any how dissolved, the delegated share in the sovereignty reverts to that delegating body, or the king and the peers, with the delegating body of the commons, are then the body wherein the sovereignty resides. So that if the commons were sovereign without the king and the peers, their present representatives in parliament would be the sovereign in effect, or would possess the entire sovereignty free from trust or obligation. The powers of the commons are delegated so absolutely to the members of the commons' house, that this representative assembly might concur with the king and the peers in defeating the principal ends for which it is elected and appointed. It might concur, for instance, in making a statute which would lengthen its own duration from seven to twenty years; or which would annihilate completely the actual constitution of the government, by transferring the sovereignty to the king or the peers from the tripartite body wherein it resides at present.

But though the commons delegate their powers in the second of the above-mentioned modes, it is clear that they might delegate them subject to a trust or trusts. The representative body, for instance, might be bound to use those powers consistently with specific ends pointed out by the electoral: or it might be bound, more generally and vaguely, not to annihilate, or alter essentially, the actual constitution of the supreme government. And if the commons were sovereign without the king and the peers, they might impose a similar trust upon any representative body to which they might delegate the entire sovereignty.

Where such a trust is imposed by a sovereign or supreme body (or by a smaller body forming a component part of it), the trust is enforced by legal, or by merely moral, sanctions. The representative body is bound by a positive law or laws: or it is merely bound by a fear that it may offend the bulk of the community, in case it shall break the engagement which it has contracted with the electoral.

And here I may briefly remark that this last is the position which really is occupied by the members of the commons' house. Adopting the language of most of the writers who have treated of the British Constitution, I commonly suppose that the present parliament, or the parliament for the time being, is possessed of the sovereignty: or I commonly suppose that the king and the lords, with the members of the commons' house, form a tripartite body which is sovereign or supreme. But, speaking accurately, the members of the commons' house are merely trustees for the body by which they are elected and appointed: and, consequently, the sovereignty always resides in the king and the peers, with the electoral body of the commons. That a trust is imposed by the party delegating, and that the party representing engages to discharge the trust, seems to be imported by the correlative expressions *delegation* and *representation*. It were absurd to suppose that the delegating empowers the representative party to defeat or abandon any of the purposes for which the latter is appointed: to suppose, for example, that the commons empower their representatives in parliament to relinquish their share in the sovereignty to the king and the lords. The supposition that the powers of the commons are delegated absolutely to the members of the commons' house probably arose from the following causes.

1. The trust imposed by the electoral body upon the body representing them in parliament is tacit rather than express: it arises from the relation between the bodies as delegating and representative parties, rather than from oral or written instructions given by the former to the latter. But since it arises from that relation, the trust is general and vague. The representatives are merely bound, generally and vaguely, to abstain from any such exercise of the delegated sovereign powers as would tend to defeat the purposes for which they are elected and appointed.
2. The trust is simply enforced by moral sanctions. In other words, that portion of constitutional law which regards the duties of the representative towards the electoral body, is positive morality merely. Nor is this extraordinary. For (as I shall show hereafter) all constitutional law, in every country whatever, is, as against the sovereign, in that predicament: and much of it, in every country, is also in that predicament, even as against parties who are subject or subordinate to the sovereign, and who therefore might be held from infringing it by legal or political sanctions.

If a trust of the kind in question were enforced by legal sanctions, the positive law binding the representative body might be made by the representative body and not by the electoral. For example: if the duties of the commons' house towards the commons who appoint it were enforced by legal sanctions, the positive law binding the commons' house might be made by the parliament: that is to say, by the commons' house itself in conjunction with the king and the peers. Or, supposing the sovereignty resided in the commons without the king and the peers, the positive law binding the commons' house might be made by the house itself as representing the sovereign or state. But, in either of these cases, the law might be abrogated by its immediate author without the direct consent of the electoral body. Nor could the electoral body escape from that inconvenience, so long as its direct exercise of its sovereign or supreme powers was limited to the election of representatives. In order that the electoral body might escape from that inconvenience, the positive law binding its representatives must be made directly by itself or with its direct concurrence. For example: in order that the members of the commons' house might be bound legally and completely to discharge their duties to the commons, the law must be made directly by the commons themselves in concurrence with the king and the lords: or, supposing the sovereignty resided in the commons without the king and the peers, the law must be made directly by the commons themselves as being exclusively the sovereign. In either of these cases, the law could not be abrogated without the direct consent of the electoral body itself. For the king and the lords with the electoral body of the commons, or the electoral body of the commons as being exclusively the sovereign, would form an extraordinary and ulterior legislature: a legislature superior to that ordinary legislature which would be formed by the parliament or by the commons' house. A law of the parliament, or a law of the commons' house, which affected to abrogate a law of the extraordinary and ulterior legislature, would not be obeyed by the courts of justice. The tribunals would enforce the latter in the teeth of the former. They would examine the competence of the ordinary legislature to make the abrogating law, as they now examine the competence of any subordinate corporation to establish a bylaw or other statute or ordinance. In the state of New York, the ordinary legislature of the state is controlled by an extraordinary legislature, in the manner which I have now described. The body of citizens appointing the ordinary legislature forms an extraordinary and ulterior legislature by which the constitution of the state was directly established: and any law of the ordinary legislature, which conflicted with a constitutional law directly proceeding from the extraordinary, would be treated by the courts of justice as a legally invalid act. That such an extraordinary and ulterior legislature is a good or useful institution, I pretend not to affirm. I merely affirm that the institution is possible, and that in one political society the institution actually obtains.

Of the distinction of sovereign, and other political powers into such as are legislative, *and such as are* executive *or* administrative

From the exercise of sovereign powers by the sovereign directly, and also by the sovereign through political subordinates or delegates, I pass to the distinction of sovereign, and other political powers, into such as are *legislative*, and such as are *executive* or *administrative*.

It seems to be supposed by many writers that legislative political powers, and executive political powers, may be distinguished precisely or, at least, with an approach to precision: and that in every society whose government is a government of a number or, at least, in every society whose government is a limited monarchy, the legislative sovereign powers, and the executive sovereign powers, belong to distinct parties. According, for example, to Sir William Blackstone, the legislative sovereign powers reside in the parliament: that is to say, in the tripartite sovereign body formed by the king, the members of the house of lords, and the members of the house of commons. But, according to the same writer, the executive sovereign powers reside in the king alone.

Now the distinction of political powers into such as are *legislative*, and such as are *executive*, scarcely coincides with the distinction of those powers into such as are *supreme* and such as are *subordinate*: for it is stated or assumed by the writers who make the former distinction that sovereign political powers (and, indeed, subordinate also) are divisible into such as are legislative and such as are executive. If the distinction of political powers into legislative and executive have any determinate meaning, its meaning must be this: the former are powers of establishing laws and of issuing other commands: whilst the latter are powers of administering, or of carrying into operation, laws or other commands already established or issued. But the distinction, as thus understood, is far from approaching to precision. For of all the instruments or means by which laws and other commands are administered or executed, laws and other commands are incomparably the most frequent: insomuch that most of the powers deemed executive or administrative are themselves legislative powers, or involve powers which are legislative. For example: as administered or executed by courts of justice, laws are mainly administered through judgments or decrees: that is to say, through commands issued in particular cases by supreme or subordinate tribunals. And, in order that the law so administered may be administered well, they must be administered agreeably to laws which are merely subservient to that purpose. Thus: all laws or rules determining the practice of courts, or all laws or rules determining judicial procedure, are purely subsidiary to the due execution of others.

That the legislative sovereign powers, and the executive sovereign powers, belong, in any society, to distinct parties is a supposition too palpably false to endure a moment's examination. Of the numerous proofs of its falsity which it were easy to produce, the following will more than suffice:

1. Of the laws or rules made by the British parliament, or by any supreme

legislature, many are subsidiary, and are intended to be subsidiary, to the due execution of others. And as making laws or rules subservient to that purpose, it is not less *executive* than courts of justice as making regulations of procedure.

2. In almost every society, *judicial* powers, commonly esteemed *executive* or *administrative*, are exercised directly by the supreme legislature. For example: the Roman emperors or princes, who were virtually sovereign in the Roman empire or world, not only issued the *edictal* constitutions which were general rules or laws, but, as forming the highest or ultimate tribunal of appeal, they also issued the particular constitutions which were styled *decreta* or judgments. *In libera republica*, or before the virtual dissolution of the free or popular government, the sovereign Roman people, then the supreme legislature, was a high court of justice for the trial of criminal causes. The powers of supreme judicature inhering in the modern parliament, or the body formed by the king and the upper and lower houses, have ever (I believe) been dormant, or have never been brought into exercise: for, as making the particular but *ex post facto* statutes which are styled acts of attainder, it is not properly a court of justice. But the ancient parliament, formed by the king and the barons, of which the modern is the offspring, was the ultimate court of appeal as well as the sovereign legislature.
3. The present British constitution affords not the slightest countenance to the supposition which I am now examining. It is absurd to say that the parliament has the legislative sovereign powers, but that the executive sovereign powers belong to the king alone. If the parliament (as Blackstone affirms) be sovereign or absolute, every sovereign power must belong to that sovereign body, or to one or more of its members as forming a part or parts of it. The powers of the king considered as detached from the body, or the powers of any of its members considered in the same light, are not sovereign powers, but are simply or purely subordinate: or (changing the phrase) if the king or any of its members, considered as detached from the body, be invested with political powers, that member as so detached is merely a minister of the body, or those political powers are merely emanations of its sovereignty. Besides, political powers which surely may be deemed *executive* are exercised by each of the houses; whilst political powers which surely may be deemed *legislative* are exercised by the king. In civil causes, the house of lords is the ultimate court of appeal; and of all the political powers which are deemed executive or administrative, judicial powers are the most important and remarkable. The executive or administrative powers which reside in the lower house are not so weighty and obvious as those which belong to the upper: but still it were easy to show that it exercises powers of the kind. For example: exercising judicature, through select committees of its members, it adjudges

> that elections of its members are legally valid or void. The political powers exercised by the king which surely may be deemed legislative, are of vast extent and importance. As captain general, for example, he makes articles of war: that is to say, laws which regard especially the discipline or government of the soldiery. As administering the law, through subordinate courts of justice, he is the author of the rules of procedure which they have established avowedly, or in the properly legislative mode: and (what is of greater importance) he is the author of that measureless system of judge-made rules of law, or rules of law made in the judicial manner, which has been established covertly by those subordinate tribunals as directly exercising their judicial functions.[5]

Of all the larger divisions of political powers, the division of those powers into *supreme* and *subordinate* is perhaps the only precise one. The former are the political powers, infinite in number and kind, which, partly brought into exercise and partly lying dormant, belong to a sovereign or state: that is to say, to the monarch properly so called, if the government be a government of one; and, if the government be a government of a number, to the sovereign body considered collectively, or to its various members considered as component parts of it. The latter are those portions of the supreme powers which are delegated to political subordinates: such political subordinates being subordinate or subject merely, or also immediate partakers in those very supreme powers of portions or shares wherein they are possessed as ministers and trustees.

The true natures of the communities or governments which are styled by writers on positive international law half sovereign states

There were formerly in Europe many of the communities or governments which are styled by writers on positive international law *half sovereign states*. In consequence of the mighty changes wrought by the French revolution, such communities or governments have wholly or nearly disappeared: and I advert to the true natures of such communities or governments, not because they are intrinsically of any importance or interest, but because the incongruous epithet *half* or *imperfectly sovereign* obscures the essence of sovereignty and independent political society. It seems to import that the governments marked with it are sovereign and subject at once.

According to writers on positive international law, a government half or imperfectly sovereign occupies the following position: in spite of its half or imperfect dependence, it has most of the political and sovereign powers which belong to a government wholly or perfectly supreme. More especially, in all or most of its foreign relations, or in all or most of its relations to foreign or external governments, it acts and is treated as a perfectly sovereign government, and not as a government in a state of subjection to another: insomuch that it makes and breaks alliances, and makes war or peace, without authority from another government, or of its own discretion. But, this notwithstanding, the government, or a member of the government, of another political society has political powers over the society deemed imperfectly independent. For example: in the Germanico-Roman or Romano-Germanic empire, the particular German governments depending on the empire immediately, or holding of the emperor by tenure *in capite* were deemed imperfectly sovereign in regard to that general government which consisted of the emperor and themselves as forming the Imperial Diet. For though in their foreign relations they were wholly or nearly independent, they were bound (in reality or show) by laws of that general government: and its tribunals had appellate judicature (substantially or to appearance) over the political and half independent communities wherein they were half supreme. Most, indeed, of the governments deemed imperfectly supreme are governments which in their origin had been substantially vassal: but which had insensibly escaped from most of their feudal bonds though they still continued apparently in their primitive state of subjection.

Now I think it will appear on analysis that every government deemed imperfectly supreme is really in one or another of the three following predicaments. It is perfectly subject to that other government in relation to which it is deemed imperfectly supreme; or it is perfectly independent of the other, and therefore is of itself a truly sovereign government; or in its own community it is jointly sovereign with the other, and is therefore a constituent member of a government supreme and independent. And if every government deemed imperfectly supreme be really in one or another of the three foregoing predicaments, there is no such political mongrel as a government sovereign and subject.

1. The political powers of the government deemed imperfectly supreme may be exercised entirely and habitually at the pleasure and bidding of the other. On which supposition, its so called half sovereignty is merely nominal and illusive. It is perfectly subject to the other government, though that its perfect subjection may be imperfect in extent. For example: although, in its own name and as of its own discretion, it makes war or peace, its power of making either is merely nominal and illusive, if the power be exercised habitually at the bidding of the other government.
2. The political powers exercised by the other government over the political society deemed imperfectly independent may be exercised through the permission, or through the authority, of the government deemed imperfectly supreme. On which supposition, the government deemed imperfectly supreme is of itself a truly sovereign government: those powers being legal

rights over its own subjects which it grants expressly or tacitly to another sovereign government. (For, as I shall show hereafter, a sovereign government, with the permission or authority of another, may possess legal rights against the subjects of the latter.) For example: the great Frederic of Prussia, as prince-elector of Brandenburg, was deemed half or imperfectly sovereign in respect of his feudal connection with the German empire. Potentially and in practice, he was thoroughly independent of the imperial government: and, supposing it exercised political powers over his subjects of the electorate, it virtually exercised them through his authority, and not through his obedience to its commands. Being in a habit of thrashing its armies, he was not in a habit of submission to his seeming feudal superior.

3. The political powers of the government deemed imperfectly supreme may not be exercised entirely and habitually at the pleasure and bidding of the other: but yet its independence of the other may not be so complete that the political powers exercised by the other over the political society deemed imperfectly independent are merely exercised through its permission or authority. For example: we may suppose that the elector of Bavaria was independent of the Imperial government, in all or most of his foreign, and in most of his domestic, relations: but that, this his independence notwithstanding, he could not have abolished completely, without incurring considerable danger, the appellate judicature of the Imperial tribunals over the Bavarian community. But on the supposition which I have now stated and exemplified, the sovereignty of the society deemed imperfectly independent resides in the government deemed imperfectly supreme together with the other government: and, consequently, the government deemed imperfectly supreme is properly a constituent member of a government supreme and independent. The supreme government of the society deemed imperfectly independent is one of the infinite forms of supreme government by a number, which result from the infinite modes wherein the sovereign number may share the sovereign powers. There is, in the case, nothing extraordinary but this: that all the constituent members of the supreme government in question are not exclusively members of the political society which it governs; since one of them is also sovereign in another political society, or is also a constituent member of another supreme government. In consequent of this anomaly, the interests and pretensions of the constituent members more or less antagonize. But in almost every case of supreme government by a number, the interests and pretensions of the members more or less antagonize, although the supreme government be purely domestic. Whether a supreme government be purely domestic, or one of its limbs be also a limb of another, the supreme government is perpetuated through the mutual concessions of its members, notwithstanding the opposition of their interests and pretensions, and the bloody or bloodless conflicts which the opposition may occasionally beget.

For the reasons produced and suggested in the course of the foregoing analysis, I believe that no government is sovereign and subject at once: that no government can be styled with propriety *half* or *imperfectly supreme.*[6]

Before I dismiss the riddle which I have now endeavoured to resolve, I must state or suggest the following difference: in numberless cases, political powers are exercised over a political community, by the government, or a member of the government, of an external political community. But the government of the former community is scarcely denominated half or imperfectly sovereign, unless the government of the latter, or the member of the government of the latter, possess those political powers as being the government of the latter, or as being a member of its government. For example: the particular German governments which depended on the empire immediately are denominated half sovereign: for the powers exercised by the Imperial government over their respective communities were exercised by that government as being that very government, or as being (at least, to appearance) the general government of Germany. But the government of the British Islands is not imperfectly sovereign in regard to the government of Hanover: nor is the government of Hanover an imperfectly sovereign government in regard to the government of the British Islands. For though the king of the British Islands is also king of Hanover, he is not king in either country as being king in the other. The powers which he exercises there have no dependence whatever on his share in the sovereignty here: nor have the powers which he exercises here, any dependence on his sovereignty (or his share in the sovereignty) there. The difference which I have now suggested is analogous to the difference, in the Roman law, between *real* and *personal* servitudes: or to the resembling difference, in the law of England, between easements *appurtenant* and easements *in gross*. A *real* right of servitude, or a right of easement *appurtenant*, belongs to the party invested with the right, as being the owner or occupier of specifically determined land. A *personal* right of servitude, or a right of easement *in gross*, does not belong to the party as being such owner or occupier, but (according to the current jargon) is annexed to, or inheres in, his person.

Before I proceed to composite states and systems of confederated states, I will try to explain a difficulty that is closely connected with the subjects which I have examined in the present section. I have remarked already, and shall endeavour to demonstrate hereafter, that all the individuals or aggregates composing a sovereign number are subject to the supreme body of which they are component parts. Now where a member of a body which is sovereign in one community is exclusively sovereign in another, how does the sovereignty of that member in the latter of the two communities consist with the subjection of that member to the body which is sovereign in the former? Supposing, for example, that our own king was monarch and autocrator in Hanover, how would his subjection to the sovereign body of king, lords, and commons consist with his sovereignty in his

German kingdom? A limb or member of a sovereign body would seem to be shorn, by its habitual obedience to the body, of the habitual independence which must needs belong to it as sovereign in a foreign community. To explain the difficulty, we must assume that the characters of sovereign, and member of the sovereign body, are practically distinct: that, as monarch (for instance) of the foreign community, a member of the sovereign body neither habitually obeys it, nor is habitually obeyed by it. For if, as monarch of the foreign community, he habitually obeyed the body, the body would be sovereign in that community, and he would be merely its minister: and, if, as monarch of the foreign community, he were habitually obeyed by the body, he, and not the body, would be sovereign in the other society. Insomuch that if the characters were practically blended, or, remaining practically distinct, thoroughly conflicted, one of the following results would probably ensue. The member would become subject, or else exclusively sovereign, in both communities: or, to preserve his sovereignty in the one, or his part sovereignty in the other, he would renounce his connection with the latter or with the former society.

Wherever a member of a body sovereign in one community is also a member of a body sovereign in another, there is the same or a similar difficulty. A state of subjection to the former, and a state of subjection to the latter, may become incompatible: just as a state of subjection may become incompatible with the independence which is one of the essentials of sovereignty.

It not unfrequently happens that two or more independent political societies become subject to a common sovereign: but that after their union, through that common subjection, they still are governed distinctly, and distinguished by their ancient titles. In this case, there is not the difficulty suggested above. The monarch or sovereign body ruling the two societies is one and the same sovereign: and, through their subjection to that common sovereign, they are one society political and independent.

The nature of a composite state *or a* supreme federal government*: with the nature of a* system of confederated states, *or a* permanent confederacy of supreme governments

It frequently happens that one society political and independent arises from a federal union of several political societies: or, rather, that one government political and sovereign arises from a federal union of several political governments. By some of the writers on positive international law, such an independent political society, or the sovereign government of such a society, is styled a *composite state*. But the sovereign government of such a society might be styled more aptly, as well as more popularly, a *supreme federal government*.

It also frequently happens that several political societies which are severally independent, or several political governments which are severally sovereign, are compacted by a permanent alliance. By some of the writers on positive international law, the several societies or governments, considered as thus compacted, are styled a *system of confederated states*. But the several governments, considered as thus compacted, might be styled more aptly, as well as more popularly, a *permanent confederacy of supreme governments*.

I advert to the nature of a composite state, and to that of a system of confederated states, for the following purposes: it results from positions which I shall try to establish hereafter, that the power of a sovereign is incapable of legal limitation. It also results from positions which I have tried to establish already, that in every society political and independent, the sovereign is *one* individual, or *one* body of individuals: that unless the sovereign be *one* individual, or *one* body of individuals, the given independent society is either in a state of nature, or is split into two or more independent political societies. But in a political society styled a composite state, the sovereignty is so shared by various individuals or bodies that the *one* sovereign body whereof they are the constituent members is not conspicuous and easily perceived. In a political society styled a composite state, there is not obviously *any* party truly sovereign and independent: there is not obviously *any* party armed with political powers incapable of legal limitation. Accordingly, I advert to the nature of a supreme federal government, to show that the society which it rules is ruled by one sovereign, or is ruled by a party truly sovereign and independent. And adverting to the nature of a composite state, I also advert to the nature of a system of confederated states. For the fallacious resemblance of those widely different objects tends to produce a confusion which I think it expedient to obviate: and, through a comparison or contrast of those widely different objects, I can indicate the nature of the former more concisely and clearly.

One. In the case of a *composite state*, or a *supreme federal government*, the several united governments of the several united societies, together with a government common to those several societies, are jointly sovereign in each of those several societies, and also in the larger society arising from the federal union. Or, since the political powers of the common or general government were relinquished and conferred upon it by those several united governments, the nature of a composite state may be described more accurately thus. As compacted by the common government which they have concurred in creating, and to which they have severally delegated portions of their several sovereignties, the several governments of the several united societies are jointly sovereign in each and all.

It will appear on a moment's reflection that the common or general government is not sovereign or supreme. It will also appear on a moment's reflection that none of the several governments is sovereign or supreme, even in the several society of which it is the immediate chief.

If the common or general government were sovereign or supreme, the several united societies, though constituting one society, would not constitute a composite state or, though they would be governed by a common and supreme government, their common and supreme government would not be federal. For in almost every case of independent political society, several political societies, governed by several governments, are comprised by the one society which is political and independent: insomuch that a government supreme and federal, and a government supreme but not federal, are merely distinguished by the following difference. Where the supreme government is not federal, each of the several governments, considered in that character, is purely subordinate: or none of the several governments, considered in that character, partakes of the sovereignty. But where the supreme government is properly federal, each of the several governments, *which were immediate parties to the federal compact*, is, in that character, a limb of the sovereign body. Consequently, although they are subject to the sovereign body of which they are constituent members, those several governments, even considered as such, are not purely in a state of subjection. But since those several governments, even considered as such, are not purely in a state of subjection, the common or general government which they have concurred in creating is not sovereign or supreme.

Nor is any of those several governments sovereign or supreme, even in the several society of which it is the immediate chief. If those several governments were severally sovereign, they would not be members of a composite state, though, if they were severally sovereign and yet were permanently compacted, they would form (as I shall show immediately) a system of confederated states.

To illustrate the nature of a composite state, I will add the following remark to the foregoing general description. Neither the immediate tribunals of the common or general government, nor the immediate tribunals of the several united governments, are bound, or empowered, to administer or execute *every* command that it may issue. The political powers of the common or general government are merely those portions of their several sovereignties which the several united governments, as parties to the federal compact, have relinquished and conferred upon it. Consequently, its competence to make laws and to issue other commands may and ought to be examined by its own immediate tribunals, and also by the immediate tribunals of the several united governments. And if, in making a law or issuing a particular command, it exceed the limited powers which it derives from the federal compact, all those various tribunals are empowered and bound to disobey. And since each of the united governments, as a party to the federal compact, has relinquished a portion of its sovereignty, neither the immediate tribunals of the common or general government, nor the immediate tribunals of the other united governments, nor even the tribunals which it itself immediately appoints, are bound, or empowered, to administer or execute *every* command that it may issue. Since each of the united governments, as a party to the federal compact, has relinquished a portion of its sovereignty, its competence to make laws and to issue other commands may and ought to be examined by all those various tribunals. And if it enact a law or issue a particular command, as exercising the sovereign powers which it has relinquished by the compact, all those various tribunals are empowered and bound to disobey.

If, then, the general government were of itself sovereign, or if the united governments were severally sovereign, the united societies would not constitute one composite state. The united societies would constitute one independent society, with a government supreme but not federal; or a knot of societies severally independent, with governments severally supreme. Consequently, the several united governments *as forming one aggregate body*, or they and the general government *as forming a similar body*, are jointly sovereign in each of the united societies, and also in the larger society arising from the union of all.

Now since the political powers of the common or general government are merely delegated to it by the several united governments, it is not a constituent member of the sovereign body but is merely its subject minister. Consequently, the sovereignty of each of the united societies, and also of the larger society arising from the union of all, resides in the united governments *as forming one aggregate body*: that is to say, as signifying their joint pleasure, or the joint pleasure of a majority of their number, agreeably to the modes or forms determined by their federal compact.

By that aggregate body, the powers of the general government were conferred and determined: and by that aggregate body, its powers may be revoked, abridged, or enlarged. To that aggregate body, the several united governments, though not merely subordinate, are truly in a state of subjection. Otherwise, those united governments would be severally sovereign or supreme, and the united societies would merely constitute a system of confederated states. Besides, since the powers of the general government were determined by that aggregate body, and since that aggregate body is competent to enlarge those powers, it necessarily determined the powers, and is competent to abridge the powers, of its own constituent members. For every political power conferred on the general government is subtracted from the several sovereignties of the several united governments. From the sovereignty of that aggregate body, we may deduce, as a necessary consequence, the fact which I have mentioned above: namely, that the competence of the general government, and of any of the united governments, may and ought to be examined by the immediate tribunals of the former, and also by the immediate tribunals of any of the latter. For since the general government, and also the united governments, are subject to that aggregate body, the respective courts of justice which they respectively appoint ultimately derive their powers from that sovereign and ultimate legislature. Consequently, those courts are ministers and trustees of that sovereign and ultimate legislature, as well as of the subject legislatures by which they are immediately appointed. And, consequently, those courts are empowered, and are even bound to disobey, wherever those subject legislatures exceed the limited powers which that sovereign and ultimate legislature has granted or left them.

The supreme government of the United States of America agrees (I believe) with the foregoing general description of a supreme federal government. I believe that the common government, or the government consisting of the congress and the president of the United States, is merely a subject minister of the united states' governments. I believe that none of the latter is properly sovereign or supreme, even in the state or political society of which it is the immediate chief. And, lastly, I believe that the sovereignty of each of the states, and also of the larger state arising from the federal union, resides in the states' governments *as forming one aggregate body*: meaning by a state's government, not its ordinary legislature, but the body of its citizens which appoints its ordinary legislature, and which, the union apart, is properly sovereign therein. If the several immediate chiefs of the several united states were respectively single individuals, or were respectively narrow oligarchies, the sovereignty of each of the states, and also of the larger state arising from the federal union, would reside in those several individuals, or would reside in those several oligarchies, *as forming a collective whole.*[7]

Two. A *composite state*, and a *system of confederated states*, are broadly distinguished by the following essential difference. In the case of a *composite state*, the several united societies are one independent society, or are severally subject to one sovereign body: which, through its minister the general government, and through its members and ministers the several united governments, is habitually and generally obeyed in each of the united societies, and also in the larger society arising from the union of all. In the case of a *system of confederated states*, the several compacted societies are not one society, and are not subject to a common sovereign: or (changing the phrase) each of the several societies is an independent political society, and each of their several governments is properly sovereign or supreme. Though the aggregate of the several governments was the framer of the federal compact, and may subsequently pass resolutions concerning the entire confederacy, neither the terms of that compact, nor such subsequent resolutions, are enforced in any of the societies by the authority of that aggregate body. To each of the confederated governments, those terms and resolutions are merely articles of agreement which it spontaneously adopts: and they owe their legal effect, in its own political society, to laws and other commands which it makes or fashions upon them, and which, of its own authority, it addresses to its own subjects. In short, a system of confederated states is not essentially different from a number of independent governments connected by an ordinary alliance. And where independent governments are connected by an ordinary alliance, none of the allied governments is subject to the allied governments considered as an aggregate body: though each of the allied governments adopts the terms of the alliance, and commonly enforces those terms, by laws and commands of its own, in its own independent community. Indeed, a system of confederated states, and a number of independent governments connected by an ordinary alliance, cannot be distinguished precisely through general or abstract expressions. So long as we abide in general expressions, we can only affirm generally and vaguely, that the compact of the former is intended to be permanent, whilst the alliance of the latter is commonly intended to be temporary: and that the ends or purposes which are embraced by the compact are commonly more numerous, and are commonly more complicated, than those which the alliance contemplates.

I believe that the German Confederation, which has succeeded to the ancient Empire, is merely a system of confederated states. I believe that the present Diet is merely an assembly of ambassadors from several confederated but severally independent governments: that the resolutions of the Diet are merely articles of agreement which each of the confederated governments spontaneously adopts; and that they owe their legal effect, in each of the compacted communities, to laws and commands which are fashioned upon them by its own immediate chief. I also believe that the Swiss Confederation was and is of the same nature. If, in the case of the German or of the Swiss Confederation, the body of confederated governments enforces its own resolutions, those confederated governments are one composite state, rather than a system of confederated states. The body of confederated governments is properly sovereign: and to that aggregate and sovereign body, each of its constituent members is properly in a state of subjection.

The limits of sovereign power

From the various shapes which sovereignty may assume or from the various possible forms of supreme government, I proceed to the limits, real and imaginary, of sovereign or supreme power.

The essential difference of a positive law

Subject to the slight correctives which I shall state at the close of my discourse, the essential difference of a positive law (or the difference that severs it from a law which is not a positive law) may be put in the following manner: every positive law, or every law simply and strictly so called, is set, directly or circuitously, by a sovereign person or body, to a member or members of the independent political society wherein that person or body is sovereign or supreme. Or (changing the expression) it is set, directly or circuitously, by a monarch or sovereign number, to a person or persons in a state of subjection to its author.

It follows from the essential difference of a positive law, and from the nature of sovereignty and independent political society, that the power of a monarch properly so called, or the power of a sovereign number in its collegiate and sovereign capacity, is incapable of legal *limitation*

Now it follows from the essential difference of a positive law, and from the nature of sovereignty and independent political society, that the power of a monarch properly so called, or the power of a sovereign number in its collegiate and sovereign capacity, is incapable of *legal* limitation. A monarch or sovereign number bound by a legal duty, were subject to a higher or superior sovereign: that is to say, a monarch or sovereign number bound by a legal duty were sovereign and not sovereign. Supreme power limited by positive law is a flat contradiction in terms.

Nor would a political society escape from legal despotism, although the power of the sovereign were bounded by legal restraints. The power of the superior sovereign immediately imposing the restraints, or the power of some other sovereign superior to that superior, would still be absolutely free from the fetters of positive law. For unless the imagined restraints were ultimately imposed by a sovereign not in a state of subjection to a higher or superior sovereign, a series of sovereigns ascending to infinity would govern the imagined community. Which is impossible and absurd.

Attempts of sovereigns to oblige themselves, or to oblige the successors to their sovereign powers

Monarchs and sovereign bodies have attempted to oblige themselves, or to oblige the successors to their sovereign powers. But in spite of the laws which sovereigns have imposed on themselves, or which they have imposed on the successors to their sovereign powers, the position that 'sovereign power is incapable of legal limitation' will hold universally or without exception.

The immediate author of a law of the kind, or any of the sovereign successors to that immediate author, may abrogate the law at pleasure. And though the law be not abrogated, the sovereign for the time being is not constrained to observe it by a legal or political sanction. For if the sovereign for the time being were legally bound to observe it, that present sovereign would be in a state of subjection to a higher or superior sovereign.

As it regards the successors to the sovereign or supreme powers, a law of the kind amounts, at the most, to a rule of positive morality. As it regards its immediate author, it is merely a law by a metaphor. For if we would speak with propriety, we cannot speak of a law set by a man to himself: though a man may adopt a principle as a guide to his own conduct, and may observe it as he would observe it if he were bound to observe it by a sanction.

The laws which sovereigns affect to impose upon themselves, or the laws which sovereigns affect to impose upon their followers, are merely principles or maxims which they adopt as guides, or which they commend as guides to their successors in sovereign power. A departure by a sovereign or state from a law of the kind in question is not illegal. If a law which it sets to its subjects conflict with a law of the kind, the former is legally valid or legally binding.

For example: the sovereign Roman people solemnly voted or resolved that they would never pass, or even take into consideration, what I will venture to denominate a *bill of pains and penalties*. For though, at the period in question, the Roman people were barbarians, they keenly felt a truth which is often forgotten by legislators in nations boasting of refinement: namely, that punishment ought to be inflicted agreeably to prospective rules, and not in pursuance of particular and *ex post facto* commands. This solemn resolution or vote was passed with the forms of legislation, and was inserted in the twelve tables in the following imperative terms: *privilegia ne irroganto*. But although the resolution or vote was passed with the forms of legislation, although it was clothed with the expressions appropriate to a law, and although it was inserted as a law in a code or body of statutes, it scarcely was a law in the proper acceptation of the term, and certainly was not a law simply and strictly so called. By that resolution or vote, the sovereign people adopted, and commended to their successors in the sovereignty, an ethical principle or maxim. The present and future sovereign which the resolution affected to oblige was not bound or estopped by it. Privileges enacted in spite of it by the sovereign Roman people, were not illegal. The Roman tribunals might not have treated them as legally invalid acts, although they conflicted with the maxim, wearing the guise of a law, *privilegia ne irroganto*.

Again: by the authors of the union between England and Scotland, an attempt was made to oblige the legislature, which, in consequence of that union, is sovereign in both countries. It is declared in the Articles and Acts, that the preservation of the Church of England, and of the Kirk of Scotland, is a fundamental condition of the union: or, in other words, that the Parliament of Great Britain shall not abolish those churches, or make an essential change in their structures or constitutions. Now, so long as the bulk of either nation shall regard its established church with love and respect, the abolition of the church by the British Parliament would be an *immoral* act; for it would violate positive morality which obtains with the bulk of the nation, or would shock opinions and sentiments which the bulk of the nation holds. Assuming that the church establishment is commended by the revealed law, the abolition would be *irreligious*: or, assuming that the continuance of the establishment were commended by general utility, the abolition, as generally pernicious, would also amount to a *sin*. But no man, talking with a meaning, would call a parliamentary abolition of either or both of the churches an *illegal* act. For if the parliament for the time being be sovereign in England and Scotland, it cannot be bound legally by that condition of the union which affects to confer immortality upon those ecclesiastical institutions. That condition of the union is not a positive law, but is counsel or advice offered by the authors of the union to future supreme legislatures.

The meanings of the epithet unconstitutional, *as it is contradistinguished to the epithet* illegal, *and as it is applied to conduct of a monarch, or to conduct of a sovereign number in its collegiate and sovereign capacity*

By the two examples which I have now adduced, I am led to consider the meanings of the epithet, *unconstitutional*, as it is contradistinguished in the epithet illegal, and as it is applied to conduct of a monarch, or to conduct of a sovereign number in its collegiate and sovereign capacity. The epithet *unconstitutional*, as thus opposed and applied, is sometimes used with a meaning which is more general and vague, and is sometimes used with a meaning which is more special and definite. I will begin with the former.

One. In every, or almost every, independent political society, there are principles or maxims which the sovereign habitually observes, and which the bulk of the society, or the bulk of its influential members, regard with feelings of approbation. Not unfrequently, such maxims are expressly adopted, as well as habitually observed, by the sovereign or state. More commonly, they are not expressly adopted by the sovereign or state, but are simply imposed upon it by opinions prevalent in the community. Whether they are expressly adopted by the sovereign or state, or are simply imposed upon it by opinions prevalent in the community, it is bound or constrained to observe them by merely moral sanctions. Or (changing the phrase) in case it ventured to deviate from a maxim of the kind in question, it would not and could not incur a legal pain or penalty, but it probably would incur censure, and might chance to meet with resistance, from the generality or bulk of the governed.

Now, if a law or other act of a monarch or sovereign number conflict with a maxim of the kind to which I have adverted above, the law or other act may be called *unconstitutional* (in that more general meaning which is sometimes given to the epithet). For example: the *ex post facto* statutes which are styled acts of attainder may be called *unconstitutional*, though they cannot be called *illegal*.

For they conflict with a principle of legislation which parliament has habitually observed and which is regarded with approbation by the bulk of the British community.

In short, when we style an act of a sovereign an *unconstitutional* act (with that more general import which is sometimes given to the epithet), we mean, I believe, this: that the act is inconsistent with some given principle or maxim: that the given supreme government has expressly adopted the principle, or, at least, has habitually observed it; that the bulk of the given society, or the bulk of its influential members, regard the principle with approbation; and that, since the supreme government has habitually observed the principle, and since the bulk of the society regard it with approbation, the act in question must thwart the expectations of the latter, and must shock their opinions and sentiments. Unless we mean this, we merely mean that we deem the act in question generally pernicious: or that, without a definite reason for the disapprobation which we feel, we regard the act with dislike.

Two. The epithet *unconstitutional* as applied to conduct of a sovereign, and as used with the meaning which is more special and definite, imports that the conduct in question conflicts with *constitutional law.*

And here I would briefly remark that I mean by the expression *constitutional law*, the positive morality, or the compound of positive morality and positive law, which fixes the constitution or structure of the given supreme government. I mean the positive morality, or the compound of positive morality and positive law, which determines the character of the person, or the respective characters of the persons, in whom, for the time being, the sovereignty shall reside: and, supposing the government in question an aristocracy or government of a number, which determines moreover the mode wherein the sovereign powers shall be shared by the constituent members of the sovereign number or body.

Now, against a monarch properly so called, or against a sovereign body in its collegiate and sovereign capacity, constitutional law is positive morality merely, or is enforced merely by moral sanctions: though, as I shall show hereafter, it may amount to positive law, or may be enforced by legal sanctions, against the members of the body considered severally. The sovereign for the time being, or the predecessors of the sovereign, may have expressly adopted, and expressly promised to observe it. But whether constitutional law has thus been expressly adopted, or simply consists of principles current in the political community, it is merely guarded, against the sovereign, by sentiments or feelings of the governed. Consequently, although an act of the sovereign which violates constitutional law may be styled with propriety *unconstitutional*, it is not an infringement of law simply and strictly so called, and cannot be styled with propriety *illegal*.

For example: from the ministry of Cardinal Richelieu down to the great revolution, the king for the time being was virtually sovereign in France. But, in the same country and during the same period, a traditional maxim cherished by the courts of justice, and rooted in the affections of the bulk of the people, determined the succession to the throne. It determined that the throne, on the demise of an actual occupant, should invariably be taken by the person who then might happen to be heir to it agreeably to the canon of inheritance which was named the Salic law. Now, in case an actual king, by a royal ordinance or law, had attempted to divert the throne to his only daughter and child, that royal ordinance or law might have been styled with perfect propriety an *unconstitutional* act. It would have conflicted with the traditional maxim which fixed the constitution of the monarchy, and which was guarded from infringement by sentiments prevalent in the nation. But *illegal* it could not have been called: for, inasmuch as the actual king was virtually sovereign, he was inevitably independent of legal obligation. Nay, if the governed had resisted the unconstitutional ordinance, their resistance would have been illegal or a breach of positive law, though consonant to the positive morality which is styled constitutional law, and perhaps to that principle of utility which is the test of positive rules.

Again: an act of the British parliament vesting the sovereignty in the king, or vesting the sovereignty in the king and the upper or lower house, would essentially alter the structure of our present supreme government, and might therefore be styled with propriety an *unconstitutional* law. In case the imagined statute were also generally pernicious, and in case it offended moreover the generality or bulk of the nation, it might be styled *irreligious* and *immoral* as well as *unconstitutional*. But to call it *illegal* were absurd: for if the parliament for the time being be sovereign in the United Kingdom, it is the author, directly or circuitously, of all our positive law, and exclusively sets us the measure of legal justice and injustice.[8]

Considered severally, the members of a sovereign body are in a state of subjection to the body, and may therefore be legally bound, even as members of the body, by laws of which it is the author

But when I affirm that the power of a sovereign is incapable of legal limitation, I always mean by a 'sovereign', a monarch properly so called, or a sovereign number in its collegiate and sovereign capacity. Considered collectively, or considered in its corporate character, a sovereign number is sovereign and independent: but, considered severally, the individuals and smaller aggregates composing that sovereign number are subject to the supreme body of which they are component parts. Consequently, though the body is inevitably independent of legal or political duty, any of the individuals or aggregates whereof the body is composed may be legally bound by laws of which the body is the author. For example: a member of the house of lords, or a member of the house of commons, may be legally bound by an act of parliament, which, as one of the sovereign legislature, he has concurred with others in making. Nay, he may be legally bound by statutes, or by rules made judicially, which have immediately proceeded from subject or subordinate legislatures: for a law which proceeds immediately from a subject or subordinate legislature is set by the authority of the supreme.

And hence an important difference between monarchies or governments of one, and aristocracies or governments of a number.

Against a monarch properly so called, or against a sovereign number in its collegiate and sovereign capacity, *constitutional law* (as I have remarked already) is enforced, or protected from infringement, by merely moral sanctions. Against a monarch properly so called, or against a sovereign number in its collegiate and sovereign capacity, constitutional law and the law of nations are nearly in the same predicament. Each is positive morality rather than positive law. The former is guarded by sentiments current in the given community, as the latter is guarded by sentiments current amongst nations generally.

But, considered severally, the members of a sovereign body, even as members of the body, may be legally bound by laws of which the body is the author, and which regard the constitution of the given supreme government. In case it be clothed with a legal sanction, or the means of enforcing it judicially be provided by its author, a law set by the body to any of its own members is properly a positive law: it is properly a positive law, or a law strictly so called, although it be imposed upon the obliged party as a member of the body which sets it. If the means of enforcing it judicially be not provided by its author, it is rather a rule of positive morality than a rule of positive law. But it wants the essentials of a positive law, not through the character of the party to whom it is set or directed, but because it is not invested with a legal or political sanction, or is a law of imperfect obligation in the sense of the Roman jurists. In case the law be invested with a legal or political sanction, and regard the constitution or structure of the given supreme government, a breach of the law, by the party to whom it is set, is not only *unconstitutional*, but is also *illegal*. The breach of the law is *unconstitutional*, inasmuch as the violated law regards the constitution of the state. The breach of the law is also *illegal*, inasmuch as the violated law may be enforced by judicial procedure.

For example: the king, as a limb of the parliament, might be punishable by act of parliament in the event of his transgressing the limits which the constitution has set to his authority: in the event, for instance, of his pretending to give to a proclamation of his own the legal effect of a statute emanating from the sovereign legislature. Or the members of either house might be punishable by act of parliament, if, as forming a limb of the parliament, they exceeded their constitutional powers: if, for instance, they pretended to give that legal effect to an ordinance or resolution of their own body.

Where, then, the supreme government is a monarchy or government of one, constitutional law, as against that government, is inevitably nothing more than positive morality. Where the supreme government is an aristocracy or government of a number, constitutional law, as against the members of that government, may either consist of positive morality, or of a compound of positive morality and positive law. Against the sovereign body in its corporate and sovereign character, it is inevitably nothing more than positive morality. But against the members considered severally, be they individuals or be they aggregates of individuals, it may be guarded by legal or political, as well as by moral, sanctions.

In fact or practice, the members considered severally, but considered as members of the body, are commonly free, wholly or partially, from legal or political restraints. For example: the king, as a limb of the parliament, is not responsible legally, or cannot commit a legal injury: and, as partaking in conduct of the assembly to which he immediately belongs, a member of the house of lords, or a member of the house of commons, is not amenable to positive law. But though this freedom from legal restraints may be highly useful or expedient, it is not necessary or inevitable. Considered severally, the members of a sovereign body, be they individuals or be they aggregates of individuals, may clearly be legally amenable, even as members of the body, to laws which the body imposes.

And here I may remark that if a member considered severally, but considered as a member of the body, be wholly or partially free from legal or political obligation, that legally irresponsible aggregate, or that legally irresponsible individual, is restrained or debarred in two ways from an unconstitutional exercise of its legally unlimited power.

1. Like the sovereign body of which it is a member, it is obliged or restrained morally: that is to say, it is controlled by opinions and sentiments current in the given community.
2. If it affected to issue a command which it is not empowered to issue by its constitutional share in the sovereignty, its unconstitutional command would not be legally binding, and disobedience to that command would therefore not be illegal. Nay, although it would not be responsible legally for thus exceeding its powers, those whom it commissioned to execute its unconstitutional command would probably be amenable to positive law if they tried to accomplish their mandate. For example: if the king or either of the houses, by way of proclamation or ordinance, affected to establish a law equivalent to an act of parliament, the pretended statute would not be legally binding, and disobedience to the pretended statute would therefore not be illegal. And although the king or the house would not be responsible legally for this supposed violation of constitutional law or morality, those whom the king or the house might order to enforce the statute, would be liable civilly or criminally, if they attempted to execute the order.

I have affirmed above, that, taken or considered severally, all the individuals and aggregates composing a sovereign number are subject to the supreme body of which they are component parts. By the matter contained in the last paragraph, I am led to clear the proposition, to which I have now adverted, from a seeming difficulty.

Generally speaking, if a member of a sovereign body, taken or considered severally, be not amenable to positive law, it is merely as a member of the body that he is free from legal obligation. Generally speaking, he is bound, in his other characters, by legal restraints. But in some of the mixed aristocracies which are styled limited monarchies, the so called limited monarch is exempted or absolved completely from legal or political duty. For example: according to a maxim of the English law, the king is incapable of committing wrong: that is to say, he is not responsible legally for aught that he may please to do, or for any forbearance or omission.

But though he is absolved completely from legal or political duty, it cannot be thence inferred that the king is sovereign or supreme, or that he is not in a state of subjection to the sovereign or supreme parliament of which he is a constituent member.

Of the numerous proofs of this negative conclusion, which it were easy to produce, the following will amply suffice.

1. Although he is free in fact from the fetters of positive law, he is not incapable of legal obligation. A law of the sovereign parliament, made with his own assent, might render himself and his successors legally responsible. But a monarch properly so called, or a sovereign number in its corporate and sovereign character, cannot be rendered, by any contrivance, amenable to positive law.
2. If he affected to transgress the limits which the constitution has set to his authority, disobedience on the part of the governed to his unconstitutional commands would not be illegal: whilst the ministers or instruments of his unconstitutional commands would be legally amenable, for their unconstitutional obedience, to laws of that sovereign body whereof he is merely a limb. But commands issued by sovereigns cannot be disobeyed by their subjects without an infringement of positive law: whilst the ministers or instruments of such a sovereign command cannot be legally responsible to any portion of the community, excepting the author of their mandate.
3. He habitually obeys the laws set by the sovereign body of which he is a constituent member. If he did not, he must speedily yield his office to a less refractory successor, or the British constitution must speedily expire. If he habitually broke the laws set by the sovereign body, the other members of the body would probably devise a remedy: though a prospective and definite

remedy, fitted to meet the contingency, has not been provided by positive law, or even by constitutional morality. Consequently, he is bound by a cogent sanction to respect the laws of the body, although that cogent sanction is not predetermined and certain. A law which is set by the opinion of the upper and lower houses (besides a law which is set by the opinion of the community at large) constrains him to observe habitually the proper and positive laws which are set by the entire parliament. But habitually obeying the laws of a determinate and sovereign body, he is not properly sovereign: for such habitual obedience consists not with that independence which is one of the essentials of sovereignty. And habitually obeying the laws of a certain and supreme body, he is really in a state of subjection to that certain and supreme body, though the other members of the body, together with the rest of the community, are commonly styled his subjects. It is mainly through the forms of procedure which obtain in the courts of justice that he is commonly considered sovereign. He is clothed by the British constitution, or rather by the parliament of which he is a limb, with subordinate political powers of administering the law, or rather of supervising its administration. Infringements of the law are, therefore, in the style of procedure, offences against the king. In truth, they are not offences against the king, but against that sovereign body of king, lords, and commons, by which our positive law is directly or circuitously established. And to that sovereign body, and not to the king, the several members of the body, together with the rest of the community, are truly subject.

The nature of political or civil liberty, together with the supposed difference between free and despotic governments

But if sovereign or supreme power be incapable of legal limitation, or if every supreme government be legally absolute, wherein (it may be asked) doth political liberty consist, and how do the supreme governments which are commonly deemed free differ from the supreme governments which are commonly deemed despotic?

I answer that political or civil liberty is the liberty from legal obligation, which is left or granted by a sovereign government to any of its own subjects: and that, since the power of the government is incapable of legal limitation, the government is legally free to abridge their political liberty, at its own pleasure or discretion. I say it is *legally* free to abridge their political liberty, at its own pleasure or discretion. For a government may be hindered by *positive morality* from abridging the political liberty which it leaves or grants to its subjects: and it is bound by the *law of God*, as known through the principle of utility, not to load them with legal duties which general utility condemns. There are kinds of liberty from legal obligation which will not quadrate with the foregoing description: for persons in a state of nature are independent of political duty, and independence of political duty is one of the essentials of sovereignty. But *political* or *civil* liberty supposes political society, or supposes a πόλις or *civitas*: and it is the liberty from legal obligation which is left by a state to its subjects, rather than the liberty from legal obligation which is inherent in sovereign power.

Political or civil liberty has been erected into an idol, and extolled with extravagant praises by doting and fanatical worshippers. But political or civil liberty is not more worthy of eulogy than political or legal restraint. Political or civil liberty, like political or legal restraint, may be generally useful, or generally pernicious; and it is not as being liberty, but as conducing to the general good, that political or civil liberty is an object deserving applause.

To the ignorant and bawling fanatics who stun you with their pother about liberty, political or civil liberty seems to be the principal end for which government ought to exist. But the final cause or purpose for which government ought to exist is the furtherance of the common weal to the greatest possible extent. And it must mainly attain the purpose for which it ought to exist by two sets of means: *first*, by conferring such rights on its subjects as general utility commends, and by imposing such relative duties (or duties corresponding to the rights) as are necessary to the enjoyment of the former: *secondly*, by imposing such absolute duties (or by imposing such duties without corresponding rights) as tend to promote the good of the political community at large, although they promote not specially the interests of determinate parties. Now he who is clothed with a legal right is also clothed with a political liberty: that is to say, he has the liberty from legal obligation which is necessary to the enjoyment of the right. Consequently, in so far as it attains its appropriate purpose by conferring rights upon its subjects, government attains that purpose through the medium of political liberty. But since it must impose a duty wherever it confers a right, and should also impose duties which have no corresponding rights, it is less through the medium of political liberty, than through that of legal restraint, that government must attain the purpose for which it ought to exist. To say that political liberty ought to be its principal end, or to say that its principal end ought to be legal restraint, is to talk absurdly: for each is merely a means to that furtherance of the common weal, which is the only ultimate object of good or beneficent sovereignty. But though both propositions are absurd, the latter of the two absurdities is the least remote from the truth. As I shall show hereafter, political or civil liberties rarely exist apart from corresponding legal restraints. Where persons in a state of subjection are free from legal duties, their liberties (generally speaking) would be nearly useless to themselves, unless they were protected, in the enjoyment of their liberties, by legal duties on their fellows: that is to say, unless they had legal rights (importing such duties on their fellows) to those political liberties which are left them by the sovereign government. I am legally free, for example, to move from place to place, in so far as I can move from place to place consistently with my legal obligations: but this my political liberty would be but a sorry liberty unless my fellow subjects were restrained by a political duty from assaulting and imprisoning my body. Through the ignorance or negligence of a sovereign government, some of the civil liberties which it leaves or grants to its subjects may not be protected against their fellows by answering legal duties: and some of those civil liberties may perhaps be protected sufficiently by religious and moral obligations. But, speaking generally, a political or civil liberty is coupled with a legal right to it: and, consequently, political liberty is fostered by that very political restraint from which the devotees of the idol liberty are so fearfully and blindly averse.[9]

From the nature of political or civil liberty, I turn to the supposed difference between free and despotic governments.

Every supreme government is *free* from legal restraints: or (what is the same proposition dressed in a different phrase) every supreme government is legally *despotic*. The distinction, therefore, of governments into *free* and *despotic* can hardly mean that some of them are freer from restraints than others: or that the subjects of the governments which are denominated free are protected against their governments by positive law.

Nor can it mean that the governments which are denominated free leave or grant to their subjects more of political liberty than those which are styled despotic. For the epithet *free* importing praise, and the epithet *despotic* importing blame, they who distinguish governments into free and despotic suppose that the first are better than the second. But inasmuch as political liberty may be generally useful or pernicious, we cannot infer that a government is better than another government because the sum of the liberties which the former leaves to its subjects exceeds the sum of the liberties which are left to its subjects by the latter. The excess in the sum of the liberties which the former leaves to its subjects may be purely mischievous. It may consist of freedom from restraints which are required by the common weal and which the government would lay upon its subjects, if it fulfilled its duties to the Deity. In consequence, for example, of that mischievous freedom, its subjects may be guarded inadequately against one another, or against attacks from external enemies.

They who distinguish governments into free and despotic probably mean this: The rights which a government confers, and the duties which it lays on its subjects, ought to be conferred and imposed for the advancement of the common weal, or with a view to the aggregate happiness of all the members of the society. But in every political society the government deviates, more or less, from that ethical principle or maxim. In conferring rights and imposing duties, it more or less disregards the common or general weal, and looks, with partial affection, to the peculiar and narrower interests of a portion or portions of the community. Now the governments which deviate less from that ethical principle or maxim are better than the governments which deviate more. But, according to the opinion of those who make the distinction in question, the governments which deviate less from that ethical principle or maxim are *popular* governments (in the largest sense of the expression): meaning by a *popular* government (in the largest sense of the expression) any aristocracy (limited monarchy or other) which consists of such a number of the given political community as bears a large proportion to the number of the whole society. For it is supposed by those who make the distinction in question that, where the government is democratical or popular, the interests of the sovereign number, and the interests of the entire community, are nearly identical, or nearly coincide: but that, where the government is properly monarchical, or where the supreme powers reside in a comparatively few, the sovereign one or number has numerous sinister interests, or interests which are not consistent with the good or weal of the general. According, therefore, to those who make the distinction in question, the duties which a government of many lays upon its subjects are more consonant to the general good than the duties which are laid upon its subjects by a government of one or a few. Consequently, though it leaves or grants not to its subjects more of political liberty than is left or granted to its subjects by a government of one or a few, it leaves or grants to its subjects more of the political liberty *which conduces to the common weal*. But, as leaving or granting to its subjects more of that *useful* liberty, a government of many may be styled *free*: whilst, as leaving or granting to its subjects less of that *useful* liberty, a government of one or a few may be styled *not free*, or may be styled *despotic* or *absolute*. Consequently, a *free* government, or a *good* government, is a democratical or popular government (in the largest sense of the expression): whilst a *despotic* government, or a bad government, is either a monarchy properly so called, or any such narrow aristocracy (limited monarchy or other) as is deemed an oligarchy.

They who distinguish governments into free and despotic are therefore lovers of democracy. By the epithet *free*, as applied to governments of many, they mean that governments of many are comparatively *good*: and by the epithet *despotic*, as applied to monarchies or oligarchies, they mean that monarchies or oligarchies are comparatively *bad*. The epithets *free* and *despotic* are rarely, I think, employed by the lovers of monarchy or oligarchy. If the lovers of monarchy or oligarchy did employ those epithets, they would apply the epithet *free* to governments of one or a few, and the epithet *despotic* to governments of many. For they think the former comparatively *good*, and the latter comparatively *bad*; or that monarchical or oligarchical governments are better adapted than popular, to attain the ultimate purpose for which governments ought to exist. They deny that the latter are less misled than the former, by interests which are not consistent with the common or general weal: or, granting that excellence to governments of many, they think it greatly outweighed by numerous other excellences which they ascribe to governments of one or to governments of a few.

But with the respective merits or demerits of various forms of government, I have no direct concern. I have examined the current distinction between free and despotic governments because it is expressed in terms which are extremely inappropriate and absurd, and which tend to obscure the independence of political or legal obligation that is common to sovereign governments of all forms or kinds.

Why it has been doubted that the power of a sovereign is incapable of legal limitation

That the power of a sovereign is incapable of legal limitation has been doubted, and even denied. But the difficulty, like thousands of others, probably arose from a verbal ambiguity. The foremost individual member of a so called limited monarchy, is styled improperly *monarch* or *sovereign*. Now the power of a monarch or sovereign, thus improperly so styled, is not only capable of legal limitations, but is sometimes actually limited by positive law. But monarchs or sovereigns, thus improperly so styled, were confounded with monarchs and other sovereigns, in the proper acceptation of the terms. And since the power of the former is capable of legal limitations, it was thought that the power of the latter might be bounded by similar restraints.

The proposition is asserted expressly by renowned political writers of opposite parties or sects

Whatever may be its origin, the error is remarkable. For the legal independence of monarchs in the proper acceptation of the term, and of sovereign bodies in their corporate and sovereign capacities, not only follows inevitably from the nature of sovereign power, but is also asserted expressly by renowned political writers of opposite parties or sects: by celebrated advocates of the governments which are decked with the epithet *free*, as by celebrated advocates of the governments which are branded with the epithet *despotic*.

> If it be objected [*says Sidney*] that I am a defender of arbitrary powers, I confess I cannot comprehend how any society can be established or subsist without them. The difference between good and ill governments is not that those of one sort have an arbitrary power which the others have not; for they all have it; but that in those which are well constituted, this power is so placed as it may be beneficial to the people.

> It appeareth plainly [*says Hobbes*] to my understanding, that the soveraign power whether placed in one man, as in monarchy, or in one assembly of men, as in popular and aristocratically commonwealths, is as great as men can be imagined to make it. And though of so unlimited a power men may fancy many evill consequences, yet the consequence of the want of it, which is warre of every man against his neighbour, is much worse. The condition of man in this life shall never be without inconveniences: but there happeneth in no commonwealth any great inconvenience, but what proceeds from the subjects' disobedience. And whosoever, thinking soveraign power too great, will seek to make it lesse, must subject himselfe to a power which can limit it: that is to say, to a greater.

> One of the opinions [*says the same writer*] which are repugnant to the nature of a commonwealth, is this: that he who hath the soveraign power is subject to the civill lawes. It is true that all soveraigns are subject to the lawes of nature; because such lawes be Divine, and cannot by any man, or by any commonwealth, be abrogated. But to the civill lawes, or to the lawes which the soveraign maketh, the soveraign is not subject: for if he were subject to the civill lawes, he were subject to himselfe; which were not subjection, but freedom. The opinion now in question, because it setteth the civill lawes above the soveraign, setteth also a judge above him, and a power to punish him: which is to make a new soveraign; and, again, for the same reason, a third to punish the second; and so continually without end, to the confusion and dissolution of the commonwealth.

> The difference [*says the same writer*] between the kinds of forms of commonwealth, consisteth not in a difference between their powers, but in a difference between their aptitudes to produce the peace and security of the people: which is their end.[10]

A sovereign government of one, or a sovereign government of a number in its collegiate and sovereign capacity, has no legal rights *(in the proper acceptation of the term)* against its own subjects

Before I discuss the origin of political government and society, I will briefly examine a topic allied to the liberty of sovereigns from political or legal restraints.

A sovereign government of one, or a sovereign government of a number in its collegiate and sovereign capacity, has no *legal rights* (in the proper acceptation of the term) *against its own subjects*.

Every legal right is the creature of a positive law: and it answers to a relative duty imposed by that positive law, and incumbent on a person or persons other than the person or persons in whom the right resides. To every legal right, there are therefore three parties: the sovereign government of one or a number which sets the positive law, and which through the positive law confers the legal right and imposes the relative duty; the person or persons on whom the right is conferred; the person or persons on whom the duty is imposed, or to whom the positive law is set or directed. As I shall show hereafter, the person or persons invested with the right are not necessarily members of the independent political society wherein the author of the law is sovereign or supreme. The person or persons invested with the right may be a member or members, sovereign or subject, of another society political and independent. But (taking the proposition with the slight correctives which I shall state hereafter) the person or persons on whom the duty is imposed, or to whom the law is set or directed, are necessarily members of the independent political society wherein the author of the law is sovereign or supreme. For unless the party burthened with the duty were subject to the author of the law, the party would not be obnoxious to the legal or political sanction by which the duty and the right are respectively enforced and protected. A government can hardly impose legal duties or obligations upon members of foreign societies: although it can invest them with legal rights by imposing relative duties upon members of its own community. A party bearing a legal right is not necessarily burthened with a legal trust. Consequently, a party may bear and exercise a legal right, though the party cannot be touched by the might or power of its author. But unless the opposite party, or the party burthened with the relative duty, could be touched by the might of its author, the right and the relative duty, with the law which confers and imposes them, were merely nominal and illusory. And (taking the proposition with the slight correctives which I shall state hereafter) a person obnoxious to the sanction enforcing a positive law is necessarily subject to the author of the law, or is necessarily a member of the society wherein the author is sovereign.

It follows from the essentials of a legal right that a sovereign government of one, or a sovereign government of a number in its collegiate and sovereign capacity, has no legal rights (in the proper acceptation of the term) against its own subjects.

To every legal right, there are three several parties: namely, a party bearing the right; a party burthened with the relative duty; and a sovereign government setting the law through which the right and the duty are respectively conferred and imposed. A sovereign government cannot acquire rights through laws set by itself to its own subjects. A man is no more able to confer a right on himself than he is able to impose on himself a law or duty. Every party bearing a right (divine, legal, or moral) has necessarily acquired the right through the might or power of another: that is to say, through a law and a duty (proper or improper) laid by that other party on a further and distinct party. Consequently, if a sovereign government had legal rights against its own subjects, those rights were the creatures of positive laws set to its own subjects by a third person or body. And, as every positive law is laid by a sovereign government on a person or persons in a state of subjection to itself, that third person or body were sovereign in that community whose own sovereign government bore the legal rights: that is to say, the community were subject to its own sovereign, and were also subject to a sovereign conferring rights upon its own. Which is impossible and absurd.[11]

But so far as they are bound by the law of God to obey their temporal sovereign, a sovereign government has *rights divine* against its own subjects: rights which are conferred upon itself, through duties which are laid upon its subjects, by laws of a common superior. And so far as the members of its own community are severally constrained to obey it by the opinion of the community at large, it has also *moral rights* (or rights arising from positive morality) against its own subjects severally considered: rights which are conferred upon itself by the opinion of the community at large, and which answer to relative duties laid upon its several subjects by the general or prevalent opinion of the same indeterminate body.

Consequently, when we say that a sovereign government, as against its own subjects, has or has not a *right* to do this or that, we necessarily mean by a *right* (supposing we speak exactly) a right *divine* or *moral*: we necessarily mean (supposing we speak exactly) that it has or has not a right derived from a law of God, or derived from a law improperly so called which the general opinion of the community sets to its members severally.

But when we say that a government, as against its own subjects, has or has not *a right* to do this or that, we not uncommonly mean that we deem the act in question *generally useful* or *pernicious*. This application of the term *right* resembles an application of the term *justice* to which I have adverted above. An act which conforms to the Divine law is styled, emphatically, just: an act which does not is styled, emphatically, unjust. An act which is generally useful conforms to the Divine law as known through the principle of utility: an act which is generally pernicious does not conform to the Divine law as known through the same exponent. Consequently, 'an act which is just or unjust', and 'an act which is generally useful or generally pernicious', are nearly equivalent expressions. An act which a sovereign government has a Divine right to do, it, emphatically, has a right to do: if it has not a Divine right it, emphatically, has not a right. An act which were generally useful, the Divine law, as known through the principle of utility, has conferred on the sovereign government a right to do: an act which were generally pernicious, the Divine law, as known through the same exponent, has not conferred on the sovereign government a right to do. Consequently, an act which the government has a right to do is an act which were generally useful: as an act which the government has not a right to do is an act which were generally pernicious.

To ignorance or neglect of the palpable truths which I have expounded in the present section, we may impute a pernicious jargon that was current in our own country on the eve of her horrible war with her North American children. By the great and small rabble in and out of parliament, it was said that the government sovereign in Britain was also sovereign in the colonies; and that, since it was sovereign in the colonies, it had a *right* to tax their inhabitants. It was objected by Mr Burke to the project of taxing their inhabitants, that the project was *inexpedient*: pregnant with probable evil to the inhabitants of the colonies, and pregnant with probable evil to the inhabitants of the mother country. But to that most rational objection, the sticklers for the scheme of taxation returned this asinine answer. They said that the British government had a *right* to tax the colonists; and that it ought not to be withheld by paltry considerations of *expediency* from enforcing its sovereign right against its refractory subjects. Now, assuming that the government sovereign in Britain was properly sovereign in the colonies, it had no legal right to tax its colonial subjects; although it was not restrained by positive law from dealing with its colonial subjects at its own pleasure or discretion. If, then, the sticklers for the scheme of taxation had any determinate meaning, they meant that the British government was empowered by the law of God to tax its American subjects. But it had not a Divine right to tax its American subjects unless the project of taxing them accorded with general utility: for every Divine right springs from the Divine law; and to the Divine law, general utility is the index. Consequently, when the sticklers for the scheme of taxation opposed *the right* to *expediency*, they opposed the right to the only test by which it was possible to determine the reality of the right itself.

From an appearance of a sovereign government before a tribunal of its own, we cannot infer that the government lies under legal duties, or has legal rights against its own subjects

A sovereign government of one, or a sovereign government of a number in its collegiate and sovereign capacity, may appear in the character of defendant, or may appear in the character of demandant, before a tribunal of its own appointment or deriving jurisdiction from itself. But from such an appearance of a sovereign government, we cannot infer that the government lies under legal duties, or has legal rights against its own subjects.

Supposing that the claim of the plaintiff against the sovereign defendant were truly founded on a positive law, it were founded on a positive law set to the sovereign defendant by a third person or body: or (changing the phrase) the sovereign defendant would be in a state of subjection to another and superior sovereign. Which is impossible and absurd. And supposing that the claim of the sovereign demandant were truly founded on a positive law, it were founded on a positive law set by a third party to a member, or members, of the society wherein the demandant is supreme: or (changing the phrase) the society subject to the sovereign demandant were subject, at the same time, to another supreme government. Which is also impossible and absurd.

Besides, where the sovereign government appears in the character of defendant, it appears to a claim founded on a so called law which it has set to itself. It therefore may defeat the claim by abolishing the law entirely, or by abolishing the law in the particular or specific case. Where it appears in the character of demandant, it apparently founds its claim on a positive law of its own, and it pursues its claim judicially. But although it reaches its purpose through a general and prospective rule, and through the medium of judicial procedure, it is legally free to accomplish its end by an arbitrary or irregular exercise of its legally unlimited power.

The rights which are pursued against it before tribunals of its own, and also the rights which it pursues before tribunals of its own, are merely *analogous* to legal rights (in the proper acceptation of the term): or (borrowing the brief and commodious expressions by which the Roman jurists commonly denote an analogy) they are legal rights *quasi*, or legal rights *uti*. The rights which are pursued against it before tribunals of its own, it may extinguish by its own authority. But, this notwithstanding, it permits the demandants to prosecute their claims. And it yields to those claims, when they are established judicially, *as if* they were truly founded on positive laws set to itself by a third and distinct party. The rights which it pursues before tribunals of its own, are powers which it is free to exercise according to its own pleasure. But, this notwithstanding, it prosecutes its claims through the medium of judicial procedure, *as if* they were truly founded on positive laws set to the parties defendant by a third person or body.[12]

The foregoing explanation of the seeming legal rights which are pursued against sovereign governments before tribunals of their own tallies with the style of judicial procedure which, in all or most nations, is observed in cases of the kind. The object of the plaintiff's claim is not demanded as of right, but is begged of the sovereign defendant as a grace or favour.

In our own country, claims pursued judicially against our own king are presented to the courts of justice in the same or similar style. The plaintiff *petitions* the royal defendant to grant him his so called right: or he *shows* to the royal defendant his so called right and injury, and prays the royal defendant to yield him fitting redress. But where a claim is pursued judicially against our own king, this mendicant style of presenting the claim is merely accidental. It arises from the mere accident to which I have adverted already: namely, that our own king, though not properly sovereign, is completely free in fact from legal or political duties. Since he is free in fact from every legal obligation, no one has a legal right (in the proper acceptation of the term) against the king: for if any had a legal right against the king, the king were necessarily subject to an answering legal duty. But seeing that our own king is merely a limb of the parliament, and is virtually in a state of subjection to that sovereign body or aggregate, he is capable of legal duties: that is to say, duties imposed upon him by that sovereign body or aggregate in its collegiate and sovereign character. For the same reason, he is capable of legal rights: that is to say, rights conferred upon him by that sovereign body or aggregate, and answering to relative duties imposed by the same body on others of its own subjects. Accordingly, the king has legal rights against others of his fellow subjects: though by reason of his actual exemption from every legal obligation, none of his fellow subjects have legal rights against him.

Though a sovereign government of one, or a sovereign government of a number in its collegiate and sovereign capacity, cannot have legal rights against its own subjects, it may have a legal right against a subject or subjects of another sovereign government

Though a sovereign government of one, or a sovereign government of a number in its collegiate and sovereign capacity, cannot have legal rights against its own subjects, it may have a legal right against a subject or subjects of another sovereign government. For seeing that a legal or political right is not of necessity saddled with a legal or political trust, the positive law conferring the right may not be set to the government on which the right is conferred. The law conferring the right (as well as the relative duty answering to the right) may be laid or imposed exclusively on the subject or subjects of the government by which the right is imparted. The possession of a legal or political right against a subject or subjects of another sovereign government, consists, therefore, with that independence which is one of the essentials of sovereignty. And since the legal right is acquired from another government, and through a law which it sets to a subject or subjects of its own, the existence of the legal right implies no absurdity. It is neither acquired through a positive law set by the government which acquires it, nor through a positive law set by another government to a member or members of the society wherein the acquirer is supreme.

The origin or causes of political government and society

I now have defined or determined the general notion of sovereignty, including the general notion of independent political society. And, in order that I might further elucidate the nature or essence of sovereignty, and of the independent political society which sovereignty implies, I have considered the possible forms of supreme political government with the limits, real or imaginary, of supreme political power. To complete my intended disquisition on the nature or essence of sovereignty, and of the independent political society that sovereignty implies, I proceed to the origin or causes of the habitual or permanent obedience which, in every society political and independent, is rendered by the bulk of the community to the monarch or sovereign number. In other words, I proceed to the origin or causes of political government and society.

The proper purpose or end of a sovereign political government, or the purpose or end for which it ought to exist, is the greatest possible advancement of human happiness. Though, if it would duly accomplish its proper purpose or end, or advance as far as is possible the weal or good of mankind, it commonly must labour directly and particularly to advance as far as is possible the weal of its own community. The good of the universal society formed by mankind is the aggregate good of the particular societies into which mankind is divided: just as the happiness of any of those societies is the aggregate happiness of its single or individual members. Though, then, the weal of mankind is the proper object of a government, or though the test of its conduct is the principle of general utility, it commonly ought to consult directly and particularly the weal of the particular community which the Deity has committed to its rule. If it truly adjust its conduct to the principle of general utility, it commonly will aim immediately at the particular and more precise, rather than the general and less determinate, end.

It were easy to show that the general and particular ends never or rarely conflict. Universally, or nearly universally, the ends are perfectly consistent, or rather are inseparably connected. An enlightened regard for the common happiness of nations implied an enlightened patriotism; whilst the stupid and atrocious patriotism which looks exclusively to country, and would further the interests of country at the cost of all other communities, grossly misapprehends and frequently crosses the interests that are the object of its narrow concern. But the topic which I now have suggested belongs to the province of ethics, rather than the province of jurisprudence. It belongs especially to the peculiar department of ethics which is concerned with international morality: which affects to determine the morality that ought to obtain between nations, or to determine the international morality commended by general utility.[13]

From the proper purpose or end of a sovereign political government, or from the purpose or end for which it ought to exist, we may readily infer the causes of that habitual obedience which would be paid to the sovereign by the bulk of an enlightened society. Supposing that a given society were adequately instructed or enlightened, the habitual obedience to its government which was rendered by the bulk of the community would exclusively arise from reasons bottomed in the principle of utility. If they thought the government perfect, or that the government accomplished perfectly its proper purpose or end, this their conviction or opinion would be their motive to obey. If they deemed the government faulty, a fear that the evil of resistance might surpass the evil of obedience would be their inducement to submit; for they would not persist in their obedience to a government which they deemed imperfect if they thought that a better government might probably be got by resistance, and that the probable good of the change outweighed its probable mischief.

Since every actual society is inadequately instructed or enlightened, the habitual obedience to its government which is rendered by the bulk of the community is partly the consequence of custom. They partly pay that obedience to that present or established government because they, and perhaps their ancestors, have been in a habit of obeying it. Or the habitual obedience to the government which is rendered by the bulk of the community, is partly the consequence of prejudices: meaning by 'prejudices', opinions and sentiments which have no foundation whatever in the principle of general utility. If, for example, the government is monarchical, they partly pay that obedience to that present or established government because they are fond of monarchy inasmuch as it is monarchy, or because they are fond of the race from which the monarch has descended. Or if, for example, the government is popular, they partly pay that obedience to that present or established government because they are fond of democracy inasmuch as it is democracy, or because the word 'republic' captivates their fancies and affections.

But though that habitual obedience is partly the consequence of custom, or though that habitual obedience is partly the consequence of prejudices, it partly arises from a reason bottomed in the principle of utility.[14] It partly arises from a perception, by the generality or bulk of the community, of the expediency of political government: or (changing the phrase) it partly arises from a preference, by the generality or bulk of the community, of any government to anarchy. If, for specific reasons, they are attached to the established government, their general perception of the utility of government concurs with their special attachment. If they dislike the established government, their general perception of the utility of government controls and masters their dislike. They detest the established government: but if they would change it for another by resorting to resistance, they must travel to their object through an intervening anarchy which they detest more.

The habitual obedience to the government which is rendered by the bulk of the community partly arises, therefore, in almost every society, from the cause which I now have described: namely, a perception, by the bulk of the community, of the utility of political government, or a preference, by the bulk of the community, of any government to anarchy. And this is the only cause of the habitual obedience in question, which is common to all societies, or nearly all societies. It therefore is the only cause of the habitual obedience in question which the present general disquisition can properly embrace. The causes of the obedience in question which are peculiar to particular societies belong to the province of statistics, or the province of particular history.

The only general cause of the *permanence* of political governments, and the only general cause of the *origin* of political governments, are exactly or nearly alike. Though every government has arisen in part from specific or particular causes, almost every government must have arisen in part from the following general cause: namely, that the bulk of the natural society from which the political was formed were desirous of escaping to a state of government from a state of nature or anarchy. If they like specially the government to which they submitted, their general perception of the utility of government concurred with their special inclination. If they disliked the government to which they submitted, their general perception of the utility of government controlled and mastered their repugnance.

The specific or particular causes of specific or particular governments are rather appropriate matter for particular history, than for the present general disquisition.

The position 'that every government continues through the people's consent*', and the position 'that every government arises through the people's* consent*', examined and explained*

According to a current opinion (or according to a current expression) the permanence and origin of every government are owing to the people's *consent*: that is to say, every government continues through the *consent* of the people, or the bulk of the political community: and every government arises through the consent of the people, or the bulk of the natural society from which the political is formed. According to the same opinion dressed in a different phrase, the power of the sovereign flows from the people, or the people is the fountain of sovereign power.

Now the permanence of every government depends on the habitual obedience which it receives from the bulk of the community. For if the bulk of the community were fully determined to destroy it, and to brave and endure the evils through which they must pass to their object, the might of the government itself, with the might of the minority attached to it, would scarcely suffice to preserve it, or even to retard its subversion. And though it were aided by foreign governments, and therefore were more than a match for the disaffected and rebellious people, it hardly could reduce them to subjection, or constrain them to permanent obedience, in case they hated it mortally and were prepared to resist it to the death. But all obedience is *voluntary* or *free*, or every party who obeys *consents* to obey. In other words, every party who obeys *wills* the obedience which he renders, or is determined to render it by some *motive* or another. That acquiescence which is purely involuntary, or which is purely the consequence of physical compulsion or restraint, is not obedience or submission. If a man condemned to imprisonment were dragged to the prison by the jailers, he would not obey or submit. But if he were liable to imprisonment in the event of his refusing to walk to it, and if he were determined to walk to it by a fear of that further restraint, the man would render obedience to the sentence or command of the judge. Moved by his dislike of the contingent punishment, he would *consent* to the infliction of the present. Since, then, a government continues through the obedience of the people, and since the obedience of the people is voluntary or free, every government continues through the *consent* of the people, or the bulk of the political society. If they like the government, they are determined to obey it habitually or to consent to its continuance, by their special inclination or attachment. If they hate the government, they are determined to obey it habitually, or to *consent* to its continuance, by their dread of a violent revolution. They consent to what they abhor because they avoid thereby what they abhor more. As correctly or truly apprehended, the position 'that every government continues through the people's *consent*', merely amounts to this: that, in every society, political and independent, the people are determined, by motives of some description or another, to obey their government habitually: and that, if the bulk of the community ceased to obey it habitually, the government would cease to exist.

But the position in question, as it is often understood, is taken with one or another of the two following meanings.

Taken with the first of those meanings, the position amounts to this: that the bulk of every community, without inconvenience to themselves, can abolish the established government: and that, being able to abolish it without inconvenience to themselves, they yet consent to its continuance or pay it habitual obedience. Or, taken with the first of those meanings, the position amounts to this: that the bulk of every community approve of the established government, or prefer it to every government which could be substituted for it: and that they consent to its continuance, or pay it habitual obedience, by reason of that their approbation or by reason of that their preference. As thus understood, the position is ridiculously false: the habitual obedience of the people in most or many communities, arises wholly or partly from their fear of the probable evils which they might suffer by resistance.

Taken with the second of those meanings, the position amounts to this: that, if the bulk of a community dislike the established government, the government *ought* not to continue: or that, if the bulk of a community dislike the established government, the government therefore is bad or pernicious, and the general good of the community requires its abolition. And, if every actual society were adequately instructed or enlightened, the position, as thus understood, would approach nearly to the truth. For the dislike of an enlightened people towards their established government would beget a violent presumption that the government was faulty or imperfect. But, in every actual society, the government has neglected to instruct the people in sound political science; or pains have been taken by the government, or the classes that influence the government, to exclude the bulk of the community from sound political science, and to perpetuate or prolong the prejudices which weaken and distort their undertakings. Every society, therefore, is inadequately instructed or enlightened. And, in most or many societies the love or hate of the people towards their established government would scarcely beget a presumption that the government was good or bad. An ignorant people may love their established government, though it positively crosses the purpose for which it ought to exist: though, by cherishing pernicious institutions and fostering mischievous prejudices, it positively prevents the progress in useful knowledge and in happiness, which its subjects would make spontaneously if it simply were careless of their good. If the goodness of an established government be proportioned to the love of the people, the priest-bestridden government of besotted Portugal or Spain is probably the best of governments: as weighed against Miguel and Ferdinand, Trajan and Aurelius, or Frederic and Joseph, were fools and malignant tyrants. And as an ignorant people may love their established government, though it positively crosses the purpose for which it ought to exist, so may an ignorant people hate their established government, though it labours strenuously and wisely to further the general weal. The dislike of the French people to the ministry of the godlike Turgot amply evinces the melancholy truth. They stupidly thwarted the measures of their warmest and wisest friend, and made common cause with his and their enemies: with the rabble of nobles and priests who strove to uphold misrule, and to crush the reforming ministry with a load of calumny and ridicule.

That the *permanence* of every government is owing to the people's consent, and that the *origin* of every government is owing to the people's consent, are two positions so closely allied, that what I have said of the former will nearly apply to the latter.

Every government has arisen through the *consent* of the people, or the bulk of the natural society from which the political was formed. For the bulk of the natural society from which a political is formed submit *freely* or *voluntarily* to the inchoate political government. Or (changing the phrase) their submission is a consequence of *motives*, or they *will* the submission which they render.

But a special approbation of the government to which they freely submit, or a preference of that government to every other government, may not be their motive to submission. Although they submit to it freely, the government perhaps is forced upon them: that is to say, they could not withhold their submission from that particular government unless they struggled through evils which they are loath to endure, or unless they resisted to the death. Determined by a fear of the evils which would follow a refusal to submit (and, probably, by a general perception of the utility of political government), they freely submit to a government from which they are specially averse.

The expression 'that every government arises through the people's *consent*', is often uttered with the following meaning: that the bulk of a natural society about to become a political, or the inchoate subjects of an inchoate political government, *promise*, expressly or tacitly, to obey the future sovereign. The expression, however, as uttered with the meaning in question, confounds *consent* and *promise*, and therefore is grossly incorrect. That the inchoate subjects of every inchoate government *will* or *consent* to obey it is one proposition: that they promise, expressly or tacitly, to render obedience is another proposition. Inasmuch as they actually obey, they will or consent to obey: or their will or consent to obey is evinced by their actual obedience. But a will to render obedience, as evinced by actual obedience, is not of necessity a tacit promise to render it: although by a promise to render obedience, a will or consent to render it is commonly expressed or intimated.

That the inchoate subjects of every inchoate government *promise* to render it obedience is a position involved by an hypothesis which I shall examine in the next section.

The hypothesis of the original covenant *or the* fundamental civil pact

In every community ruled by a monarch, the subject members of the community lie under duties to the monarch; and in every community ruled by a sovereign body, the subject members of the community (including the several members of the body itself), lie under duties to the body in its collective and sovereign capacity. In every community ruled by a monarch, the monarch lies under duties towards his subjects: and in every community ruled by a sovereign body, the collective and sovereign body lies under duties to its subjects (including its own members considered severally).

The duties of the subjects towards the sovereign government are partly religious, partly legal, and partly moral.

The religious duties of the subjects towards the sovereign government are creatures of the Divine law as known through the principle of utility. If it thoroughly accomplish the purpose for which it ought to exist, or further the general weal to the greatest possible extent, the subjects are bound religiously to pay it habitual obedience. And, if the general good which probably would follow submission outweigh the general good which probably would follow resistance, the subjects are bound religiously to pay it habitual obedience, although it accomplish imperfectly its proper purpose or end. The legal duties of the subjects towards the sovereign government are creatures of positive laws which itself has imposed upon them, or which are incumbent upon them by its own authority and might. The moral duties of the subjects towards the sovereign government are creatures of positive morality. They mainly are creatures of laws (in the improper acceptation of the term) which the general opinion of the community itself sets to its several members.

The duties of the sovereign government towards the subjects are partly religious and partly moral. If it lay under legal duties towards the subjects, it were not a supreme, but were merely a subordinate government.

Its religious duties towards the subjects are creatures of the Divine law as known through the principle of utility. It is bound by the Divine law, as known through the principle of utility, to advance as far as is possible the weal or good of mankind: and, to advance as far as is possible the weal or good of mankind, it commonly must labour directly and particularly to advance as far as is possible the happiness of its own community. Its moral duties towards the subjects are creatures of positive morality. They mainly are creatures of laws (in the improper acceptation of the term) which the general opinion of its own community lays or imposes upon it.

It follows from the foregoing analysis that the duties of the subjects towards the sovereign government, with the duties of the sovereign government towards the subjects, originate respectively in three several sources: namely, the Divine law (as indicated by the principle of utility), positive law, and positive morality. And, to my understanding, it seems that we account sufficiently for the origin of those obligations when we simply refer them to those their obvious fountains. It seems, to my understanding, that an ampler solution of their origin is not in the least requisite, and, indeed, is impossible. But there are many writers on political government and society who are not content to account for their origin by simply referring them to those their manifest sources. It seems to the writers in question that we want an ampler solution of the origin of those obligations, or, at least, of the origin of such of them as are imposed by the law of God. And, to find that ampler solution which they believe requisite, those writers resort to the hypothesis of the *original covenant* or *contract*, or the *fundamental civil pact*.[15]

By the writers who resort to it, this renowned and not exploded hypothesis is imagined and rendered variously. But the purport or effect of the hypothesis, as it is imagined and rendered by most of those writers, may be stated generally thus:

To the formation of every society political and independent, or to the institution of every πόλις or *civitas*, all its future members then in being are joint or concurring parties: for all are parties to an agreement in which it then originates, and which is also the basis whereon it afterwards rests. As being the necessary source of the independent political society, or as being a condition necessarily preceding its existence, this agreement of all is styled the *original covenant*: as being the necessary basis whereon the *civitas* afterwards rests, it is styled *pactum civile fundamentale*. In the process of making this covenant or pact, or the process of forming the society political and independent, there are three several stages, which three several stages may be described in the following manner.

One. The future numbers of the community, just about to be created, jointly resolve to unite themselves into an independent political society: signifying and determining withal the paramount purpose of their union, or even more or fewer of its subordinate or instrumental ends. And here I must briefly remark that the paramount purpose of their union, or the paramount purpose of the community just about to be created, is the paramount purpose (let it be what it may) for which a society political and independent ought to be founded and perpetuated. By the writers who resort to the hypothesis, this paramount purpose or absolute end is conceived differently, their several conceptions of this purpose or end differing with the several natures of their respective ethical systems. To writers who admit the system which I style the theory of utility, this purpose or end is the advancement of human happiness. To a multitude of writers who have flourished and flourish in Germany, the following is the truly magnificent though somewhat mysterious object of political government and society: namely, the extension over the earth, or over its human inhabitants, of the empire of right or justice. It would seem that this right or justice, like the good Ulpian's justice, is absolute, eternal, and immutable. It would seem that this right or justice is not a creature of law: that it was anterior to every law; exists independently of every law; and is the measure or test of all law and morality. Consequently, it is not the right or justice which is a creature of the law of God, and to which the name of 'justice' is often applied emphatically. It rather is a something, perfectly self-existent, to which his law conforms, or to which his law should conform. I, therefore, cannot understand it, and will not affect to explain it. Merely guessing at what it may be, I take it for the right or justice mentioned in a preceding note: I take it for general utility darkly conceived and expressed. Let it be what it may, it doubtless is excellently good, or is superlatively fair or high, or (in a breath) is pre-eminently worthy of praise. For, compared with the extension of its empire over mankind, the mere advancement of their happiness is a mean and contemptible object.

Two. Having resolved to unite themselves into an independent political society, all the members of the inchoate community jointly determine the constitution of its sovereign political government. In other words, they jointly determine the member or members in whom the sovereignty shall reside: and, in case they will that the sovereignty shall reside in more than one, they jointly determine the mode wherein the sovereign number shall share the sovereign powers.

Three. The process of forming the independent political society, or the process of forming its supreme political government, is completed by promises given and accepted: namely, by a promise of the inchoate sovereign to the inchoate subjects, by promises of the latter to the former, and by a promise of each of the latter to all and each of the rest. The promise made by the sovereign, and the promises made by the subjects, are made to a common object: namely, the accomplishment of the paramount purpose of the independent political society and of such of its subordinate purposes as were signified by the resolution to form it. The purport of the promise made by the sovereign, and the purport of the promises made by the subjects, are, therefore, the following. The sovereign promises generally to govern to the paramount end of the independent political society: and, if any of its subordinate ends were signified by the resolution to form it, the sovereign moreover promises specifically to govern specifically to those subordinate ends. The subjects promise to render to the sovereign a qualified or conditional obedience: that is to say, to render to the sovereign all the obedience which shall consist with that paramount purpose and those subordinate purposes. The resolution of the members to unite themselves into an independent political society is styled *pactum unionis*. Their determination of the constitution or structure of the sovereign political government is styled *pactum constitutionis* or *pactum ordinationis*. The promise of the sovereign to the subjects, with the promises of the subjects to the sovereign and to one another, are styled *pactum subjectionis*: for, through the promises of the subjects, or through the promises of the subjects coupled with the promise of the sovereign, the former are placed completely in a state of subjection to the latter, or the relation of subjection and sovereignty arises between the parties. But of the so called *pact of union*, the so called *pact constituent*, and the so called *pact of subjection*, the last only is properly a convention. The so called pact of union and the so called pact constituent are properly resolves or determinations introductory to the pact of subjection, the pact of subjection being the original covenant or the fundamental civil pact. Through this original covenant, or this fundamental pact, the sovereign is bound (or at least is bound religiously) to govern as is mentioned above: and the subjects are bound (or, at least, are bound religiously) to render to the sovereign for the time being the obedience above described. And the binding virtue of this fundamental pact is not confined to the founders of the independent political society. The binding virtue of this fundamental pact extends to the following members of the same community. For the promises which the founders of the community made for themselves respectively, import similar promises which they make for their respective successors. Through the promise made by the original sovereign, following sovereigns are bound (or at least, are bound religiously) to govern as is mentioned above. Through the promises made by the original subjects, following subjects are bound (or at least, are bound religiously) to render to the sovereign for the time being the obedience above described. In every society political and independent, the duties of the sovereign towards the subjects (or the religious duties of the sovereign towards the subjects) spring from an original covenant like that which I now have delineated: and in every society political and independent, the duties of the subjects towards the sovereign (or the religious duties of the subjects towards the sovereign) arise from a similar pact. Unless we suppose that such an agreement is incumbent on the sovereign and subjects, we cannot account adequately for those their respective obligations. Unless the subjects were held to render it by an agreement that they shall render it, the subjects would not be obliged, or would not be obliged sufficiently, to render to the sovereign the requisite obedience: that is to say, the obedience requisite to the accomplishment of the proper purpose or end of the independent political society. Unless the sovereign were held by an agreement to govern as is mentioned above, the sovereign would not be obliged, or would not be obliged sufficiently, from governing despotically or arbitrarily: that is to say, governing with little or no regard to the proper purpose or end of a supreme political government.

Such, I believe, is the general purport of the hypothesis, as it is imagined and rendered by most of the writers who resort to it.

But, as I have remarked above, the writers who resort to the hypothesis imagine and render it variously. According, for example, to some of those writers, the original subjects, covenanting for themselves and their followers, promise obedience to the original and following sovereigns. But the original sovereign is not a promising party to the fundamental civil pact. The original sovereign does not agree with the subjects that the sovereign powers shall be used to a given end or ends, or that those powers shall be used in a given mode or modes. And by the different writers who render the hypothesis thus, the purport of the subjects' promises is imagined. For example: some suppose that the obedience promised by the subjects is the qualified or conditional obedience briefly described above; whilst others suppose that the obedience promised by the subjects is an obedience passive or unlimited. The writers, in short, who suppose an original covenant think variously concerning the nature of the end for which a supreme government ought to exist. They think moreover variously concerning the extent of the obedience which a supreme government ought to receive from its subjects. And to his own opinion concerning the nature of that end, or to his own opinion concerning the extent of that obedience, each of the writers in question endeavours to shape the hypothesis. But though the writers who resort to the hypothesis imagine and render it variously, they concur in this: that the duties of the subjects towards the sovereign (or the religious duties of the subjects towards the sovereign) are creatures of the original covenant. And the writers who fancy that the original sovereign was a promising party to the pact also concur in this:

that the duties of the sovereign towards the subjects (or the religious duties of the sovereign towards the subjects) are engendered by the same agreement.

A complete though concise exposition of the various forms or shapes in which various writers imagine and render the hypothesis would fill a considerable volume. Besides, the ensuing strictures apply exactly, or may be fitted easily, to any original covenant that has been or can be conceived; although they are directed more particularly to the fancied original covenant which I have delineated above. My statement of the purport of the hypothesis, I, therefore, conclude here. And I now will suggest shortly a few of the conclusive objections to which the hypothesis is open.

One. To account for the duties of subjects towards their sovereign government, or for those of the sovereign government towards its subjects, or for those of each of the parties towards the other, is the scope of every writer who supposes an original covenant. But, to account for the duties of subjects towards their sovereign government, or for those of the sovereign government towards its subjects, we need not resort to the hypothesis of a fundamental civil pact. We sufficiently account for the origin of those respective obligations when we refer them simply (or without the supposition of an original covenant) to their apparent and obvious fountains: namely, the law of God, positive law, and positive morality. Besides, although the formation of an independent political society were really preceded by a fundamental civil pact, scarce any of the duties lying thereafter on the subjects, or of the duties lying thereafter on the sovereign, would be engendered or influenced by that foregoing convention. The hypothesis, therefore, of an original covenant is needless and is worse than needless. It affects to assign the cause of certain phænomena: namely, the duties of subjects towards their sovereign government, or the duties of the sovereign government towards its subjects, or the duties of each of the parties towards the other. But the cause which it assigns is superfluous; inasmuch as there are other causes which are at once obvious and adequate: and that superfluous cause is inefficient as well as superfluous, or could not have produced the phænomena whereof it is the fancied source.

It will appear from the following analysis that, although the formation of an independent political society were really preceded by an original covenant, scarce any of the duties lying thereafter on the subjects, or of the duties lying thereafter on the sovereign, would be engendered or affected by that foregoing agreement. In other words, the covenant would hardly oblige (*legally*, *religiously*, or *morally*) the original or following subjects, or the original or following sovereigns.

Every convention which obliges legally (or every contract properly so called) derives its legal efficacy from a positive law. Speaking exactly, it is not the convention that obliges legally, or that engenders the legal duty: but the law obliges legally, or engenders the legal duty, through the convention. In other words, the positive law annexes the duty to the convention: or it determines that duties of the given class shall follow conventions of the given description. Consequently, if the sovereign government were bound *legally* by the fundamental civil pact, the legal duty lying on the government were the creature of a positive law: that is to say, the legal duty lying on the government were the creature of a positive law annexing the duty to the pact. And, seeing that a law set by the government to itself were merely a law through a metaphor, the positive law annexing the duty to the pact would be set to the sovereign government by another and superior sovereign. Consequently, the sovereign government legally bound by the pact would be in a state of subjection. Through a positive law set by their own sovereign, the subjects might be bound legally to keep the original covenant. But the legal or political duty thus incumbent on the subjects would properly proceed from the law set by their own sovereign, and not from the covenant itself. If they were bound legally to keep the original covenant without a positive law set by their own sovereign, the subjects would be bound legally to keep the original covenant through a positive law set by another sovereign: that is to say, they would be in a state of subjection to their own sovereign government, and also to a sovereign government conferring rights upon their own.

Every convention which obliges (properly or improperly) derives its efficacy from law (proper or improper) As obliging legally, a convention derives its efficacy from law positive: as obliging religiously or morally, it derives its efficacy from the law of God or from positive morality. Consequently, if the sovereign or subjects were bound *religiously* by the fundamental civil pact, the religious duty lying on the sovereign, or the religious duty lying on the subjects, would properly proceed from the Divine law, and not from the pact itself. The party bound religiously would be bound by the law of God through the original covenant: or the religious duty lying on the party would be annexed to the original covenant by the law of God.

Now the proper absolute end of an independent political society, and the nature of the index to the law of God, are conceived differently by different men. But whatever be the absolute end of an independent political society, and whatever be the nature of the index to the law of God, the sovereign would be bound religiously, without an original covenant, to govern to that absolute end: whilst the subjects would be bound religiously, without an original covenant, to render to the sovereign the obedience which the accomplishment of the end might require. Consequently, whether it consisted or conflicted with that proper absolute end, the original covenant would not oblige religiously either of the two parties. If the original covenant consisted with that absolute end, the original covenant would be superfluous, and therefore would be inoperative. The religious duties lying on the sovereign and subjects would not be effects or consequences, mediately or immediately, of the fundamental civil pact. Inasmuch as the Divine law would impose those religious duties, although the pact had not been made, they would not be effects or consequences annexed to the pact by the law, or would not be imposed by the law through the pact. If the original covenant conflicted with that absolute end, it would also conflict with the law which is the source of religious obligations, and would not oblige religiously the sovereign government or its subjects.

For example: let us suppose that the principle of utility is the index to the law of God; and that, since the principle of utility is the index to the law of God, the greatest possible advancement of the common happiness or weal is the proper absolute end of an independent political society. Let us suppose, moreover, that the accomplishment of this absolute end was the scope of the original covenant. Now no religious obligation would be laid on the sovereign or subjects through the fundamental pact. For the sovereign would be bound religiously, without the fundamental pact, to govern to the very end at which its authors had aimed: whilst the subjects would be bound religiously, without the fundamental pact, to render to the sovereign the obedience which the accomplishment of the end might require. And if the accomplishment of this same end were not the scope of the pact, the pact would conflict with the law as known through the principle of utility, and would not oblige religiously either of the two parties. To make a promise which general utility condemns is an offence against the law of God: but to break a promise of a generally pernicious tendency is the fulfilment of a religious duty.

And though the original sovereign or the original subjects might have been bound religiously by the original covenant, why or how should it bind religiously the following sovereigns or subjects? Duties to the subjects for the time being would be laid by the law of God on all the following sovereigns; and duties to the sovereign for the time being would be laid by the law of God on all the following subjects: but why should those obligations be laid on those following parties, through the fundamental pact? Through or in consequence of a pact made without their authority, and even without their knowledge? Legal obligations often lie upon parties (as, for example, upon heirs or administrators) through or in consequence of promises made by other parties whose legal representatives they are: whose faculties or means of fulfilling obligations devolve or descend to them by virtue of positive law. And I perceive readily why the legal obligations which are consequent on those promises extend from the makers of the promises to the parties who legally represent them. It is expedient, for various reasons, that positive law should impose obligations on the makers of certain promises: and for the same, or nearly the same, reasons, it is expedient that the legal duties which are laid on the makers themselves, should pass to the parties who legally represent them, and who take their faculties or means. But I am unable to perceive why or how a promise of the original sovereign or subjects should bind religiously the following sovereigns or subjects: though I see that the cases of legal obligation to which I now have adverted probably suggested the groundless conceit to those who devised the hypothesis of a fundamental civil pact.

If the sovereign were bound *morally* to keep the original covenant, the sovereign would be bound by opinions current amongst the subjects to govern to the absolute end at which its authors had aimed: and if the subjects were bound *morally* to keep the original covenant, the subjects would be bound severally by opinions of the community at large to render to the sovereign the obedience which the accomplishment of the end might require. But the moral obligations thus incumbent on the sovereign, with the moral obligations thus incumbent on the subjects, would not be engendered or affected by the original covenant. They would not be imposed by the positive morality of the community, through or in consequence of the pact. For the opinions obliging the sovereign to govern to that absolute end, with the opinions obliging the subjects to render that requisite obedience, would not be consequents of the pact, but would have been its antecedents: inasmuch as the pact itself would have been made by the founders of the community because those very opinions were held by all or most of them.

We may, if we like, imagine and assume that the fancied original covenant was conceived and constructed by its authors, with some particularity and precision: that, having determined the absolute end of their union, it specified some of the ends positive or negative, or some of the means or modes positive or negative, through which the sovereign government should rule to that absolute end. The founders, for example, of the independent political society (like the Roman people who adopted the Twelve Tables), might have adverted specially to the monstrous and palpable mischiefs of *ex post facto* legislation: and therefore the fancied covenant might have determined specially that the sovereign government about to be formed should forbear from legislation of the kind. And if any of those positive or negative ends were specified by the original covenant, the promise of the subjects to render obedience to the sovereign was made with special reservations; it was not extended to any of the cases wherein the sovereign might deviate from any of the subordinate ends which the covenant determined specially.

Now the bulk or generality of the subjects, in an independent political community, might think alike or uniformly concerning the absolute end to which their sovereign government ought to rule: and yet their uniform opinions concerning that absolute end might bind or control their sovereign very imperfectly. Notwithstanding the uniformity of their opinions concerning that absolute end, the bulk of the subjects might think variously concerning the conduct of their sovereign: since the proper absolute end of a sovereign political government, or the absolute end for which it ought to exist, is inevitably conceived in a form, or is inevitably stated in expressions, extremely abstract and vague. For example: the bulk or generality of the subjects might possibly concur in thinking that the proper absolute end of their sovereign political government was the greatest possible advancement of the general or common weal: but whether a positive law made by it *ex post facto* did or did not comport with its proper absolute end is clearly a question which they might answer variously, notwithstanding the uniformity of their opinions concerning that paramount purpose. Unless, then, the bulk of the subjects thought alike or uniformly concerning more or fewer of its proper subordinate ends, they hardly would oppose to the government, in any particular case, a uniform, simultaneous, and effectual resistance. Consequently, the sovereign government would not be affected constantly by the fear of an effectual resistance from the subject members of the community: and, consequently, their general and uniform opinions concerning its paramount purpose would bind or control it feebly. But if the mass of the subjects thought alike or uniformly concerning more or fewer of its proper subordinate ends, the uniform opinions of the mass, concerning those subordinate ends, would probably control it potently. Speaking generally, the proper subordinate ends of a sovereign political government (let those ends or means be what they may) may be imagined in forms, or may be stated in expressions, which are neither extremely abstract nor extremely vague. Consequently, if the government ventured to deviate from any of the subordinate ends to which those uniform opinions were decidedly favourable, the bulk or generality of the subjects would probably unite in resenting, and even in resisting, its measures: for if they tried its measures by one and the same standard, and if that standard or test were determinate and not dubious, their respective opinions concerning its measures would exactly or nearly tally. Consequently, a fear of encountering an effectual resistance, in case it should venture to deviate from any of those ends, would constantly hold the government to all the subordinate ends which the uniform opinions of the mass decidedly favoured. The extent to which a government is bound by the opinions of its subjects, and the efficacy of the moral duties which their opinions impose upon it, therefore depend mainly on the two following causes: first, the number of its subordinate ends (or the number of the ends subserving its absolute end) concerning which the mass of its subjects think alike or uniformly; secondly, the degree of clearness and precision with which they conceive the ends in respect whereof their opinions thus coincide. The greater is that number, and the greater is that degree, the more extensively, and the more effectually, is the government bound or controlled by the positive morality of the community.

Now it follows from what I have premised that, if an original covenant had determined clearly and precisely some of the subordinate ends whereto the sovereign should rule, the sovereign would be bound effectually by the positive morality of the community to rule to the subordinate ends which the covenant had thus specified: supposing (I, of course, understand) that those same subordinate ends were favoured by opinions and sentiments which the mass of the subjects for the time being held and felt. And here (it might be argued) the sovereign would be bounded morally to rule to those same ends, through the fundamental pact, or in consequence of the fundamental pact. For (it might be said) the efficacy of the opinions binding the sovereign government would mainly arise from the clearness and precision with which those same ends were conceived by the mass of the subjects; whilst the clearness and precision of their conceptions would mainly arise from the clearness and precision with which those same ends had been specified by the original covenant. It will, however, appear on a moment's reflection that the opinions of the generality of the subjects, concerning those same ends, would not be engendered by, but rather would have engendered, the covenant: for if most of the subject founders of the independent political society had not been affected by opinions exactly similar, why were those same ends specially determined by the covenant of which those subject founders were the principal authors? And, granting that the clearness with which they were specified by the covenant would impart an answering clearness to the conceptions of the following subjects, that effect on the opinions held by the following subjects would not be wrought by the covenant as being *a covenant or pact*: that is to say, as being *a promise, or mutual promises, proffered and accepted*. That effect would be wrought by the covenant as being a luminous statement of those same subordinate ends. And any similar statement which might circulate widely (as a similar statement, for example, by a popular and respected writer) would work a similar effect on the opinions of the following subjects. Stating clearly and precisely those same subordinate ends, it would naturally give to their conceptions of those same subordinate ends a corresponding clearness and precision.

The following (I think) is the only, or nearly the only, case wherein an original covenant, as being a covenant or pact, might generate or influence any of the duties lying on the sovereign or subjects.

It might be believed by the bulk of the subjects, that an agreement or convention (or a promise proffered and accepted) has that mysterious efficacy which is expressly or tacitly ascribed to it by those who resort to the hypothesis of a fundamental civil pact. It might be believed by the bulk of the subjects that, unless their sovereign government had *promised* so to govern, it would not be bound by the law of God, or would not be bound sufficiently by the law of God, to govern to what they esteemed its proper absolute end. It might be believed moreover by the bulk of the subjects that the promise made by the original sovereign was a promise made in effect by each of the following sovereigns, and therefore it might be believed by the bulk of the subjects that their sovereign government was bound religiously to govern to that absolute end, rather because it had *promised* to govern to that absolute end, than by reason of the intrinsic worth belonging to the end itself. Now, if the mass of the subjects potently believed these positions, the duties of the government toward its subjects, which the positive morality of the community imposed upon it, would be engendered or affected by the original covenant. They would be imposed upon it, wholly or in part, because the original covenant had preceded or accompanied the institution of the independent political society. For if it departed from any of the ends determined by the original covenant, the mass of its subjects would be moved to anger (and perhaps to eventual rebellion) by its breach of its *promise*, real or supposed, rather than by that misrule of which they esteemed it guilty. Its breach of its promise, as being a breach of a promise, would be the cause of their offence, wholly or in part. For they would impute to the promise, real or supposed, a proper and absolute worth; or they would care for the promise, real or supposed, without regard to its scope and tendency.

It appears from the foregoing analysis that, although the formation of the independent political society had really been preceded by a fundamental civil pact, none of the *legal* or *religious* duties lying on the sovereign or subjects could be engendered or influenced by that preceding convention: that there is only a single case, or are only a few cases, wherein it could engender or influence any of the *moral* duties lying on the same parties. It will appear from the following analysis that, where it might engender or influence any of those *moral* duties, that preceding convention would probably be pernicious.

Of the duties of the sovereign towards the subjects, and of the duties of the subjects towards the sovereign, it is only those which are moral, or are imposed by positive morality, that any original covenant could possibly affect. And, considered with reference to those, an original covenant would be simply useless, or would be positively pernicious.

An original covenant would be simply useless if it merely determined the absolute end of the sovereign political government: if it merely determined that the absolute end of the government was the greatest possible advancement of the common happiness or weal. For though the covenant might give uniformity to the opinions of the mass of the subjects, it would only affect their opinions concerning that absolute end: and, as I have shown already, the uniformity of their opinions concerning the paramount purpose would hardly influence the conduct of their sovereign political government.

But the covenant might specify some of the means, or some of the subordinate or instrumental ends, through which the government should rule to that its absolute end, or through which it should so rule as to further the common weal. And as specially determining any of those means, or any of the subordinate ends to which the government should rule, the original covenant would be simply useless, or would be positively pernicious.

For the opinions of the following members of the independent political community, concerning the subordinate ends to which the government should rule, would or would not be affected by the covenant or pact of the founders.

If the covenant of the founders of the community did not affect the opinions of its following members, the covenant would be simply useless.

If the covenant of the founders of the community did affect the opinions of its following members, the covenant probably would be positively pernicious. For the opinions of the following members would probably be affected by the covenant as being a covenant or pact made by the founders. They probably would impute to the subordinate ends specified by the original covenant, a worth extrinsic and arbitrary, or independent of their intrinsic merits. A belief that the specified ends were of a useful or beneficent tendency, or were ends tending to the furtherance of the common happiness or weal, would not be their reason, or would not be their only reason, for regarding the ends with respect. They probably would respect the specified ends, or probably would partly respect them, because the venerable founders of the independent political society (by the venerable covenant or pact which was the basis of the social fabric) had determined that those same ends were some of the ends or means through which the weal of the community might be furthered by its sovereign government. Now the venerable age or times wherein the community was founded would probably be less enlightened (notwithstanding its claims to veneration) than any of the ensuing and degenerate ages through which the community might endure. Consequently, the following pernicious effect would be wrought by the original covenant. The opinions held in an age comparatively ignorant, concerning the subordinate ends to which the government should rule, would influence, more or less, through the medium of the covenant, the opinions held, concerning those ends, in ages comparatively knowing. Let us suppose, for example, that the formation of the British community was preceded by a fundamental pact. Let us suppose (a 'most unforced' supposition), that the ignorant founders of the community deemed foreign commerce hurtful to domestic industry. Let us, therefore, suppose, moreover, that the government about to be formed promised, for itself and its successors, to *protect* the industry of its own society by forbidding and preventing the importation of foreign manufactures. Now if the fundamental pact made by our worthy ancestors were devoutly reverenced by many of ourselves, it would hinder the diffusion of sound œconomical doctrines through the present community. The present sovereign government would, therefore, be prevented by the pact from legislating wisely and usefully in regard to our commercial intercourse with other independent nations. If the government attempted to withdraw the restrictions which the laws of preceding governments have laid on our foreign commerce, the fallacies which now are current, and the nonsense which now is in vogue, would not be the only fallacies, and would not be the only nonsense, wherewith the haters of improvement would belabour the audacious innovators. All who delighted in 'things ancient' would certainly accuse it of infringing a principle which was part of the very basis whereon the community rested: which the wise and venerable authors of the fundamental pact itself had formerly adopted and consecrated. Nay, the lovers of darkness assuredly would affirm, and probably would potently believe, that the government was *incompetent* to withdraw the restrictions which the laws of preceding governments have laid on our foreign commerce: that being, as it were, a *privy* of the first or original government, it was *estopped* by the solemn promise which that government had given.

Promises or oaths on the part of the original sovereign, or promises or oaths on the part of succeeding sovereigns, are not the efficient securities, *moral or religious*, for beneficent government or rule. The best of *moral* securities, or the best of the securities yielded by positive morality, would arise from a wide diffusion, through the mass of the subjects, of the soundest political science which the lights of the age could afford. If they conceived correctly the paramount end of their government, with the means or subordinate ends through which it must accomplish that end, none of its measures would be grossly foolish or wicked, and its conduct, positive and negative, would commonly be wise and beneficent. The best of *religious* securities, or the best of the securities yielded by religious convictions, would arise from worthy opinions, held by rulers and subjects, concerning the wishes and purposes of the Good and Wise Monarch, and concerning the nature of the duties which he lays upon earthly sovereigns.

Two. It appears from the foregoing strictures on the hypothesis of the original covenant that the hypothesis is needless and is worse than needless: that we are able to account sufficiently, without resorting to the hypothesis, for the duties of subjects towards their sovereign government, with the duties of the sovereign government towards its subjects; and that, though the formation of the independent political society had really been preceded by a fundamental civil pact, scarce any of those obligations would be engendered or influenced by that preceding agreement. It will appear from the following strictures that the hypothesis of the fundamental pact is not only a fiction, but is a fiction approaching to an impossibility: that the institution of a πόλις or *civitas*, or the formation of a society political and independent, was never preceded or accompanied, and could hardly be preceded or accompanied, by an original covenant properly so called, or by aught resembling the idea of a proper original covenant.

Every convention properly so called, or every pact or agreement properly so called, consists of a *promise* (or mutual promises) *proffered and accepted.* Wherever mutual promises are proffered and accepted, there are, in strictness, two or more conventions; for the promise proffered by each, and accepted by the other of the agreeing parties, is of itself an agreement. But where the performance of either of the promises is made by either to depend on the performance of the other, the several conventions are cross or implicated conventions, and commonly are deemed, therefore, one convention. Where one only of the agreeing parties gives or passes a promise, the promise which is proffered by the one, and which is accepted by the other, is, in the language of jurists, 'a convention *unilateral*'. Where each of the agreeing parties gives or passes a promise, and the performance of either of the promises is made to depend on the performance of the other, the several promises respectively proffered and accepted are, in the language of jurists, a 'convention *bilateral*'. Where each of the agreeing parties gives or passes a promise, and the performance of either of the promises is not made to depend on the performance of the other, each of the several conventions is a separate unilateral convention, although the several conventions be made at one time. For example: if I promise you to render you a service, and if you accept the proffered promise, the promise proffered and accepted forms a convention unilateral. If I promise *you* to render you a service, and you promise *me* to render me a service *therefor*, the promises respectively proffered, if they are respectively accepted, form a convention bilateral. If each of us promise the other to render the other a service, but the render of either of the services is not made to depend on the render of the other, the promises proffered and accepted are separate unilateral conventions, although they be proffered and accepted at one and the same time. Since, then, a convention bilateral is formed by the implication of several unilateral conventions, every convention is properly a unilateral convention, or *a promise proffered and accepted.*

The essentials of a convention may be stated generally thus.

1. The promisor, or the party who proffers the promise, promises the promisee, or the party to whom it is proffered, that he will do or perform some given act or acts, or will forbear or abstain from some given act or acts, or will do or perform and also forbear or abstain. And the acts or forbearances which he promises, or the acts and forbearances which he promises, may be styled the object of his promise, and also the object of the convention.
2. The promisor *signifies* to the promisee that he intends to do the acts, or to observe the forbearances, which form the object of his promise. If he signifies this his intention by spoken or written words (or by signs which custom or usage has rendered equivalent to words) his proffered promise is *express*. If he signifies this his intention by signs of another nature, his proffered promise is still a genuine promise, but is *implied* or *tacit*. If, for example, I receive goods from a shopkeeper, telling him that I mean to pay for them, I promise expressly to pay for the goods which I receive: for I signify an intention to pay for them, through spoken or written language. Again: having been

accustomed to receive goods from the shopkeeper, and also to pay for the goods which I have been accustomed to receive, I receive goods which the shopkeeper delivers at my house, without signifying by words spoken or written (or by signs which custom or usage has rendered equivalent to words), any intention or purpose of paying for the goods which he delivers. Consequently, I do not promise expressly to pay for the particular goods. I promise, however, tacitly. For by receiving the particular goods, under the various circumstances which have preceded and accompanied the reception, I signify to the party who delivers them my intention of paying for the goods, as decidedly as I should signify it if I told him that I meant to pay. The only difference between the express, and the tacit or implied, promise lies in the difference between the natures of the signs through which the two intentions are respectively signified or evinced.

3. The promisee *accepts* the proffered promise. In other words, he *signifies* to the promisor, expressly or tacitly, his *belief* or *expectation* that the latter will do or forbear agreeably to the intention or purpose which the latter has expressed or intimated. Unless the promise be accepted, or such a belief or expectation be signified expressly or tacitly, the promise is not a convention. If the acts or forbearances which form the object of the promise be afterwards done or observed, they are done or observed spontaneously by the promising party, or not by reason of the promise considered as such: for the promise would not be enforced (legally or morally) by a rational supreme government or a sane public opinion. In the technical language of the Roman jurists, and by most of the modern jurists who are familiar with that technical language, a promise proffered but not accepted is styled *a pollicitation*.

Consequently, the main essentials of a convention are these: first, a *signification* by the promising party of his *intention* to do the acts, or to observe the forbearances, which he promises to do or observe: secondly, a *signification* by the promisee that he *expects* the promising party will fulfil the proffered promise. And that this signification of intention and this signification of expectation are of the very essence of a proper convention or agreement will appear on a moment's reflection.

The conventions enforced by positive law or morality are enforced legally or morally for various reasons. But of the various reasons for enforcing any convention, the following is always one. Sanctions apart, a convention *naturally* raises in the mind of the promisee (or a convention *tends* to raise in the mind of the promisee) an *expectation* that its object will be accomplished: and to the expectation naturally raised by the convention, he naturally shapes his conduct. Now, as much of the business of human life turns or moves upon conventions, frequent disappointments of those expectations which conventions naturally excite, would render human society a scene of baffled hopes and of thwarted projects and labours. To prevent disappointments of such expectations is therefore a main object of the legal and moral rules whose direct and appropriate purpose is the enforcement of pacts or agreements. But the promisee would not entertain the expectation unless the corresponding intention were signified by the promising party: and, unless the existence of the expectation were signified by the promisee, the promising party would not be apprised of its existence, although the proffered promise had actually raised it. Without the signification of the intention, there were no promise properly so called: without the signification of the expectation, there were no sufficient reason for enforcing the genuine promise which really may have been proffered.[16]

It follows from the foregoing statement of the main essentials of a convention that an original covenant properly so called, or aught resembling the idea of a proper original covenant, could hardly precede the formation of an independent political society.

According to the hypothesis of the original covenant, in so far as it regards the promise of the original sovereign, the sovereign promises to govern to the absolute end of the union (and, perhaps, to more or fewer of its subordinate or instrumental ends). And the promise is proffered to, and is accepted by, all the original subjects. In case the inchoate government be a government of one, the promise passes from the monarch to all the members of the community (excepting the monarch himself). In case the inchoate government be a government of a number, it passes from the sovereign body (in its collective and sovereign capacity) to all the subject members of the inchoate community (including the members of the body considered severally). According to the hypothesis of the original covenant, in so far as it regards the promise of the original subjects, they promise to render to the sovereign a passive and unlimited obedience, or they promise to render to the sovereign such a qualified obedience as shall consist with a given end or with given ends. And the promise of the subjects passes from *all* the subjects: from all and each of the subjects to the monarch or sovereign body, or from each of the subjects to all and each of the rest. In case the inchoate government be a government of one, it passes from all the members of the inchoate community (excepting the monarch). In case the inchoate government be a government of a number, it passes from all the members of the inchoate community (including the several members of the sovereign body).

Now it appears from the foregoing statement of the main essentials of a convention, that the promise of the sovereign to the subjects would not be a covenant properly unless the subjects *accepted* it. But the subjects could hardly accept it unless they apprehended its object. Unless they apprehended its object, it hardly could raise in their minds any determinate expectation: and unless it raised in their minds a determinate expectation, they hardly could signify virtually any determinate expectation, or could hardly accept virtually the proffered promise. The signs of acceptance which might actually fall from them would not be signs of virtual acceptance, but would be in reality unmeaning noise or show. Now the ignorant and weaker portion of the inchoate community (the portion, for example, which was not adult) could hardly apprehend the object of the sovereign's promise, whether the promise were general or special: whether the sovereign promised generally to govern to the absolute end of the independent political society, or promised moreover specially to govern specially and directly to certain subordinate ends. We know that the great majority, in any actual community, have no determinate notions concerning the absolute end to which their sovereign government ought to rule: that they have no determinate notions concerning the ends or means through which it should aim at the accomplishment of that its paramount purpose. It surely, therefore, were absurd to suppose that all or many of the members of any inchoate community would have determinate notions (or notions approaching to determinateness) concerning the scope of their union, or concerning the means to its attainment. Consequently, most or many of the original subjects would not apprehend the object of the original sovereign's promise: and, not apprehending its object, they would not accept it in effect, although they might accept it in show. With regard to most or many of the original subjects, the promise of the original sovereign were hardly a covenant or pact, but were rather a pollicitation.

The remarks which I now have made on the promise of the original sovereign will apply, with a few adaptations, to the promise of the original subjects. If really they proffered to the sovereign (or if really they proffered to one another) that promise to render obedience which the hypothesis supposes or feigns, they would signify expressly or tacitly an *intention* of fulfilling it. But such a signification of intention could not be made by all of them, or even by most or many of them: for by most or many of them, the object of the fancied promise would not be apprehended determinately, or with a distant approach to determinateness. If you feign that the promise to obey passes from the subjects to the subjects, you thicken the absurdity of the fiction. You fancy that a promise is proffered by parties to whom the object of the promise is nearly or quite unintelligible: and, seeing that the promisors are also the promisees, you fancy that the promise is accepted by parties to whom the object of the promise is equally incomprehensible.

If you would suppose an original covenant which as a mere hypothesis will hold water, you must suppose that the society about to be formed is composed entirely of adult members: that all these adult members are persons of sane mind, and even of much sagacity and much judgment; and that being very sagacious and very judicious, they also are perfectly familiar, or at least are passably acquainted, with political and ethical science. On these bare possibilities, you may build an original covenant which shall be a coherent fiction.

It hardly is necessary to add that the hypothesis of the original covenant, in any of its forms or shapes, has no foundation in actual facts. There is no historical evidence that the hypothesis has ever been realised: that the formation of any society political and independent has actually been preceded by a proper original covenant, or by aught approaching to the idea.

In a few societies political and independent (as, for example, in the Anglo-American States) the sovereign political government has been determined at once, and agreeably, to a scheme or plan. But, even in these societies, the parties who determined the constitution (either as scheming or planning, or as simply voting or adopting it) were merely a slender portion of the whole of the independent community, and were virtually sovereign therein before the constitution was determined: insomuch that the constitution was not constructed by the whole of an inchoate community, but rather was constructed by a fraction of a community, already consummate or complete. If you would show me an actual case exactly squaring with the idea of a proper original covenant, you must show me a society political and independent, with a government political and sovereign, which all the members of the society who were then in existence jointly founded and constituted. You must show me, also, that all the subject or sovereign authors of this society and government were parties expressly or tacitly to a true or genuine convention resembling the original covenants which I have mentioned above. In most societies political and independent, the constitution of the supreme government has *grown*. By which fustian but current phrase, I intend not to intimate that it hath come of itself, or is a marvellous something fashioned without hands. For though we say of governments which we mean to praise, 'that they are governments of laws, and not governments of men', all human governments are governments of men: and, without men to make them, and without men to enforce them, human laws were just nothing at all, or were merely idle words scribbled on paper or parchment. I intend to intimate, by the phrase in question, that the constitution of the supreme government has not been determined at once, or agreeably to a scheme or plan: that positive moral rules of successive generations of the community (and, perhaps, positive laws made by its successive sovereigns) have determined the constitution, with more or less of exactness, slowly and unsystematically. Consequently, the supreme government was not constituted by the original members of the society: its constitution has been the work of a long series of authors, comprising the original members and many generations of their followers. And the same may be said of most of the ethical maxims which opinions current with the subjects constrain the sovereign to observe. The original sovereign government could not have promised its subjects to govern by those maxims. For the current opinions which actually enforce those maxims are not coeval with the independent political society, but rather have arisen insensibly since the society was formed. In some societies political and independent, oaths or promises are made by rulers on their accession to office. But such an oath or promise, and an original covenant to which the original sovereign is a promising party, have little or no resemblance. That the formation of the society political and independent preceded the conception of the oath itself is commonly implied by the terms of the latter. The swearing party, moreover, is commonly a limited monarch, or occupies some position like that of a limited monarch: that is to say, the swearing party is not sovereign, but is merely a limb or member of a sovereign body.

And if actual original covenants might be detected in history, they would not sustain the hypothesis. For, according to the hypothesis, an original covenant *necessarily* precedes the formation of an independent political society. And in numerous cases of independent political society, the formation of the society, as we know from history, was *not* preceded by an original covenant: or, at least, the formation of the society, as we know from history, was *not* preceded by an *express* original covenant.

It is said, however, by the advocates of the hypothesis (for the purpose of obviating the difficulty which these negative cases present), that a *tacit* original covenant preceded the formation of the society, although its formation was not preceded by an *express* covenant of the kind.

Now (as I have shown above) an actual signification of intention on the part of the promisor, with an actual acceptance of the promise on the part of the promisee, are of the very essence of a *genuine* convention or pact, be it express or be it tacit. The only difference between an express, and a tacit or implied, convention lies in this: that, where the convention is express, the intention and acceptance are signified by language, or by signs which custom or usage has rendered equivalent to language; but that, where the convention is tacit or implied, the intention and acceptance are not signified by words, or by signs which custom or usage has made tantamount to words.[17]

Most or many, therefore, of the members of the inchoate society could not have been parties, as promisors or promisees, to a tacit original covenant. Most or many of the members could not have signified virtually the requisite intention or acceptance: for they could not have conceived the object (as I have shown above) with which, according to the hypothesis, an original covenant is concerned.

Besides, in many of the negative cases to which I now am adverting, the position and deportment of the original sovereign government, and the position and deportment of the bulk of the original subjects, exclude the supposition of a tacit original covenant. For example: where the original government begins in a violent conquest, it scarcely promises tacitly, by its violences towards the vanquished, that it will make their weal the paramount end of its rule. And a tacit promise to render obedience to the intrusive and hated government scarcely passes from the reluctant subject. They presently *will* to obey it, or presently *consent* to obey it, because they are determined to obey it by their fear of its military sword. But the *will* or *consent* to obey it presently, to which they are thus determined, is scarcely a tacit *promise* (or a tacit manifestation of intention) to render it future obedience. For they intimate pretty significantly, by the reluctance with which they obey it, that they would kick with all their might against the intrusive government if the military sword which it brandishes were not so long and fearful.

By the recent and present advocates of the hypothesis of the original covenant (who chiefly are German writers on political government and society), it commonly is admitted that original covenants are not historical facts: that an actual original covenant never preceded the formation of any actual society political and independent. But they zealously maintain, notwithstanding this sweeping admission, that the only sufficient basis of an independent political society is a fundamental civil pact. Their doctrine, therefore, touching the original covenant amounts to this: namely, that the original covenant hath not preceded the formation of any society political and independent: but that though it hath not preceded the formation of *any*, it yet precedeth inevitably the formation of *every*. Such is a taste or sample of the high ideal philosophy which the Germans oppose exultingly to the philosophy of Bacon and Locke: to the earthly, grovelling, *empirical* philosophy which deigns to scrutinise facts, or stoops to observation and induction.

It would seem that the propounders of this lucid and coherent doctrine mean to insist on one or another of the two following positions.

1. That an *express* original covenant has not preceded the formation of any society political and independent: but that a *tacit* original covenant (or an original covenant imported by the fact of the formation) necessarily precedes the formation of every society of the kind.
2. That the formation of a society political and independent *must* have been preceded by a fundamental civil pact, if the sovereign political government be *rightful*, *lawful*, or *just* 'wenn es *rechtsbeständig* sein soll': meaning by 'rightful', 'lawful', or 'just', consonant to the law of God (as known somehow or other), or consonant to the right or justice (mentioned in foregoing pages) which exists independently of law, and is the test of all law.

On which of these positions they mean to insist I cannot determine: for they waver impartially between the two, or evince a perceptible inclination to neither. And an attempt to determine the position on which they mean to insist were profitless labour: seeing that both positions are false and absurd. As I have shown above, a tacit original covenant could scarcely precede the formation of an independent political society. And, granting the second of the two positions, no sovereign government has been or can be lawful. For, according to their own admission, the formation of a society political and independent was never preceded actually by a fundamental civil pact. And, as I have shown above, a proper original covenant, or aught approaching to the idea, could scarcely precede the formation of any society of the kind.[18]

Three. I close my strictures on the hypothesis of the original covenant with the following remark:

It would seem that the hypothesis was suggested to its authors by one or another of these suppositions.

1. Where there is no convention, there is no duty. In other words, whoever is obliged, is obliged through a promise given and accepted.
2. Every convention is necessarily followed by a duty. In other words, wherever a promise is given and accepted, the promising party is obliged through the promise, let its object and tendency be what they may. It is assumed, expressly or tacitly, by Hobbes, Kant, and others, that he who is bound has necessarily given a promise, and that he who has given a promise is necessarily bound.

It follows from the first supposition that, unless the sovereign and subjects were bound through a pact, neither of the parties would lie under duties to the other. It follows from the second supposition that, if the sovereign and subjects were parties to an original covenant (either immediately, or as representing the founders of the community), each of the parties would be bound to the other, assuredly and indissolubly. As the duties of each towards the other would be imposed through a pact, they would possess a certain sacredness which perhaps they might want if they were imposed otherwise.

But both suppositions are grossly and obviously false. Of religious, legal, and moral duties, some are imposed by the laws which are their respective sources, through or in consequence of conventions. But others are annexed to facts which have no resemblance to a convention, or to aught that can be deemed a promise. Consequently, a sovereign government might lie under duties to its subjects, and its subjects might lie under duties towards itself, though neither it nor its subjects were bound through a pact. And as duties are annexed to facts which are not pacts or conventions, so are there pacts or conventions which are not followed by duties. Conventions are not enforced by divine or human law, without reference to their objects and tendencies. There are many conventions which positive morality reprobates. There are many which positive law will not sustain, and many which positive law actively annuls. There are many which conflict with the law of God, inasmuch as their tendencies are generally pernicious. Consequently, although the sovereign and subjects were parties to an original covenant, neither the sovereign nor subjects would of necessity be bound by it.

The distinction of sovereign governments into governments de jure *and governments* de facto

From the origin or causes of political government and society, I pass to the distinction of sovereign governments into governments *de jure* and governments *de facto*. For the two topics are so connected, that the few brief remarks which I shall make on the latter may be placed aptly at the end of my disquisition on the former.

In respect of the distinction now in question, governments are commonly divided into three kinds: first, governments which are governments *de jure* and also *de facto*; secondly, governments which are governments *de jure* but not *de facto*; thirdly, governments which are governments *de facto* but not *de jure*. A government *de jure* and also *de facto* is a government deemed lawful, or deemed rightful or just, which is present or established: that is to say, which receives presently habitual obedience from the bulk or generality of the members of the independent political community. A government *de jure* but not *de facto* is a government deemed lawful, or deemed rightful or just, which, nevertheless, has been supplanted or displaced: that is to say, which receives not presently (although it received formerly) habitual obedience from the bulk of the community. A government *de facto* but not *de jure* is a government deemed unlawful, or deemed wrongful or unjust which, nevertheless, is present or established: that is to say, which receives presently habitual obedience from the bulk of the community. A government supplanted or displaced, and not deemed lawful, is neither a government *de facto* nor a government *de jure*. Any government deemed lawful, be it established or be it not, is a government *de jure*. By a government, however, *de jure*, we often mean a government which is deemed lawful, but which, nevertheless, has been supplanted or displaced. Any established government, be it deemed lawful or be it deemed unlawful, is a government *de facto*. By a government, however, *de facto*, we often mean, a government which is deemed unlawful, but which, nevertheless, is established or present. It scarcely is necessary to add that every government properly so called is a government *de facto*. In strictness, a so called government *de jure* but not *de facto* is not a government. It merely is that which was a government once, and which (according to the speaker) ought to be a government still.

In respect of *positive law*, a sovereign political government which is established or present is neither lawful nor unlawful. In respect of *positive law*, it is neither rightful nor wrongful; it is neither just nor unjust. Or (changing the expression) a sovereign political government which is established or present is neither *legal* nor *illegal*.

In every society political and independent, the actual positive law is a creature of the actual sovereign. Although it was positive law under foregoing sovereigns, it is positive law presently, or *is* positive law, through the power and authority of the present supreme government. For though the present government may have supplanted another, and though the supplanted government be deemed the lawful government, the supplanted government is stripped of the might which is requisite to the enforcement of the law considered as positive law. Consequently, if the law were not enforced by the present supreme government, it would want the appropriate sanctions which are essential to positive law, and, as positive law, would not be law imperative: that is to say, as positive law, it would not be law. To borrow the language of Hobbes, 'The legislator is he (not by whose authority the law was first made, but) by whose authority it continues to be law'.

Consequently, an established sovereign government, in respect of the positive law of its own independent community, is neither lawful nor unlawful. If it were lawful or unlawful, in respect of the positive law of its own independent community, it were lawful or unlawful by law of its own making, or were lawful or unlawful by its own appointment. Which is absurd. And if it were lawful or unlawful, in respect of the positive law of another independent community, it were lawful or unlawful by the appointment of another sovereign: that is to say, it were not an actual supreme, but an actual subordinate government. Which also is absurd.

In respect of the positive law of that independent community wherein it once was sovereign, a so called government *de jure* but not *de facto* is not, and cannot be, a lawful government: for the positive law of that independent community is now positive law by the authority of the government *de facto*. And though it now were positive law by the authority of the displaced government, the displaced government, in respect of this law, were neither lawful nor unlawful: for if, in respect of this law, the displaced government were lawful or unlawful, it were lawful or unlawful by law of its own making, or were lawful or unlawful by its own appointment. The truth is that, in respect of the positive law of that independent community, the supplanted government, though deemed *de jure*, is unlawful: for, being positive law by the authority of the government *de facto*, this positive law proscribes the supplanted government, and determines that attempts to restore it are legal wrongs. In respect of the positive law of another independent community, a so called government *de jure* but not *de facto* is neither lawful nor unlawful. For if, in respect of this law, it were lawful or unlawful, it were lawful or unlawful by the appointment of the law-maker; that is to say, it were not an ousted supreme, but an ousted subordinate government.

In respect, then, of *positive law*, the distinction of sovereign governments into lawful and unlawful is a distinction without a meaning. For, as tried by this test, or as measured by this standard, a so called government *de jure* but not *de facto* cannot be lawful: and, as tried by the same test, or measured by the same standard, a government *de facto* is neither lawful nor unlawful.

In respect, however, of *positive morality*, the distinction of sovereign governments into lawful and unlawful is not a distinction without a meaning. For, in respect of positive morality, a government not *de facto* is not of necessity unlawful. And, in respect of positive morality, the term 'lawful' or 'unlawful', as applied to a government *de facto*, is not of necessity jargon.

A government *de facto* may be lawful, or a government *de facto* may be unlawful, in respect of the positive morality of that independent community wherein it is established. If the opinions of the bulk of the community favour the government *de facto*, the government *de facto* is morally lawful in respect of the positive morality of that particular society. If the opinions of the bulk of the community be adverse to the government *de facto*, it is morally unlawful in respect of the same standard. The bulk, however, of the community may regard it with indifference: or a large portion of the community may regard it with favour, whilst another considerable portion regards it with aversion. And, in either of these cases, it is neither morally lawful, nor morally unlawful, in respect of the positive morality of that independent community wherein it is established. And what I have said of a government *de facto*, in regard to the morality of the community wherein it is established, may also be said of a government not a government *de facto*, in regard to the morality of the community wherein it formerly ruled.

And a government *de facto*, or a government not *de facto*, may be morally lawful, or morally unlawful, in respect of the positive morality which obtains between nations or states. Though positive international morality looks mainly at the possession, every government in possession, or every government *de facto*, is not acknowledged of course by other established governments. In respect, therefore, of positive international morality, a government *de facto* may be unlawful, whilst a government not *de facto* may be a government *de jure*.

A government, moreover, *de facto*, or a government not *de facto*, may be lawful or unlawful in respect of the law of God. Tried by the Divine law, as known through the principle of utility, a sovereign government *de facto* is lawfully a sovereign government if the general happiness or weal requires its continuance: tried by the same law, as known through the same index, a sovereign government *de facto* is not lawfully sovereign if the general happiness or weal requires its abolition. Tried by the Divine law, as known through the principle of utility, a government not *de facto* is yet a government *de jure* if the general happiness or weal requires its restoration. Tried by the same law, as known through the same exponent, a government not *de facto* is also not *de jure* if the general happiness or weal requires its exclusion.

A general definition of a positive law: or a general statement of the essential difference by which it is severed from a law not a positive law

A positive law may be defined generally in the following manner: or the essential difference of a positive law (or the difference which severs it from a law not a positive law) may be stated generally in the following manner. Every positive law (or every law simply and strictly so called) is set, directly or circuitously, by a sovereign individual or body, to a member or members of the independent political society wherein its author is supreme. In other words, it is set, directly or circuitously, by a monarch or sovereign number, to a person or persons in a state of subjection to its author.

This definition of a positive law is assumed expressly or tacitly throughout the foregoing lectures. But it only approaches to a perfectly complete and perfectly exact definition. And, consequently, the determination of the province of jurisprudence, which is attempted in the foregoing lectures, only approaches to a perfectly complete and perfectly exact determination

This definition of a positive law is assumed expressly or tacitly throughout the foregoing lectures. But it only approaches to a perfectly complete and perfectly exact definition. It is open to certain correctives which I now will briefly suggest.

The party or parties to whom a law is set, or the party or parties on whom a duty is laid, are necessarily obnoxious to the sanction which enforces the law and the duty. In other words, every law properly so called is set by a superior to an inferior or inferiors: it is set by a party armed with might, to a party or parties whom that might can reach. If the party to whom it is set could not be touched by the might of its author; its author would signify to the party a wish or desire, but would not impose on the party a proper and imperative law. Now (speaking generally) a party who is obnoxious to a legal sanction, or to the might of the author of the law which the legal sanction enforces, is a member of the independent community wherein the author is sovereign. In other words, a party who is obnoxious to a legal sanction is a subject of the author of the law to which the sanction is annexed. But as none but members of the community wherein the law obtains are obnoxious to the legal sanction which enforces a positive law, the positive law is imposed exclusively on a member or members of that independent community. Although the positive law may affect to oblige strangers (or parties who are not members of that independent community), none but members of that independent community are virtually or truly bound by it. Besides, if the positive law of one independent community bound legally the members of another, the other independent community were not an independent community but were merely a subordinate community forming a limb of the first. If it bound the sovereign government of the other independent community, that sovereign government would be in a state of subjection to the sovereign author of the law. If it bound the subject members of the other independent community, the sovereign author of the law would usurp the functions and authority of their own sovereign government: or their own sovereign government would be displaced or supplanted by the foreign and intrusive lawgiver. So that if the positive law of every independent community bound legally the members of others, the subjects in every community would be subject to all sovereigns, and every sovereign government would be sovereign in all societies. In other words, the subject members of every independent community would be in a state of subjection to every supreme government; whilst every supreme government would be the subject of the rest, and, at the same time, would be their sovereign.

Speaking, then, generally, we may say that a positive law is set or directed exclusively to a subject or subjects of its author: or that a positive law is set or directed exclusively to a member or members of the community wherein its author is sovereign. But, in many cases, the positive law of a given independent community imposes a duty on a *stranger*: on a party who is *not* a member of the given independent community, or is only a member to certain limited purposes. For such, in these cases, is the position of the stranger, that, though he is properly a member of a foreign independent community, and therefore is properly a subject of a foreign supreme government, he yet is obnoxious to the sanction by which the duty is enforced, or to the might of the author of the law through which the duty is imposed. And such, in these cases, is also the position of the stranger, that the imposition of the legal duty consists with the sovereignty of the government of which he is properly a subject. Although the legal duty is laid on one of its subjects, it is not laid on the foreign government itself: nor does the author of the law, by imposing the legal duty, exercise sovereign power in the community of the foreign government, or over one of its subjects as being one of its subjects. For example: a party not a member of a given independent community, but living within its territory and within the jurisdiction of its sovereign, is bound or obliged, to a certain limited extent, by its positive law. Living within the territory, he is obnoxious to the legal sanctions by which the law is enforced. And the legal duties imposed upon him by the law are consistent with the sovereignty of the foreign government of which he is properly a subject. For the duties are not imposed upon the foreign government itself, or upon a party within its independent community: nor are they laid upon the obliged party as being one of its subjects, but as being a member, to certain limited purposes, of the community wherein he resides. Again: if a stranger not residing within the given community be the owner of land or moveables lying within its territory, a convention of the stranger, with any of its members or a stranger, may be enforced against him by its positive law. For if he be sued on the agreement, and judgment be given for the plaintiff, the tribunal may execute its judgment by resorting to the land or moveables, although the defendant's body is beyond the reach of its process. And this execution of the judgment consists with the sovereignty of the government of which the stranger is properly a subject. For the judgment is not executed against that foreign government, or within the independent community of which it is the chief: nor is it executed against the defendant as being one of its subjects, but as owning land or moveables within the jurisdiction of the tribunal. If the judgment were executed within the jurisdiction of the foreign supreme government, the execution would wound the sovereignty of the foreign supreme government unless the judgment were executed through its permission and authority. And if the judgment were executed through its permission and authority, the duty enforced against the defendant would be imposed in effect by the law of his own community: the law of his own community adopting the law of the other, by reason of a special convention between the respective governments, or of a rule of international morality which the governments acknowledge and observe. In all the cases, therefore, which I now have noted and exemplified, the positive law of a given independent society may impose a duty on a stranger. By reason of the obstacles mentioned in the last paragraph, the binding virtue of the positive law cannot extend generally to members of foreign communities. But in the cases which I now have noted and exemplified, those obstacles do not intervene. For the stranger is obnoxious to the sanctions by which the law is enforced: and the enforcement of the law against the stranger is not inconsistent with the sovereignty of a foreign supreme government.

The definition, therefore, of a positive law, which is assumed expressly or tacitly throughout the foregoing lectures, is not a perfectly complete and perfectly exact definition. In the cases noted and exemplified in the last paragraph, a positive law obliges legally, or a positive law is set or directed to, a *stranger* or *strangers*: that is to say, a person or persons *not* of the community wherein the author of the law is sovereign or supreme. Now, since the cases in question are omitted by that definition, the definition is too narrow, or is defective or inadequate. To render that definition complete or adequate, a comprehensive summary of these anomalous cases (or, perhaps, a full enumeration of these anomalous cases) must be tacked to the definition in the way of supplement. But positive law, the subject of the definition, is the subject of the foregoing attempt to determine the province of jurisprudence. And since the definition is defective or inadequate, and is assumed expressly or tacitly throughout the foregoing lectures, the determination of the province of jurisprudence, which is attempted in those discourses, is not a perfectly complete and perfectly exact determination.

But I think that the foregoing attempt to determine the province of jurisprudence, and the definition of a positive law which the attempt assumes throughout, have as much of completeness and exactness as the scope of the attempt requires. To determine the province of jurisprudence is to distinguish positive law (the appropriate matter of jurisprudence) from the various objects (noted in the foregoing lectures) to which it is allied or related in the way of resemblance or analogy. But so numerous are the ties by which it is connected with those objects, or so numerous are the points at which it touches those objects, that a perfect determination of the province of jurisprudence were a perfect exposition of the science in all its manifold parts. An adequate exposition of the science (the only adequate determination of the province of jurisprudence) is really the ambitious aim of the entire Course of Lectures of which the foregoing attempt is merely the opening portion. But a perfect determination of the province of jurisprudence is not the purpose of the attempt itself. Its purpose is merely to *suggest* (with as much of completeness and exactness as consist with generality and brevity) the subject of that adequate exposition of the science of jurisprudence, or the subject of that adequate determination of the province of jurisprudence, which is the purpose of the entire Course. Since such is the scope of the foregoing attempt, the definition of a positive law which it assumes throughout has as much of completeness and exactness as its scope requires. To render that definition complete or adequate, a comprehensive summary of the anomalous cases in question (or, perhaps, a full enumeration of the anomalous cases in question) must be tacked to the definition in the way of supplement. But these anomalous cases belong to the departments of my Course which are concerned with the detail of the science. They hardly were appropriate matter for the foregoing *general* attempt to determine the province of jurisprudence: for the foregoing attempt to *suggest* the subject of the science, with as much of completeness and exactness as consist with generality and brevity. Accordingly, the definition or notion of a positive law, which is assumed expressly or tacitly throughout the preceding lectures, omits entirely the anomalous cases in question. And the truth of the positions and inferences contained by the preceding lectures is not, I believe, impaired, or is not impaired materially, by this omission and defect.

And though the definition is not complete, it approaches nearly to completeness. Allowing for the omission of the anomalous cases in question, it is, I believe, an adequate definition of its subject. I hardly could have rendered a juster definition of the subject, in brief and abstract expressions: that is to say, unless I had descended from the generals to the detail of the science of jurisprudence.

An explanation of a seeming defect in the foregoing definition of independent political society

Defining sovereignty and independent political society (or stating their characters or distinguishing marks), I have said that a given society is a society political and independent if the bulk or generality of its members habitually obey the commands of a determinate and independent party: meaning by 'a determinate and independent party' a determinate individual, or a determinate body of individuals, not obeying habitually the express or tacit commands of a determinate human superior. But who are the members of a given society? By what characters, or by what distinguishing marks, are its members severed from persons who are not of its members? Or how is a given person determined to a given community? By the foregoing general definition of independent political society (or the foregoing general statement of its characters or distinguishing marks), the questions which I now have suggested are not resolved or touched: and it may seem, therefore, that the foregoing general definition is not complete or adequate. But, for the following reasons, I believe that the foregoing definition, considered as a general definition, is, notwithstanding, complete or adequate: that a general definition of independent political society (or such a definition as is applicable to every society of the kind) could hardly resolve the questions which I have suggested above.

One. It is not through one mode, or it is not through one cause, that the members of a given society are members of that community. In other words, it is not through one mode, or it is not through one cause, that they are subjects of the person or body sovereign therein. A person may be a member of a given society, or a person may be determined to a given society, by any of numerous modes, or by any of numerous causes: as, for example, by birth within the territory which it occupies; by birth without its territory, but of parents being of its members; by simple residence within its territory; or by naturalisation.[19] Again: a subject member of one society may be, at the same time, a subject member of another. A person, for example, who is naturalised in one independent society may yet be a member completely, or to certain limited purposes, of that independent society which he affects to renounce: or a member of one society who simply resides in another may be a member completely of the former society, and, to limited purposes, a member of the latter. Nay, a person who is sovereign in one society may be, at the same time, a subject member of another. Such, for example, would be the plight of a so called limited monarch, if he were monarch and autocrator in a foreign independent community. Now if the foregoing definition of independent political society had affected to resolve the questions which I have suggested above, I must have discussed the topics which I have touched in the present paragraph. I must have gone from the generals into the details of jurisprudence; and therefore I must have wandered from the proper purpose or scope of the foregoing general attempt to determine the province of the science.

Two. By a general definition of independent political society (or such a definition as is applicable to every society of the kind), I could not have resolved completely the questions suggested above, although I had discussed the topics touched in the last paragraph. For the modes through which persons are members of particular societies (or the causes by which persons are determined to particular societies) differ in different communities. These modes are fixed differently in different particular societies, by their different particular systems of positive law or morality. In some societies, for example, a person born of aliens within the territory of the community is, *ipso jure*, or without an act of his own, a perfect member of the community within whose territory he is born; but, in other societies, he is not a perfect member (or is merely a resident alien) unless he acquire the character by fulfilling certain conditions. (See the French Code, Article 9.) It therefore is only in relation to a given particular society that the questions suggested above can be completely resolved.

Restrictions or explanations of the two following positions: namely, that a sovereign government cannot be bound legally, *and that it cannot have* legal rights *against its own subjects*

I have assumed expressly or tacitly throughout the foregoing lectures that a sovereign government of one, or a sovereign government of a number in its collective and sovereign capacity, cannot be *bound legally*. In the sense with which I have assumed it, the position will hold universally. But it needs a slight restriction, or rather a slight explanation, which may be placed conveniently at the close of my present discourse.

It is true universally that, as being the sovereign of the community wherein it is sovereign, a sovereign government cannot be bound legally: and this is the sense with which I have assumed the position throughout the foregoing lectures. But, as being a subject of a foreign supreme government (either generally or to certain limited purposes), it may be bound by laws (simply and strictly so called) of that foreign supreme government. In the case which I now am supposing, the sovereign political government bound by positive laws bears two characters, or bears two persons: namely, the character or person of sovereign in its own independent society, and the character or person of subject in the foreign independent community. And in order to the existence of the case which I now am supposing, its two characters or two persons must be distinct in practice, as well as in name and show. The laws which are laid upon it by the foreign supreme government may really be laid upon it as chief in its own society: and, on this supposition, it is subject (in that character) to the sovereign author of the laws, in case the obedience which it yields to them amounts to a *habit* of obedience. But if the laws be exclusively laid upon it as subject in the foreign community, its sovereignty is not impaired by the obedience which it yields to them, although the obedience amounts to a *habit*. The following cases will amply illustrate the meaning which I have stated in general expressions. Let us suppose that our king is properly monarch in Hanover: and that our own king, as limited monarch in Britain, is not absolved completely from legal obligation. Now if, as chief in

Hanover, he be not in a habit of obedience to the sovereign British parliament, the legal duties incumbent upon him consist with his sovereignty in his German kingdom. For the duties are incumbent upon him (not as autocrator there), but as limited monarch here: as member of the sovereign body by which he is legally bound. Before the French Revolution, the sovereign government of the Canton of Bern had money in the English funds: and if the English law empowered it to hold lands, it might be the owner of lands within the English territory as well as the owner of money in the English funds. Now, assuming that the government of Bern is an owner of lands in England, it also is subject to the legal duties with which property in land is saddled by the English law. But by its subjection to those duties, and its habitual observance of the law through which those duties are imposed, its sovereignty in its own Canton is not annulled or impaired. For the duties are incumbent upon it (not as governing there), but as owning lands here: as being, to limited purposes, a member of the British community, and obnoxious, through the lands, to the process of the English tribunals.

I have said in a preceding section that a sovereign government of one, or a sovereign government of a number in its collective and sovereign capacity, cannot have *legal rights* (in the proper acceptation of the term) against its own subjects. In the sense with which I have advanced it, the position will hold universally. But it needs a slight restriction, or rather a slight explanation, which I now will state or suggest.

It is true universally that against a subject of its own, as being a subject of its own, a sovereign political government cannot have legal rights: and this is the sense with which I have advanced the position. But against a subject of its own, as being generally or partially a subject of a foreign government, a sovereign political government may have legal rights. For example: let us suppose that a Russian merchant is resident and domiciled in England: that he agrees with the Russian emperor to supply the latter with naval stores: and that the laws of England, or the English tribunals, lend their sanctions to the agreement. Now, according to these suppositions, the emperor bears a right, given by the law of England, against a Russian subject. But the emperor has not the right through a law of his own, or against a Russian subject in that capacity or character. He bears the legal right against a subject of his own, through the positive law of a foreign independent society; and he bears it against his subject (not as being his subject), but as being, to limited purposes, a subject of a foreign sovereign. And the relative legal duty lying on the Russian merchant consists with the emperor's autocracy in all the Russias. For since it lies upon the merchant as resident and domiciled in England, the sovereign British parliament, by imposing the duty upon him, does not interfere with the autocrat in his own independent community.

Notes

1. If every member of an independent political society were adult and of sound mind, every member would be naturally competent to exercise sovereign powers: and if we suppose a society so constituted, we may also suppose a society which strictly is governed by itself, or in which the supreme government is strictly a government of all. But in every actual society, many of the members are naturally incompetent to exercise sovereign powers: and even in an actual society whose government is the most popular, the members naturally incompetent to exercise sovereign powers are not the only members excluded from the sovereign body. If we add to the members excluded by reason of natural incompetency, the members (women, for example) excluded without that necessity, we shall find that a great majority even of such a society is merely in a state of subjection. Consequently, though a government of all is not impossible, every actual society is governed by one of its members, or by a number of its members which lies between one and all.
2. In every monarchy, the monarch renders habitual deference to the opinions and sentiments held and felt by his subjects. But in almost every monarchy, he defers especially to the opinions and sentiments, or he consults especially the interests and prejudices, of some especially influential though narrow portion of the community. If the monarchy be military, or if the main instrument of rule be the sword, this influential portion is the military class generally, or a select body of the soldiery. If the main instrument of rule be not the sword, this influential portion commonly consists of nobles, or of nobles, priests, and lawyers. For example: in the Roman world, under the sovereignty of the princes or emperors, this influential portion was formed by the standing armies, and, more particularly, by the Prætorian guard: as, in the Turkish empire, it consists, or consisted, of the corps of Janizaries. In France, after the kings had become sovereign, and before the great revolution, this influential portion was formed by the nobility of the sword, the secular and regular clergy, and the members of the parliaments or higher courts of justice.

   Hence it has been concluded that there are no monarchies properly so called: that every supreme government is a government of a number: that in every community which seems to be governed by one, the sovereignty really resides in the seeming monarch or autocrator, with that especially influential though narrow portion of the community to whose opinions and sentiments he especially defers. This, though plausible, is an error. If he habitually obeyed the *commands* of a determinate portion of the community, the sovereignty would reside in the miscalled monarch, with that determinate body of his miscalled subjects: or the sovereignty would reside exclusively in that determinate body, whilst he would be merely a minister of the supreme government. For example: in case the corps of Janizaries, acting as an organised body, habitually addressed commands to the Turkish sultan, the Turkish sultan, if he habitually obeyed those commands, would not be sovereign in the Turkish empire. The sovereignty would reside in the corps of Janizaries, with the miscalled sultan or monarch: or the sovereignty would reside exclusively in the corps of Janizaries, whilst he would be merely their vizier or prime minister. But habitual deference to opinions of the community, or habitual and especial deference to opinions of a portion of the community, consists with that independence which is one of the essentials of sovereignty. If it did not, none of the governments deemed supreme would be truly sovereign; for habitual deference to opinions of the community, or habitual and especial deference to opinions of a portion of the community, is rendered by every aristocracy, or by every government of a number, as well as by every monarch. Nay, supreme government would be impossible: for if the sovereignty resided in the portion of the community to whose opinions and sentiments the sovereign especially deferred, it would reside in a body uncertain (that is to say, nowhere), or in a certain body not in a habit of command. A confusion of laws properly so called with laws improper imposed by opinion is the source of the error in question. The habitual independence which is one of the essentials of sovereignty is merely habitual independence of laws imperative and proper. By laws which opinion imposes, every member of every society is habitually determined.

3. 'The government of a kingdom wherein the king is limited is by most writers called monarchy. Such a king, however, is not soveraign, but is a minister of him or them who truly have the soveraign power.' 'The king whose power is limited is not the soveraign of the assembly which hath the power to limit it. The soveraignty, therefore, is in that assembly which hath the power to limit him. And, by consequence, the government is not monarchy, but aristocracy or democracy.' In these extracts from Hobbes' *Leviathan*, the true nature of the supreme governments which are styled limited monarchies is well stated. It cannot, however, be said, with perfect precision, that the so called limited monarch is merely a minister of the sovereign. He commonly, it is true, has subordinate political powers, or is a minister of the sovereign body: but, unless he also partook in the supreme powers, or unless he were a member, as well as a minister of the body, he would hardly be complimented with the magnificent name of monarch, and the sovereign government of which he was merely a servant would hardly be styled a monarchy. I shall revert to the character or position of a so called limited monarch when I come to consider the limits of sovereign power.

4. *Various meanings of the following terms: 1. The term 'sovereign', or* 'the *sovereign'; 2. The term 'republic', or 'commonwealth'; 3. The term 'state', or* 'the *state'; 4. The term 'nation'*

The present is a convenient place for the following remarks upon terms.

The term 'sovereign', or '*the* sovereign', applies to a sovereign body as well as to a sovereign individual. 'Il sovrano' and 'le souverain' are used by Italian and French writers with this generic and commodious meaning. I say *commodious*: for supreme government, abstracted from form is frequently a subject of discourse. 'Die *Obrig*keit' (the person or body *over* the community) is also applied indifferently, by German writers, to a sovereign individual or a sovereign number: though it not unfrequently signifies the aggregate of the political superiors who in capacities supreme and subordinate govern the given society. But though 'sovereign' is a generic name for sovereign individuals and bodies, it is not unfrequently used as if it were appropriate to the former: as if it were synonymous with 'monarch' in the proper acceptation of the term. 'Sovereign', as well as 'monarch', is also often misapplied to the foremost individual member of a so called limited monarchy. Our own king, for example, is neither 'sovereign' nor 'monarch': but, this notwithstanding, he hardly is mentioned oftener by his appropriate title of 'king', than by those inappropriate and affected names.

'Republic', or 'commonwealth', has the following amongst other meanings:

1. Without reference to the form of the government, it denotes the main object for which a government should exist. It denotes the weal or good of an independent political society: that is to say, the aggregate good of all the individual members, or the aggregate good of those of the individual members whose weal is deemed by the speaker worthy of regard.
2. Without reference to the form of the government, it denotes a society political and independent.
3. Any aristocracy, or government of a number, which has not acquired the name of a limited monarchy is commonly styled a republican government, or, more briefly, a republic. But the name 'republican government', or the name 'republic', is applied emphatically to such of the aristocracies in question as are deemed democracies or governments of many.
4. 'Republic' also denotes an independent political society whose supreme government is styled republican.

The meanings of 'state', or '*the* state', are numerous and disparate: of which numerous and disparate meanings the following are the most remarkable:

1. '*The* state' is usually synonymous with '*the* sovereign'. It denotes the individual person, or the body of individual persons, which bears the supreme powers in an independent political society. This is the meaning which I annex to the term, unless I employ it expressly with a different import.
2. By the Roman lawyers, the expression '*status* reipublicæ' seems to be used in two senses. As used in one of those senses, it is synonymous with 'republic', or 'commonwealth', in the first of the four meanings which I have enumerated above: that is to say, it denotes the weal or good of an independent political society. As used in the other of those senses, it denotes the individual or body which is sovereign in a given society, together with the subject individuals and subject bodies who hold political rights from that sovereign one or number. Or (changing the phrase) it denotes the respective conditions of the several political superiors who, with sovereign and delegated powers, govern the community in question. And the 'status republicæ', as thus understood, is the appropriate subject of *public law* in the definite meaning of the term: that is to say, the portion of a *corpus juris* which is concerned with political conditions, or with the powers, rights, and duties of political superiors. It is hardly necessary to remark that the expression 'status republicæ' is not coextensive or synonymous with the expression 'status'. The former is a collective name for political or public

conditions, or for the powers, rights, and duties of political superiors. The latter is synonymous with the term 'condition', and denotes a private condition as well as a political or public.

3. Where a sovereign body is compounded of minor bodies, or of one individual person and minor bodies, those minor bodies are not unfrequently styled 'states' or 'estates'. For example: before the kings of France had become substantially sovereign, the sovereignty resided in the king with the three *estates* of the realm.
4. An independent political society is often styled a 'state', or a 'sovereign and independent state'.

An independent political society is often styled a 'nation', or a 'sovereign and independent nation'. But the term 'nation', or the term '*gens*', is used more properly with the following meaning. It denotes an aggregate of persons, exceeding a single family, who are connected through blood or lineage, and, perhaps, through a common language. And, thus understood, a 'nation' or '*gens*' is not necessarily an independent political society.

5. Division of governments according to *forma imperii* (Monarchy, Aristocracy, and Democracy), or *forma regiminis* (despotic or republican). The latter is founded on a fancied distinction between executive and legislative. See Kant, *Entwurf zum ewigen Frieden*, pp. 25–30. Krug, *Allgemeines Handwörterbuch der Philosophie*, Vol. IV, p. 37. Politz, *Staatswissenschaft*, Vol. I, MS note.
6. The application of the epithet *half sovereign* seems to be capricious. For example: over most of the political communities wherein the Roman Catholic is the prevalent and established religion, legislative and judicial powers are exercised by the Pope: that is to say, by an external government, or a member of an external government. But those political communities, or their domestic and temporal governments, are not denominated, therefore, by writers on international law, half independent or half supreme. It seems to be supposed by such writers that, in every political community occupying that position, those powers are merely exercised by the authority of the domestic government, or the domestic government and the Pope are jointly sovereign. On the first of which suppositions, the former is of itself perfectly sovereign: and on the last of which suppositions, the former is a constituent member of a government supreme and independent.

According, indeed, to some of such writers, if those powers be exclusively exercised in matters strictly ecclesiastical, the sovereignty of the domestic government is not impaired by the exercise, though they are not merely exercised through its permission or authority. And, consequently, it is not necessary to suppose that it shares the sovereignty with the Pope, or to mark it with the incongruous epithet of half or imperfectly supreme. But though those powers be exclusively exercised in matters strictly ecclesiastical, still they are legislative and judicial powers. And how is it possible to distinguish precisely matters which are strictly ecclesiastical from matters which are not: the powers of ecclesiastical regiment which none but the church should wield from the powers of ecclesiastical regiment (or the *jus circa sacra*) which secular and profane governments may handle without sin?

7. The Constitution of the United States, or the constitution of their general government, was framed by deputies from the several states in 1787. It may (I think) be inferred from the fifth article, that the sovereignty of each of the states, and also of the larger state arising from the federal union, resides in the states' governments as *forming one aggregate body*. It is provided by that article that 'the congress, whenever two-thirds of both houses shall deem it necessary, shall propose amendments to this constitution: or, on the application of the legislatures of two-thirds of the several states, shall call a convention for proposing amendments: which amendments, in either case, shall be valid to all intents and purposes, as part of this constitution, *when ratified by the legislatures* of three-fourths *of the several states, or by convention in* three-fourths *thereof*'. See also the tenth section of the first article: in which section some of the disabilities of the several states' governments are determined expressly.
8. *The meaning of Hobbes's proposition, that 'no law can be unjust'*. Just *or* unjust, justice *or* injustice, *is a term of relative and varying import*

It is affirmed by Hobbes, in his masterly treatises on government, that 'no law can be unjust': which proposition has been deemed by many, an immoral or pernicious paradox. If we look at the scope of the treatises in which it occurs, or even at the passages by which it is immediately followed, we shall find that the proposition is neither pernicious nor paradoxical, but is merely truism put in unguarded terms. His meaning is obviously this: that 'no *positive* law is *legally* unjust'. And the decried proposition, as thus understood, is indisputably true. For positive law is the measure or test of legal justice and injustice: and, consequently, if positive law might be legally unjust, positive law might be unjust as measured or tried by itself. In the passages immediately following, he tells us that positive law may be generally pernicious: that is to say, may conflict with the Divine law which general utility indicates, and, as measured or tried by that law, may be unjust. He might have added that it also may be unjust as measured by positive morality, although it must needs be just as measured by itself, and although it happen to be just as measured by the law of God.

For *just* or *unjust*, *justice* or *injustice*, is a term of relative and varying import. Whenever it is uttered with a determinate meaning, it is uttered with relation to a determinate law which the speaker assumes as a standard of comparison. This is hinted by Locke at the end of the division of laws which I have inserted in my fifth lecture; and it is, indeed, so manifest, on a little sustained reflection, that it hardly needs the authority of that great and venerable name.

By the epithet *just*, we mean that a given object, to which we apply the epithet, accords with a given law to which we refer it as to a test. And as that which is *just* conforms to a determinate law, *justice* is the conformity of a given object to the same or a similar measure: for *justice* is the abstract term which corresponds to the epithet just. By the epithet *unjust*, we mean that the given object conforms not to the given law. And since the term *injustice* is merely the corresponding abstract, it signifies the non-conformity of the given and compared object to that determinate law which is assumed as the standard of comparison. And since such is the relative nature of justice and injustice, one and the same act may be just and unjust as tried by different measures. Or (changing the expression) an act may be just as agreeing with a given law, although the act itself, and the law with which it agrees, are both of them unjust as compared with a different rule. For example: where positive law conflicts with positive morality, that which is just as tried by the former is also unjust as tried by the latter: or where law or morality conflicts with the law of God, that which is just as tried by the human rule, is also unjust as tried by the Divine.

Though it signifies conformity or non-conformity to any determinate law, the term *justice* or *injustice* sometimes denotes, emphatically, conformity or non-conformity to the ultimate measure or test: namely, the law of God. This is the meaning annexed to justice when law and justice are opposed: when a positive human rule is styled unjust. And when it is used with this meaning, *justice* is nearly equivalent to *general utility*. The only difference between them consists in this: that, as agreeing immediately with the *law of God*, a given and compared action is just; whilst, as agreeing immediately with the *principle* which is the index to the law of God, that given and compared action is *generally useful*. And hence it arises that, when we style an action just or unjust, we not uncommonly mean that it is generally useful or pernicious.

9. Political or civil liberties are left or granted by sovereigns in two ways; namely, through permissions coupled with commands, or through simple permissions. If a subject possessed of a liberty be clothed with a legal right to it, the liberty was granted by the sovereign through a permission coupled with a command: a permission to the subject who is clothed with the legal right, and a command to the subject or subjects who are burthened with the relative duty. But a political or civil liberty left or granted to a subject may be merely protected against his fellows by religious and moral obligations. In other words, the subject possessed of the political liberty may not be clothed with a legal right to it. And, on that supposition, the political or civil liberty was left or granted to the subject through a simple permission of the sovereign or state.

10. By his modern censors, French, German, and even English, Hobbes's main design in his various treatises on politics is grossly and thoroughly mistaken. With a marvellous ignorance of the writings which they impudently presume to condemn, they style him 'the apologist of *tyranny*': meaning by the rant, that his main design is the defence of monarchical government. Now, though he prefers monarchical, to popular or oligarchical, government, it is certain that his main design is the establishment of these propositions:

    1. That sovereign power, *whether it reside in one, or in many or a few*, cannot be limited by positive law:
    2. That a present or established government, *be it a government of one, or a government of many or a few*, cannot be disobeyed by its subjects consistently with the common weal, or consistently with the law of God as known through utility or the scriptures.

    That his principal purpose is not the defence of monarchy is sufficiently evinced by the following passages from his *Leviathan*.

> The prosperity of a people ruled by an aristocraticall or democraticall assembly, cometh not from aristocracy or democracy, but from the obedience and concord of the subjects: nor do the people flourish in a monarchy, because they are ruled by one man, but because they obey him. Take away in a state of any kind, the obedience, and consequently the concord of the people, and they shall not only not flourish, but in short time be dissolved. And they that go about by disobedience to doe no more than reforme the commonwealth, shall find that they doe thereby destroy it.

> In monarchy one man is supreme; and all other men who have power in the state, have it by his commission, and during his pleasure. In aristocracy or democracy there is one supreme assembly; which supreme assembly hath the same unlimited power that in monarchy belongeth to the monarch. And which is the best of these three kinds of government, is not to be disputed there where any of them is already established.

So many similar passages occur in the same treatise, and also in his treatise *De Cive*, that they who confidently style him 'the apologist of tyranny or monarchy' must have taken their notion of his purpose from mere hearsay. A dip here or there into either of the decried books would have led them to withhold their sentence. To those who have really read, although in a cursory manner, these the most lucid and easy of profound and elaborate compositions, the current conception of their object and tendency is utterly laughable.

The capital errors in Hobbes's political treatises are the following:

1. He inculcates too absolutely the religious obligation of obedience to present or established government. He makes not the requisite allowance for the anomalous and excepted cases wherein disobedience is counselled by that very principle of utility which indicates the duty of submission. Writing in a season of civil discord, or writing in apprehension of its approach, he naturally fixed his attention to the glaring mischiefs of resistance, and scarcely adverted to the mischiefs which obedience occasionally engenders. And although his integrity was not less remarkable than the gigantic strength of his understanding, we may presume that his extreme timidity somewhat corrupted his judgment and inclined him to insist unduly upon the evils of rebellion and strife.
2. Instead of directly deriving the existence of political government from a perception by the bulk of the governed of its great and obvious expediency, he ascribes the origin of sovereignty, and of independent political society, to a fictitious agreement or covenant. He imagines that the future subjects covenant with one another, or that the future subjects covenant with the future sovereign,

to obey without reserve every command of the latter. And of this imaginary covenant, immediately preceding the formation of the political government and community, the religious duty of the subjects to render unlimited submission, and the divine right of the sovereign to exact and receive such submission, are, according to Hobbes, necessary and permanent consequences. He supposes, indeed, that the subjects are induced to make that agreement by their perception of the expediency of government, and by their desire to escape from anarchy. But, placing his system immediately on that interposed figment, instead of resting it directly on the ultimate basis of utility, he often arrives at his conclusions in a sophistical and quibbling manner, though his conclusions are commonly such as the principle of utility will warrant. The religious duty of the subjects to render unlimited obedience, and the divine right of the sovereign to exact and receive such obedience, cannot, indeed, be reckoned amongst those of Hobbes's conclusions which that principle will justify. In truth, the duty and the right cannot be inferred logically even from his own fiction. For, according to his own fiction, the subjects were induced to promise obedience by their perception of the utility of government: and, since their inducement to the promise was that perception of utility, they hardly promised to obey in those anomalous cases wherein the evils of anarchy are surpassed by the evils of submission. And though they promised to obey even in those cases, they are not religiously obliged to render unlimited obedience; for as the principle of general utility is the general index to religious obligations, no religious obligation can possibly arise from a promise whose tendency is generally pernicious. Besides, though the subject founders of the political community were religiously obliged by their mischievous promise, a religious obligation would hardly be imposed upon their followers by virtue of a mischievous agreement to which their followers were strangers. The last objection, however, is not exclusively applicable to Hobbes's peculiar fiction. That, or a like objection, may be urged against all the romances which derive the existence of government from a fancied original contract. Whether we suppose, with Hobbes, that the subjects were the only promisers, or we suppose, with others, that the sovereign also covenanted: whether we suppose, with Hobbes, that they promised unlimited obedience, or we suppose, with others, that their promise contained reservations; we can hardly suppose that the contract of the founders, unless it be presently useful, imposes religious obligations on the present members of the community.

If these two capital errors be kept in mind by the reader, Hobbes's extremely celebrated but extremely neglected treatises may be read to great advantage. I know of no other writer (excepting our great contemporary Jeremy Bentham) who has uttered so many truths, at once new and important, concerning the necessary structure of supreme political government and the larger of the necessary distinctions implied by positive law. And he is signally gifted with the talent, peculiar to writers of genius, of inciting the mind of the student to active and original thought.

The authors of the antipathy with which he is commonly regarded were the papistical clergy of the Roman Catholic Church, the high church clergy of the Church of England, and the Presbyterian clergy of the true blue complexion. In matters ecclesiastical (a phrase of uncertain meaning, and therefore of measureless compass), independence of secular authority was more or less affected by churchmen of each of those factions. In other words they held that their own church was co-ordinate with the secular government: or that the secular government was not of itself supreme, but rather partook in the supreme powers with one or more of the clerical order. Hobbes's unfailing loyalty to the present temporal sovereign was alarmed and offended by this anarchical pretension: and he repelled it with a weight of reason, and an aptness and pungency of expression, which the aspiring and vindictive priests did bitterly feel and resent. Accordingly, they assailed him with the poisoned weapons which are ministered by malignity and cowardice. All of them twitted him (agreeably to their wont) with flat atheism; whilst some of them affected to style him an apologist of tyranny or misrule, and to rank him with the perverse writers (Machiavelli, for example) who really have applauded tyranny maintained by ability and courage. By these calumnies, those conspiring and potent factions blackened the reputation of their common enemy. And so deep and enduring is the impression which they made upon the public mind that 'Hobbes the Atheist', or 'Hobbes the apologist of tyranny' is still regarded with pious, or with republican horror, by all but the extremely few who have ventured to examine his writings.

Of positive atheism; of mere scepticism concerning the existence of the Deity; or of, what is more impious and mischievous than either, a religion imputing to the Deity human infirmities and vices; there is not, I believe, in any of his writings, the shadow of a shade.

It is true that he prefers monarchical (though he intimates his preference rarely) to popular or oligarchical government. If, then, tyranny be synonymous with monarchy, he is certainly an apologist and fautor of tyranny, inasmuch as he inclines to the one, rather than the many or the few. But if tyranny be synonymous with misrule, or if tyranny be specially synonymous with monarchical misrule, he is not of the apologists and fautors of tyranny, but may rank with the ablest and most zealous of its foes. Scarcely a single advocate of free or popular institutions, even in these latter and comparatively enlightened ages, perceives and inculcates so clearly and earnestly as he, the principle cause and preventive of tyrannous or bad government. The principal cause of tyrannous or bad government is ignorance on the part of the multitude of sound *political science* (in the largest sense of the expression): that is to say, *political economy*, with the two great branches of *ethics*, as well as *politics* (in the strict acceptation of the term). And if such be the principal cause of tyrannous or bad government, the principal preventive of the evil must lie in the diffusion of such knowledge throughout the mass of the community. Compared with this, the best political constitution that the wit of man could devise were surely a poor security for good or beneficent rule. Now in those departments of his treatises on politics, which are concerned with 'the *office* (or duty) of the sovereign', Hobbes insists on the following propositions: *that good and stable government is simply or nearly impossible, unless the fundamentals of political science be known by the bulk of the people*: that the bulk of the people are as capable of receiving such science as the loftiest and proudest of their superiors in station, wealth, or learning: that to provide for the diffusion of such science throughout the bulk of the people, may be classed with the weightiest of the duties which the Deity lays upon the sovereign: that he is bound to hear their complaints, and even to seek their advice, in order that he may better understand the nature of their wants, and may better adapt his institutions to the advancement of the general good: that he is bound to render his laws as compendious and clear as possible, and also to promulge a knowledge of their more important provisions through every possible channel: that if the bulk of his people know their duties imperfectly, for want of the instruction which he is able and bound to impart, he is responsible religiously for all their breaches of the duties whereof he hath left them in ignorance.

In regard to the respective aptitudes of the several forms of government to accomplish the ultimate purpose for which government ought to exist, Hobbes's opinion closely resembles the doctrine which, about the middle of the eighteenth century, was taught by the French philosophers who are styled emphatically the *Œconomists*. In order, say the Œconomists, to the being of a good government, two things must pre-exist:

1. Knowledge by the bulk of the people, of the elements of political science (in the largest sense of the expression);
2. A numerous body of citizens versed in political science, and not misled by interests conflicting with the common weal, who may shape the political opinions, and steer the political conduct, of the less profoundly informed, though instructed and rational, multitude. Without that knowledge in the bulk of the people, and without that numerous body of 'gens *lumineux*', the government, say the Œconomists, will surely be bad, be it a government of one or a few, or be it a government of many. If it be a government of one or a few, it will consult exclusively the peculiar and narrow interests of a portion or portions of the community: for it will not be constrained to the advancement of the general or common good by the general opinion of a duly instructed society. If it be a government of many, it may not be diverted from the advancement of the general or common good by partial and sinister regard for peculiar and narrow interests: but, being controlled by the general opinion of the society, and that society not being duly instructed, it will often be turned from the paths leading to its appropriate end by the restive and tyrannous prejudices of an ignorant and asinine multitude. But, given that knowledge in the bulk of the people, and given that numerous body of '*light-diffusing* citizens', the government, say the Œconomists, let the form be what it may, will be strongly and steadily impelled to the furtherance of the general good by the sound and commanding morality obtaining throughout the community. And, for numerous and plausible reasons (which my limits compel me to omit), they affirm that, in any society thus duly instructed,

> monarchical government would not only be the best, but would surely be chosen by that enlightened community in preference to a government of a few, or even to a government of many.

Such is the opinion (stated briefly, and without their peculiar phraseology) which was taught by Quesnai and the other Œconomists about the middle of the last century. And such is also the opinion (although he conceived it less clearly, and less completely, than they) which was published by their great precursor, in the middle of the century preceding.

The opinion taught by the Œconomists is rather, perhaps, defective than positively erroneous. Their opinion, perhaps, is sound, so far as it reaches: but they leave an essential consideration uncanvassed and nearly untouched. In a political community not duly instructed, a government good and stable is, I believe, impossible: and in a political community duly instructed, monarchy, I incline to believe, were better than democracy. But in a political community not duly instructed, is not popular government, with all its awkward complexness, less inconvenient than monarchy? And, unless the government be popular, can a political community not duly instructed emerge from darkness to light: from the ignorance of political science, which is the principal cause of misrule, to the knowledge of political science, which were the best security against it? To these questions, the Œconomists hardly advert: and, unhappily, the best of possible governments for a society already enlightened is, when compared with these, a question of little importance. The Œconomists, indeed, occasionally admit 'que dans *l'état d'ignorance* l'autorité est plus dangereuse dans les mains d'un seul, qu'elle ne l'est dans les mains de plusieurs'. But with this consideration they rarely meddle. They commonly infer or assume that, since in *the state of ignorance* the government is inevitably bad, the form of the government, during that state, is a matter of consummate indifference. Agreeing with them in most of their premises, I arrive at an inference extremely remote from theirs; namely, that in a community already enlightened, the form of the government were nearly a matter of indifference; but that where a community is still in *the state of ignorance*, the form of the government is a matter of the highest importance.

The political and œconomical system of Quesnai and the other Œconomists, is stated concisely and clearly by M Mercier de la Rivière in his *L'Ordre naturel et essential des Sociétés politiques*.

11. *'Right is might'*

It has often been affirmed that 'right is might', or that 'might is right'. But this paradoxical proposition (a great favourite with shallow scoffers and buffoons) is either a flat truism, affectedly and darkly expressed, or is thoroughly false and absurd.

If it mean that a party who possesses a right possesses the right through might or power of his own, the proposition is false and absurd. For a party who possesses a right necessarily possesses the right through the might or power of another: namely, the author of the law by which the right is conferred, and by which the duty answering to the right is laid on a third and distinct party. Speaking generally, a person who is clothed with a right is weak rather than mighty; and unless he were shielded from harm by the might of the author of the right, he would live, by reason of his weakness, in ceaseless insecurity and alarm. For example: such is the predicament of persons clothed with legal rights, who are merely subject members of an independent political society, and who owe their legal rights to the might and pleasure of their sovereign.

If it mean that right and might are one and the same thing, or are merely different names for one and the same object, the proposition in question is also false and absurd. My physical ability to move about, when my body is free from bonds, may be called *might* or *power*, but cannot be called a right: though my ability to move about *without hindrance from you* may doubtless be styled *a right*, with perfect precision and propriety, if I owe the ability to a law imposed upon you by another.

If it mean that every right is a creature of might or power, the proposition is merely a truism disguised in paradoxical language. For every right (divine, legal, or moral) rests on a relative duty; that is to say, a duty lying on a party or parties other than the party or parties in whom the right resides. And, manifestly, that relative duty would not be a duty substantially if the law which affects to impose it were not sustained by might.

I will briefly remark, before I conclude the note, that 'right' has two meanings which ought to be distinguished carefully.

The noun substantive '*a* right' signifies that which jurists denominate 'a faculty': that which resides in a determinate party or parties, by virtue of a given law; and which avails against a party or parties (or answers to a duty lying in a party or parties) other than the party or parties in whom it resides. And the noun substantive 'rights' is the plural of the noun substantive '*a* right'. But the expression 'right', when it is used as an adjective, is equivalent to the adjective 'just': as the adverb 'rightly' is equivalent to the adverb 'justly'. And when it is used as the abstract name corresponding to the adjective 'right', the noun substantive 'right' is synonymous with the noun substantive 'justice'. If, for example, I owe you a hundred pounds, you have '*a* right' to the payment of the money: a right importing an obligation to pay the money, which is incumbent upon me. Now in case I make the payment to which you have '*a* right', I do that which is 'right' or just, or I do that which consists with 'right' or justice. Again: I have '*a* right' to the quiet enjoyment of my house: a right importing a duty to forbear from disturbing my enjoyment, which lies upon other persons generally, or lies upon the world at large. Now they who practise the forbearance to which I have '*a* right', conduct themselves therein 'rightly' or justly. Or so far as they practise the forbearance to which I have '*a* right', their conduct is 'right' or just. Or so far as they practise the forbearance to which I have '*a* right', they are observant of 'right' or justice.

It is manifest that 'right' as signifying 'faculty', and 'right' as signifying 'justice', are widely different, though not unconnected, terms. But, nevertheless, the terms are confounded by many of the writers who attempt a definition of 'right:' and their attempts to determine the meaning of that very perplexing expression are, therefore, sheer jargon. By many of the German writers on the science of law and morality (as by Kant, for example, in his *Metaphysical Principles of Jurisprudence*), 'right' in the one sense is blended with 'right' in the other. And through the disquisition on 'right' or 'rights' which occurs in his *Moral Philosophy*, Paley obviously wavers between the dissimilar meanings.

'Right' as meaning 'faculty', 'right' as meaning 'justice', and 'right' as meaning 'law'

An adequate definition of '*a* right', or of 'right' as signifying 'faculty' cannot, indeed, be rendered easily. In order to a definition of '*a* right', or of 'right' as signifying 'faculty', we must determine the respective differences of the principal kinds of rights, and also the respective meanings of many intricate terms which are implied by the term to be defined.

The Italian 'diritto', the French 'droit', the German 'recht', and the English 'right', signify 'right' as meaning 'faculty', and also signify 'justice': though each of those several tongues has a name which is appropriate to 'justice', and by which it is denoted without ambiguity.

In the Latin, Italian, French, and German, the name which signifies 'right' as meaning 'faculty' also signifies 'law': 'jus', 'diritto', 'droit', or 'recht' denoting indifferently either of the two objects. Accordingly, the 'recht' which signifies 'law', and the 'recht' which signifies 'right' as meaning 'faculty', are confounded by German writers on the philosophy or *rationale* of law, and even by German expositors of particular systems of jurisprudence. Not perceiving that the two names are names respectively for two disparate objects, they make of the two objects, or make of the two names, one 'recht'. Which one 'recht', as forming a *genus* or kind, they divide into two *species* or two sorts: namely, the 'recht' equivalent to 'law', and the 'recht' equivalent to 'right' as meaning 'faculty'. And since the strongest and wariest minds are often ensnared by ambiguous words, their confusion of those disparate objects is a venial error. Some, however, of these German writers are guilty of a grave offence against good sense and taste. They thicken the mess which that confusion produces with a misapplication of terms borrowed from the Kantian philosophy. They divide 'recht', as forming the *genus* or kind, into '*recht* in the *objective* sense', and '*recht* in the *subjective* sense': denoting by the former of those unapposite phrases, 'law'; and denoting by the latter, 'right' as meaning 'faculty'.

The confusion of 'law' and 'right' our own writers avoid: for the two disparate objects which the terms respectively signify are *commonly* denoted in our own language by palpably distinct marks. I say that they are *commonly* denoted in our own language by palpably distinct marks: for the modern English 'right' (which probably comes from the Anglo Saxon, and therefore is allied to the German 'recht') means, in a few instances, 'law'.[a]

[a]Hale and Blackstone are misled by this double meaning of the word *jus*. They translate *jus* personarum et rerum, '*rights* of persons and things': which is mere jargon. [MS note inserted by R. Campbell.]

12. A good government will not arbitrarily (or by *ex post facto* commands) abrogate quasi rights which it has conferred. And, where possible, will accomplish its ends by prospective rules. [MS note inserted by R. Campbell.]

13. *The proper purpose or end of political government and society, or the purpose or end for which they ought to exist*

The proper purpose or end of a sovereign political government, or the purpose or end for which it ought to exist, is conceived inadequately, or is conceived obscurely, by most or many of the speculators on political government and society.

To advance as far as is possible the weal or good of mankind is more generally but more vaguely its proper purpose or end: to advance as far as is possible the weal of its own community is more particularly and more determinately the purpose or end for which it ought to exist. Now if it would accomplish the general object, it commonly must labour directly to accomplish the particular: and it hardly will accomplish the particular object unless it regard the general. Since, then, each of the objects is inseparably connected with the other, either may be deemed the paramount object for which the sovereign government ought to exist. We therefore may say, for the sake of conciseness, that its proper paramount purpose, or its proper absolute end, is 'the greatest possible advancement of *the common happiness or weal*': meaning indifferently by 'the common happiness or weal', the common happiness or weal of its own particular community, or the common happiness or weal of the universal community of mankind. (Here I may remark that in my fourth lecture, from page 61, I shortly examined a current misconception of the theory of general utility; and that the brief suggestions which I then threw out may easily be fitted to the topic on which I now have touched.)

To advance as far as is possible the weal or good of mankind, or to advance as far as is possible the weal of its own community, is, then, the paramount or absolute end for which a sovereign government ought to exist. We may say of the government itself what Bacon says of the law which it sets to its subjects: 'Finis et scopus quem intueri debet, non alius est, quam ut cives feliciter degant.' The way, indeed, of the government to the attainment of its absolute end lies through the attainment of ends which may be styled subordinate or instrumental. Or, in order that the government may accomplish its proper absolute end the government must accomplish ends subserving that absolute end, or serving as means to its accomplishment. But the subordinate or instrumental ends through which the government must accomplish its paramount or absolute end will hardly admit of a complete description, or a description approaching to completeness. Certainly they are not to be determined, and are not to be suggested justly, by a short and sweeping definition. For, assuming that the government accomplished thoroughly its paramount or absolute purpose, its care would extend (as Bacon adequately affirms) 'ad *omnia* circa bene esse civitatis': its care would extend to *all* the means through which it probably might minister to the furtherance of the common weal.

But, by most or many of the speculators on political government and society, one or a few of the instrumental ends through which a government must accomplish its proper absolute end, are mistaken for that paramount purpose.

For example: it is said by many of the speculators on political government and society that 'the end of every government is to institute and protect property'. And here I must remark, by the by, that the propounders of this absurdity give to the term 'property' an extremely large and not very definite signification. They mean generally by the term 'property', legal rights, or legal faculties: and they mean not particularly by the term 'property', the legal rights, or legal faculties, which are denominated strictly 'rights of property or dominion'. If they limited the term 'property' to legal rights of dominion, their proposition would stand thus: 'The creation and protection of legal rights of dominion is the end of every government; but the creation of legal rights which are not rights of dominion (as legal rights, for example, which are properly effects of contracts) is not parcel of its end, or falls not within its scope.' Consequently, their proposition amounts to this: 'To confer on its subjects legal rights, and to preserve those rights from infringement, is the end of every government.'

[The maintenance of the Rights which are vested in private individuals (i.e. in the governed) is not the only end for which Government ought to exist. It is often expedient that it should be invested with powers which neither directly nor indirectly subserve that end, though they minister to that ultimate purpose for which Rights themselves should exist: viz the general well being. ('Neque tamen jus publicum ad hoc tantum spectat, ut addatur tanquam custos juri privato, ne illud violetur atque cessent injuriæ; sed extenditur etiam ad religionem et arma et disciplinam et ornamenta et opes, *denique ad omnia circa* BENE ESSE civitatis.') (e.g. powers to construct roads, etc.) See Hugo, *Lehrbuch des Naturrechts*, p. 183. MS notes inserted by R. Campbell.]

Now the proper paramount purpose of a sovereign political government, is not the creation and protection of legal rights or faculties, or (in the terms of the proposition) the institution and protection of property. If the creation and protection of legal rights were its proper paramount purpose, its proper paramount purpose might be the advancement of misery, rather than the advancement of happiness; since many of the legal rights which governments have created and protected (as the rights of masters, for example, to and against slaves) are generally pernicious, rather than generally useful. To advance as far as is possible the common happiness or weal, a government must confer on its subjects legal rights: that is to say, a government must confer on its subjects *beneficent* legal rights, or such legal rights as general utility commends. And, having conferred on its subjects beneficent legal rights, the government, moreover, must preserve those rights from infringement, by enforcing the corresponding sanctions. But the institution and protection of beneficent legal rights, or of the kinds of property that are commended by general utility, is merely a subordinate and instrumental end through which the government must accomplish its paramount or absolute purpose.

As affecting to determine the absolute end for which a sovereign government ought to exist, the proposition in question is, therefore, false. And, considered as a definition of the means through which the sovereign government must reach that absolute end, the proposition in question is defective. If the government would duly accomplish its proper paramount purpose, it must not confine its care to the creation of legal rights, and to the creation and enforcement of the answering relative duties. There are absolute legal duties, or legal duties without corresponding rights, that are not a whit less requisite to the advancement of the general good than legal rights themselves with the relative duties which they imply. Nor would a government accomplish thoroughly its proper paramount purpose if it merely conferred and protected the requisite rights, and imposed and enforced the requisite absolute duties: that is to say, if it merely established and issued the requisite laws and commands, and looked to their due execution. The sum of the subordinate ends which may subserve its absolute end is scarcely comprised by a good legislation and a good administration of justice: though a good legislation with a good administration of justice, or good laws well administered, are doubtless the chief of the means through which it must attain to that end, or (in Bacon's figurative language) are the *nerves* of the common weal.

The prevalent mistake which I now have stated and exemplified is committed by certain of the writers on the science of political œconomy, whenever they meddle incidentally with the connected science of legislation. Whenever they step from their own into the adjoining province, they make expressly, or they make tacitly and unconsciously, the following assumption: that the proper absolute end of a sovereign political government is to further as far as is possible the growth of the national wealth. If they think that a political institution fosters production and accumulation, or that a political institution damps production and accumulation, they pronounce, without more, that the institution is good or bad. They forget that the wealth of the community is not the weal of the community, though wealth is one of the means requisite to the attainment of happiness. They forget that a political institution may further the weal of the community, though it checks the growth of its wealth; and that a political institution which quickens the growth of its wealth may hinder the advancement of its weal.

Mistakes like those of political œconomists are made by utilitarians, only of a more general nature. Instead of confounding (specifically) some subordinate end of government with the paramount end of the same, they take a part of human happiness, or a part of the means towards it, for the whole of human happiness, or the whole of those means. (*e.g.* The exclusion of poetry or the fine arts, or the degrading them to 'the agreeable'. Their eminent utility. The wisdom to be got from poets.)

This partial view of human happiness, or of means towards it, will always be taken till a system of ethical teleology be constructed: *i.e.* an analysis of happiness, the means towards it, and therefore the ends to be pursued directly. [MS fragment inserted by R. Campbell.]

14. As connected with the proper purpose or end of political government and society, I may mention one cause which always will make political government (or political government *quasi*) necessary or highly expedient: namely, the uncertainty, scantiness, and imperfection of positive moral rules. Hence the necessity for a common governing (or common guiding) head to whom the community may in *concert* defer.

It is possible to conceive a society in which legal sanctions would lie dormant, or in which *quasi* government would merely recommend, or utter laws of *imperfect obligation* (in the sense of Roman jurists). But however perfect and universal the inclination to act up to rules tending to the general good, it is impossible to dispense with a governing or guiding head.

(Uncertainty of existence of positive moral rules: want of the precision and detail required by dispositions regarding the objects about which positive law is conversant. Hence Godwin, Fichte, and others have made a great mistake.)

In many cases, however, notwithstanding its defectiveness, it is necessary to abandon acts to positive morality. (See p. 140, n. 4.) [MS fragment inserted by R. Campbell.]

15. I style the supposed covenant 'the original *covenant* or *convention*', rather than 'the original *contract*'. Every convention, agreement, or pact is not a contract properly so called: though every contract properly so called is a convention, agreement, or pact. A contract properly so called is a convention which binds legally the promising party or parties. But admitting the hypothesis, the supposed '*original* covenant' would not and could not engender legal or political duties.
16. The incidental statement, in the text, of the essentials of a convention or pact is sufficient for the limited purpose to which I have there placed it. If I were expounding directly the rationale of the doctrine of contracts, I should annex to the general statement which I have placed in the text, many explanations and restrictions which now I must pass in silence. A good exposition of that *rationale* (which jargon and bad logic have marvellously perplexed and obscured) would involve a searching analysis of the following intricate expressions: promise; pollicitation; convention, agreement or pact; contract; quasi-contract.

   But I will add to the statement in the text, before I conclude the note, the following remark on that *consent* which is of the essence of a convention. That *consent* which is of the essence of a convention is formed of the intention signified by the promisor, and of the corresponding expectation signified by the promisee. This intention with this expectation is styled the *consensus* of the parties, because the intention and expectation chime or go together, or because they are directed to a common object; namely, the acts of forbearances which form the object of the convention. But the term *consent*, as used with a wider meaning, signifies any compliance with any wish of another. And, taking the term with this wider meaning, subjects (as I have shown already) *consent* to obey their sovereign, whether they promise or not to render obedience, and whatever be the nature of the motives by which they are determined to render it.
17. Quasi-contracts, or contracts *quasi* or *uti*, ought to be distinguished carefully from tacit or implied contracts. A tacit or implied contract is a genuine contract: that is to say, a genuine convention which binds legally, or to which positive law annexes an obligation. But a quasi-contract is not a genuine convention, and, by consequence, is not a genuine contract. It is some fact or event, not a genuine convention, to which positive law annexes an obligation, *as if* (*quasi* or *uti*) it *were* a genuine convention. And the analogy between a contract and a contract *quasi* or *uti* merely lies in the resemblance between the two obligations which are annexed respectively to the two facts or events. In other respects the two facts are dissimilar. For example: the payment and receipt of money erroneously supposed to be owed is a fact or event amounting to a contract *quasi*. There is nothing in the fact or event that savours of a convention or pact; for the fulfilment of an existing obligation, and not the creation of a future obligation, is the scope or design of the transaction between the payor

and payee. But since the money is not owed, and is not given as a gift, a legal obligation to return it lies upon the payee from the moment of the erroneous payment. Although he is not obliged *ex contractu*, he is obliged *quasi ex contractu*, *as if* he truly had contracted to return the money. The payee is obliged to return it, *as* he might have been obliged *if* he had promised to return it and the payor had accepted his promise.

In the language of English jurisprudence, facts or events which are contracts *quasi* or *uti* are styled *implied contracts*, or *contracts which the law implies*: that is to say, contracts *quasi* or *uti*, and genuine though tacit contracts are denoted by a common name, or by names nearly alike. And, consequently, contracts *quasi* or *uti*, and implied or tacit contracts, are commonly or frequently confounded by English lawyers. See, in particular, Sir William Blackstone's *Commentaries*, Bk II, ch 30 and Bk III, ch 9.

Rights of one great class are rights *in personam certam*: that is to say, rights which avail exclusively against persons determined specifically, or which answer to duties that lie exclusively on persons determined specifically. To the duties answering to such rights, the Roman lawyers limit the expression *obligationes*: and since they have no name appropriate to rights of the class, they apply that expression to the rights themselves as well as to the answering duties which the rights import. Now rights *in personam*, or *obligationes*, arise principally from facts of two classes: namely, geniune *contracts* express or tacit, and *delicts* or injuries. But besides contracts and delicts, there are facts or events, *not* contracts or delicts, to which positive law annexes *obligationes*. By the Roman lawyers, these facts or events are styled *quasi*-contracts: or the obligations annexed to these facts or events are styled obligations *quasi ex contractu*. These facts or events are styled *quasi*-contracts, for two reasons.

1. Inasmuch as the obligations annexed to them resemble the obligations annexed to contracts, they are, in that respect, *analogous* to contracts.
2. The only resemblance between their *species* or *sorts* lies in the resemblance between the obligations which are respectively annexed to them.

Consequently, the common name of *quasi*-contracts is applied to the *genus* or *kind*, for want of a generic term more apt and significant. As the expression is employed by the Roman lawyers, 'obligationes *quasi* ex contractu' is equivalent to '*anomalous* obligations', or to '*miscellaneous* obligations': that is to say, *obligationes*, or rights *in personam*, which are annexed to facts that are neither *contracts* nor *delicts*; and which, being annexed to facts that are neither contracts nor delicts, cannot be brought under either of those two principal classes into which rights *in personam* are aptly divisible. 'Obligationes (say the Digests) aut ex contractu nascuntur, aut ex maleficio (sive delicto), aut *proprio quodam jure ex variis causarum figuris*.' The confusion of quasi-contracts with tacit yet genuine contracts is certainly not imputable to the Roman jurists. But with modern lawyers (how, I cannot conjecture) this gross confusion of ideas is extremely frequent. It is, indeed, the cause of most of the nonsense and jargon which have covered the nature of conventions with nearly impenetrable obscurity.

18. For the notions or language, concerning the original covenant, of recent German writers on political government and society, I refer the curious reader to the following books:

    1. Kant's *Metaphysical Principles of Jurisprudence*. For the original covenant, see the head *Das Staatsrecht*.
    2. A well made *Philosophical Dictionary* (in four octavo volumes), by Professor Krug of the University of Leipzig. For the original covenant, see the article *Staatsursprung*.
    3. *An Exposition of the Political Sciences* (*Staatswissenschaften*), by Professor Pölitz of the same University: an elaborate and useful work in five octavo volumes. For the original covenant, see the head *Staats und Staatenrecht*.
    4. Friedrich von Gentz, a celebrated servant of the Austrian government in *The Historical Journal* for November 1799.

    For, in Germany, the lucid and coherent doctrine to which I have adverted in the text is not maintained exclusively by mere metaphysical speculators, and mere university-professors, of politics and jurisprudence. We are gravely assured by Gentz that the original covenant (meaning this same doctrine touching the original covenant) is the very basis of the science of politics: that, without a correct conception of the original covenant, we cannot judge soundly on any of the questions or problems which the science of politics presents. 'Der gesellschaftliche Vertrag (says he) ist die Basis der allgemeinen Staatswissenschaft. Eine richtige Vorstellung von diesem Vertrage ist das erste Erforderniss zu einem reinen Urtheile über alle Fragen und Aufgaben der Politik.' Nay, he thinks that this same doctrine touching the original covenant is probably the happiest result of the newer German philosophy; insomuch that the fairest product of the newer German philosophy is the conceit of an original covenant which never was made anywhere, but which is the necessary basis of political government and society. Warmly admiring German literature, and profoundly respecting German scholarship, I cannot but regret the proneness of German philosophy to vague and misty abstraction.

19. The following brief explanation may be placed pertinently here.

    Generally speaking, a society political and independent occupies a determined territory. Consequently, when we imagine an independent political society, we commonly imagine it in that plight. And, according to the definition of independent political society which is assumed expressly or tacitly by many writers, the occupation (by the given society) of a determined territory, or seat, is of the very essence of a society of the kind. But this is an error. History presents us with societies of the kind which have been, as it were, *in transitu*. Many, for example, of the barbarous nations which invaded and settled in the Roman Empire were not, for many years before their final establishment, occupants of determined seats.

INDEX

INDEX OF PRINCIPAL SUBJECTS

INDEX OF PRINCIPAL PROPER NAMES